Communism, The Highest Stage of Ecology

Communism, The Highest Stage of Ecology

Guillaume Suing

Original Translation and Foreword by
**Henry Hakamäki &
Salvatore Engel-Di Mauro**

iskra books
olympia | london | dublin

Published by *Iskra Books* © 2025

Originally published as *L'écologie réelle: Une histoire soviétique et cubaine* by *Éditions Delga* © 2018

All rights reserved.
The moral rights of the author have been asserted.

ISKRA BOOKS
U.S. | Britain | Ireland
WWW.ISKRABOOKS.ORG

Iskra Books is an independent scholarly publisher—publishing original works of revolutionary theory, history, education, and art, as well as edited collections, new translations, and critical republications of older works.

ISBN-13 (*Hardcover*) 979-8-3485-3874-3
ISBN-13 (*Softcover*) 979-8-3485-3829-3

British Library Cataloguing in Publication Data
A catalogue record for this book is available from the British Library.

Library of Congress Cataloguing-in-Publication Data
A catalog record for this book is available from the Library of Congress.

Editing and Proofing by DAVID PEAT
Typesetting by DAVID PEAT & BEN STAHNKE
Cover Art and Book Design by BEN STAHNKE
Cover Art Inspired by the Design of H. KAPITZKI, IDZ BERLIN
Interior Figures, Tables, and Maps by TAYLOR R. GENOVESE & BEN STAHNKE

Contents

Translators' Foreword (Henry Hakamäki & Salvatore Engel-Di Mauro) xi

Original Foreword (Viktor Dedaj) 1

Introduction 5
  —From Utopian Ecosocialism to Scientific Socialism 8
  —Protecting Nature: A Matter for Scientists, not Shamans 10
  —Behind "Degrowth," the Reactionary Malthus... 14
  —Ecological USSR versus Productivist USA 17
  —Not all that Moves is Red, not all that is Green is Sincere 19

Agroecology: A Little-Known Socialist Achievement 25
  —A Workers' Victory for the Environment is Better than a Dozen Kyoto Protocols 25
  —The Cuban Example; Agroecology "In One Country" 27
  —Why it Works in Cuba and not Elsewhere 36
  —The First Historical Overcoming of the Town-Country Contradiction 38
  —Hydrocarbons: An Energy "NEP" for Certain Anti-

IMPERIALIST STATES **41**

—THE INCONSEQUENTIALITY OF GREEN TROTSKYISM **43**

—THE "ECO-ANARCHIST" MUTATION OF PART OF THE KURDISH NATIONAL MOVEMENT **47**

THE SOVIET UNION: THE STORY OF A GREEN REVOLUTION! **51**

—WAS THE USSR REALLY "PRODUCTIVIST"? **51**

—SOVIET AGRICULTURE BEFORE KHRUSHCHEV'S "CHEMICALIZATION" **60**

—SOVIET SOIL: A NATIONAL ASSET TO BE PROTECTED **82**

—ENERGY POLICY: THE PREMIUM ON RENEWABLES **96**

DIALECTICAL MATERIALISM: BRAKE OR BOOST FOR AGROBIOLOGY? **107**

—A HANDFUL OF CRYPTO-LYSENKOISTS SHAKE UP CONVENTIONAL AGRICULTURE **107**

—IDEALISTIC GENETICS VERSUS PROTO-DIALECTICAL MATERIALISM: A DRAW? **114**

—FROM THE SOVIET PREHISTORY OF EPIGENETICS TO THE SEEDS OF TOMORROW **140**

—BETWEEN CONSERVATION AND EVOLUTION: A DIALECTIC OF LIFE AND ENVIRONMENT **151**

—DIALECTICS OF NATURE YESTERDAY AND TODAY **159**

CONCLUSION **167**

—PROGRESSIVE DEGROWTHERS AND PRODUCTIVIST COMMUNISTS? **167**

APPENDIX 1: "TREES ARE THE MASTERS OF THE SOIL" **173**

APPENDIX 2: EPIGENETIC VERNALIZATION OF CEREALS IN THE USSR **177**

APPENDIX 3: HOW IS A SCIENTIFIC THEORY BORN? **183**

APPENDIX 4: CUBAN SOCIALISM AND AGROECOLOGY: MUTUALLY

Reinforcing **187**

Timeline **193**

References (In Chronological Order of Publication) **197**

For Yafa,
my little wonder.

—*Guillaume Suing*

The history of nature and the history of men
are dependent on each other so long as men exist.

—KARL MARX & FRIEDRICH ENGELS, *The German Ideology*

♧?↑

TRANSLATORS' FOREWORD
REFLECTIONS ON SOCIALISM AND ENVIRONMENTAL PROTECTION

HENRY HAKAMÄKI & SALVATORE ENGEL-DI MAURO

IN THE FACE OF ESCALATING ENVIRONMENTAL CRISES, the urgent need for a paradigm shift in humanity's relationship with the rest of nature has become increasingly apparent. The interplay between social and environmental justice is a topic of profound significance, especially when considering the historical and theoretical frameworks that have informed our understanding of these issues. Yet, despite this, hegemonic narratives around the supposed "destructive" nature of communism on the environment pervade and inhibit exploration of radical alternatives to the truly destructive capitalist world system we are already living in. The work of French scholar Guillaume Suing, now translated into English for the first time, offers a timely and insightful contribution to this discourse, and aims to shatter these hegemonic narratives that have been implanted into popular consciousness as a means of stifling, if not subverting, revolutionary fervor in the environmental movement. *Communism, the Highest Stage of Ecology* is a meticulously researched and powerfully argued analysis that challenges these hegemonic narratives surrounding communism and environmentalism, revealing a rich tapestry of interconnections that have long been overlooked or misunderstood. This introduction aims to provide a synthesis of the key arguments presented in the book, highlighting the relevance of a dialectical materialist perspective in addressing the pressing ecological concerns of our time.

The text's narrative begins with a preface by Viktor Dedaj that underscores the imperative of socialist planning in the context of energy and environmental policies. Drawing upon the experiences of various socialist and capitalist countries, Dedaj critically examines the strategic and tactical choices made by these systems. The distinction between transitional and long-term energy strategies is crucial, as it reflects the underlying priorities and constraints inherent in each system. Socialist countries, striving for independence and development, have often pursued the establishment of sovereignty over energy systems to break free from the shackles of imperialist control. The book argues that only socialist planning can effectively address the looming fossil fuel shortage and contribute to global environmental protection in the long run. This analysis is set against the backdrop of "green capitalism," which is critiqued for its potential to serve as a tool for maintaining the status quo and hindering the development of emerging powers such as China, Russia, Brazil, and India. The historical and political implications of energy provision strategies are thus situated within the broader context of national sovereignty and social transformation.

The concept of "productivism," which is central to the critique of capitalism's environmental record, is also a focal point of the book. Certainly, socialist countries, especially the USSR and the PRC, have been accused of productivism, both from the right and left. Suing engages with the perspectives of environmental activists, communists, and socialists, dissecting the nuances of this term and its relation to energy choices. Productivism, as traditionally understood, involves the relentless pursuit of economic growth through increased production and technological innovation, often at the expense of environmental considerations. However, the author shows that a dialectical approach can reveal the complexities of this concept, describing how it has been shaped by the specific conditions of each society and the historical epochs in which it has been applied. The transitional nature of socialist economies is underscored, as they grapple with the legacy of underdevelopment and the imperatives of modernization, while simultaneously striving to achieve a harmonious balance with the environment. This is why the charge of productivism against socialist states is out of place. When such accusation comes from pro-capitalist environmentalists, it is tantamount to projection, since it is an inexhaustible hunger for profit that drives productivism.

Chapter 1 delves into the concrete example of Cuba's agroecological revolution. This case study exemplifies how socialist planning can lead to sustainable agriculture and environmental protection. Cuba's nationalization of resources, particularly agricultural resources, has allowed for the funding of comprehensive education and health systems, which in turn have supported the development of agroecological practices.

The chapter highlights Cuba's success in achieving food sovereignty, increasing agricultural production, and ensuring equitable social distribution, all while maximizing seed biodiversity and employing organic farming techniques for, among others, soil health improvement and pest control. Cuba's commitment to political independence and environmental conservation is also underscored, with significant investments in renewable energy and the expansion of forested areas and protected species. Given the high rate of urbanization in Cuba, cities have not been exempted from the process. Cuba, as a direct result of coordination among multiple segments of society and the socialization of the means of production, has turned into a world leader in ecologically sustainable urban farming techniques and production levels, along with successes in creating synergies between town and country. Thereby, socialism as developed in Cuba prefigures degrowth in practice. It demonstrates a pathway towards achieving degrowth in its leftist understanding, reducing throughputs while increasing living standards.

Moving on to discussing the Soviet Union, Chapter 2 provides a historical analysis of agricultural practices and policies, particularly in the period of the Stalin administration following the Second World War. Suing documents the complexities of the Soviet Union's approach to agriculture, characterized by the tension between intensive production and the preservation of individual plots for personal use, as well as tensions over the use of biological or chemical agricultural methods, methods that were hotly debated within the halls of Soviet academies. The chapter also delves into the ideological clashes within the scientific community, notably the confrontation between Trofim Lysenko's "proletarian science" and the more Western-oriented scientific approaches of the time. The Lysenko affair, while often vilified in the West, is presented as a reflection of the broader struggle to reconcile the imperatives of socialist development with the demands of scientific truth and environmental stewardship. The Khrushchev-led descent into an ecologically more destructive path, tied to a policy of catching up to the US farming model, exemplifies one outcome of this struggle, which is discussed in Chapter 2 as a contrast to what happened in Cuba. Suing's insightful and comparative discussion underscores the need for a dialectical understanding that transcends simplistic dichotomies of East versus West, tradition versus innovation, and productivism versus conservation.

The third chapter of the book takes us into the realm of life itself, exploring the fundamental contradictions of heredity and evolution through the lens of epigenetics. Here, the dialectical materialist approach is essential in making sense of the intricate dance between self-preservation and the mechanisms that drive species to diversify and evolve. The historical and ideological confrontations within the field of ecology are laid bare, as the author contends that for a true synthesis of ecological thought Marxist methodology must be embraced. The need for a collective endeavor to re-envision our future is emphasized, one that transcends the limitations of both scientific disciplines and political ideologies.

The conclusion of the book brings us back to the contemporary landscape of environmental politics, addressing the fraught relationship between communism and ecology. The author identifies the historical misunderstandings that have divided these two movements and advocates for a genuine integration capable of overcoming the conceptual impasses that have hindered their unity. The text critically assesses the limitations of ecosocialism generally and calls for a deeper engagement with Marxist thought, especially of the sort that has evolved in socialist countries, to inform environmental policy. It challenges the dichotomy of progress and degrowth, suggesting that a revolutionary orientation is necessary to transcend the limitations imposed by the capitalist mode of production. The unprecedented nature of the ecological crisis is underscored, as many in future generations may have to live more modestly than their ancestors, many of whom already live in devastated environments, under threats of disasters, and in conditions of chronic deprivation.

Communism, the Highest Stage of Ecology is a critical intervention in the debate surrounding the compatibility of socialist and environmentalist agendas. It demonstrates that the core principles of communism—collective ownership of the means of production, democratic planning, and the centrality of human and environmental well-being—are not only compatible with but also necessary for a sustainable ecological future. By examining historical examples and engaging with the complexities of scientific knowledge, the author provides a compelling argument for the potential of socialist systems to lead the way in addressing the current environmental challenges.

The book is particularly relevant in an era where the limitations of market-based solutions to environmental issues are becoming increasingly evident even in the mainstream. The neoliberal model of "green capitalism" has been shown to be insufficient in addressing the systemic causes of ecological degradation. Instead, a radical rethinking of our relationship with nature is required, one that acknowledges the interdependence of social and environmental justice. Suing's work suggests that this is not only possible but also historically and theoretically grounded in the principles of communism.

So, where does this leave us? How should revolutionary scholars and activists alike make use of this text? Suing's work serves as a clarion call to integrate ecological concerns into the very fabric of our socialist projects, drawing from what has already been accomplished historically in socialist countries. It is a reminder that the struggle for a better world is not merely an economic or political endeavor but also a profoundly ecological one. By embracing a dialectical understanding of the complexities inherent in environmental policy and practice, we can forge a path forward that is both scientifically rigorous and ideologically sound.

One could start from numerous entry points to achieve this. One that we have found particularly inspiring with respect to the current conjuncture is the development and spread of agroecologically informed farming in Cuba. Suing ably recounts the success attained so far in raising food productivity in both town and country. It could be added as well that the advances made in linking and coordinating food production in both urban and rural areas. All the while, the relative progress in raising the level of nutritious food access to all Cubans has been reached while minimizing negative impacts, if not even bringing about improvements in ecosystem health (especially in urban ecosystems). The need to add that the successes have been relative is due to the brutal US blockade now exceeding 60 years and intensifying as well as the great efforts that have had to be devoted towards overcoming centuries of Spanish and US colonialism and associated plantation systems, subtended as they were by genocides and slavery systems. The objective conditions of capitalist imperialist siege and colonial histories must always be borne in mind when assessing the environmental and social records of socialist countries. The fact that in Cuba such strides have been by way of agroecology, urban food production, and reconciling town and country food production systems points to the decisive advantages of applying Marxist principles to guide the biophysical sciences with the support of a socialist state, without which no such progress is achievable.

Examples of the socialist state's key role in improving people's lives as well as, eventually and necessarily, raising a society's ecological sustainability level can also be found where socialist revolutions have been crushed. Burkina Faso features importantly, even if fleetingly, in Suing's discussion of a successful implementation of ecologically mindful policies under socialism, working out solutions in parallel with Cuba during roughly the same time period. For similar reasons, Burkina Faso would have headed in similar directions as Cuba had it not been for the 1987 French colonial intervention in backing a violent coup, installing a dictatorship only overthrown by 2014.

This experience of agroecology, and an effort to establish food security, flies directly in the face of what the bulwarks of the imperialist capitalist world system foster their self-aggradising actions—political, economic, and food insecurity in the global periphery. Take, for example, the way that Western development scholars, analysts, and consultants lecture developing nations on how to develop their economies through resource extraction and the selling of primary commodities with the aim of developing other industries in the future. What does this look like in practice? Among other impacts is the overfocusing on extraction, which leads to massive distortions of national economies, often leading to a sidelining of agricultural production. For instance, in the case of Nigeria, a major oil boom took place beginning in the 1960s, and continued its acceleration through the 1970s. However, at the same time, the amount of cultivated land in the country decreased by a disconcerting 60% in just the period of 1975-1978.[1] Furthermore, entire regions like the Niger Delta were effectively taken out of agricultural production as a result of lasting pollution from oil and gas extraction, involving the assassinations of local activists, such as Ken Saro Wiwa, who dared to oppose the systematic upending of their lands. The result of this was a once food self-sufficient country having to turn to food imports, to the extent that Nigeria was importing over $1 billion annually in rice alone.[2] Without food sovereignty, politi-

---

[1] Shaxson (2008).

[2] Sourced from the International Trade Administration.

cal sovereignty is also always a tenuous line to hold, as the moment that a developing country reaches a crisis point, the imperialist West sees more opportunities for extraction and exploitation. As Henry Kissinger candidly put it, "To give food aid to a country just because they are starving is a pretty weak reason."[3] A neo-colonised country in crisis, to imperialists, is simply more fodder for capital accumulation.

The Burkinabé revolutionaries analyzed the imperialist system brilliantly, and took steps, informed by Cuba's ongoing experimentation, to seek not only political sovereignty, but also ecologically sensitive food sovereignty. It is no wonder then that a Western backed coup cut this project short. Think of the threat that sovereignty in the Global Periphery poses to the Imperialist Core. As a more recent example, take the case of Niger, a country that within the last year has begun revoking French licenses at uranium mines in the country. This is a country in which only 19% of the population has access to electricity,[4] yet whose uranium, "covers 30% of [France's] civilian needs, and 100% of [France's] military needs,"[5] and which produces huge profits within France. This relationship is exactly that which the Burkinabé Revolutionaries were not only criticizing, but were struggling against. No wonder that the Alliance of Sahel States is portrayed in witheringly negative light within the media apparatuses of the Imperial Core. Nevertheless, despite the twisting of narratives by imperialists in both this contemporary example and the historical examples that this book analyses, the Burkinabé experiment and Cuba's revolutionary agroecological experimentation remain a shining examples of what can be attempted when the shackles of capitalist imperialism are shorn and a new political and economic horizon can be explored.

Communism, the Highest Stage of Ecology is a germinal work that not only contributes to the theoretical debate on the relationship between communism and environmentalism but also provides practical insights into the strategies and policies that can lead to a sustainable future. Guillaume Suing's combined historical analysis, scientific inquiry, and political critique offers a refreshing perspective that challenges readers to think

---

3 NACLA (1975), p. 12.
4 World Bank (2023).
5 Le Monde (2022).

critically about the future of our planet and the systems that govern it. This book is a useful tool for those seeking to break the hegemonic narratives that have dominated discussions of environmental policy and to build a world that prioritizes the common good over the short-term interests of the few.

References

"L'Afrique est notre avenir," information report N° 104 (2013-2014) by Jeanny Lorgeoux and Jean-Marie Bockel, on behalf of the Committee on Foreign Affairs, Defence and Armed Forces, submitted on 29 October 2013. https://www.senat.fr/rap/r13-104/r13-1041.pdf pg.237

International Trade Administration. https://www.trade.gov/country-commercial-guides/nigeria-agriculture-sector

NACLA (1975). "U.S. Grain Arsenal." *NACLA's Latin America and Empire Report*, 9(7).

Shaxson, Nicholas. *Poisoned Wells: The Dirty Politics of African Oil.* New York and Basingstoke: Palgrave Macmillan, 2008.

World Bank (2023). "Access to electricity (% of population)—Niger." https://data.worldbank.org/indicator/EG.ELC.ACCS.ZS?locations=NE, accessed 15 December 2024.

ORIGINAL FOREWORD

Viktor Dedaj

In the beginning, there was the tomato. Then, they made the shitty tomato. And instead of calling it the "shitty tomato," they called it "tomato." While the tomato, the one that tasted like a tomato and had grown as such, became the "organic tomato." From then on, it was all downhill.

—Unknown

So, you would like to save the planet? I can understand you well. It would be a shame to do without it. So I do what you do: I pay attention. To what? That depends on my level of awareness and commitment. When I bought my 4x4, I made sure it came with a catalytic converter. And big rubber tires. And leather seats. And lots of metal and plastic all around. I'm also careful to use only "clean" gas (the kind you extract with a feather duster and white gloves). When I take it to the supermarket to do my shopping, I only buy products stamped "organic," like these freshly hand-picked fruits flown to my plate. Oh yes, and I also sort my garbage (it's amazing how much waste we produce). In short, I'm all about "ecology," "sustainable development" and all that. Even capitalism has gone green. According to the law of supply and demand, all you have to do is demand. That's it.

On a more serious note, there was a time, not so long ago, when we heard with horror how megacities were suffocating under a blanket of pollution. But here we are at the beginning of the 21st century, and pollution alerts now punctuate our days. What horrified us only a short time ago has become our daily routine.

Bulletins announcing how "breathable" the air is, vegetables that no longer taste of anything, suffocating transport, and unliveable megacities. As if these simple observations weren't enough to convince everyone

2 COMMUNISM, THE HIGHEST STAGE OF ECOLOGY

of the urgency of the situation, now we've got to sound the alarm too.

Relying on capitalism to save our environment is like relying on arms dealers to ensure world peace. Of course, one will say that capitalism is no fool, and its interest is the same as ours: survival. Which presupposes a minimum of interest in the long or medium term, or in collective well-being.

And, clever as it is, capitalism drapes itself in green, looking for ways to take advantage of this (belated) awareness. But between questioning the consumer society to save the air and the opportunity to boost consumption by selling gas masks (made from recycled products, it goes without saying), what do you think capitalism will *naturally* choose? And if you've never heard of the head of a multinational food company recently declaring that he sees no reason why access to drinking water should be a right, it's probably because you've been reading the wrong newspaper.

And as with any well-thought-out scam, the first thing to do is to control the narrative. But what do you do when history contradicts narrative? You've probably guessed it: simply rewrite history. And that's how (let's put it schematically) ecology came into being in our part of the world, during the 1970s, as an "apolitical" movement (an indicative choice, for those in the know). A sort of "meta-movement" that proclaimed itself (as you prefer) outside, above, or alongside parties and ideologies, a veritable eruption on the political scene of a "response" to a "new" and ... unforeseen problem. Yes, unforeseen, because who could have imagined *before* that capitalism would lead us, through the dynamics of its internal logic, towards a pre-ordained catastrophe? Who knows, perhaps understood by those who had long ago analyzed this dynamic and had thought up alternatives?

Rewriting history means reinventing the past, but it also means concealing part of the present. Like, for example, the reality of a large Caribbean island that has managed to plan—remember that word—the redesign of its development to become the one and only example in the world, still to this day, of a concrete model of sustainable development. If you've never heard of it, it's probably because you haven't been reading the right newspaper.

In this book, Guillaume Suing has taken up the welcome initiative of setting a few things straight and overturning a number of preconceived ideas, helping us to (re)discover past thinkers—that some would have us forget—and lift the veil on a certain present—that the same people would have us ignore.

—Viktor Dedaj

INTRODUCTION

> Did you not see the helpless infirmity, no better than a dream, in which the blind generation of men is shackled? Never shall the counsels of mortal men transgress the ordering of Zeus.
>
> —AESCHYLUS, *Prometheus Bound*

THE FACT THAT GREEN JOINS RED on the flags of today's Left[1] reflects both a step forward in the unity of the militant anti-capitalist front and a kind of political misunderstanding that neither the environmentalists nor, indeed, the communists seem to want to dispel. The relative youth of political ecology and its social base partly explain why its anti-capitalist character is only just emerging today. But the disqualification of illusions linked to the trend towards "green capitalism" and the "Marxization"[2] of what we usually call *ecosocialism* is a recent and still largely unfinished business.[3]

---

1   The phenomenon is fairly widespread, at least in Europe at the start of this century, with parties such as *Syriza* in Greece, *Izquierda Unida* in Spain, *Os Verdes* in Portugal, *Ensemble* and the *Parti de Gauche* in France.

2   A philosopher in vogue today, Moishe Postone, claims to regenerate Marxism on the basis of Marx's posthumously published *Grundrisse*. This new ecosocialist Althusser evokes what "escaped" the Bolshevik founders of the Soviet Union in an outline of "anti-productivist" thinking, based on the double contradiction: Capital-Nature and Capital-Labor.

3   **Translators' Note:** The term 'ecosocialist' has differing meanings inside and outside particular Marxist tendencies and schools of thought. Throughout this text Suing is using it to mean to movements (e.g. the IV Internationalists in France, like Loewy), mainly intellectual in nature, that unite environmentalism and political struggle or views environmental issues as political, albeit in abstracted and utopian ways. These movements typically avoid questions of the practicalities of political power, the realities of bringing about meaningful ecological restoration, and have the tendency to be dismissive of, if not antagonistic to, socialist countries. Another term for these could be "utopian environmentalism."

The communist movement, for its part, seems to be getting used to a defensive position in the face of this new "green" social-democratic spirit, including in terms of concepts, when on the contrary it should be taking the lead and fighting on the ideological front, drawing unashamedly from the Soviet heritage. This was not only theoretical, but also to a large extent practical, as explained below. It is in total contradiction with the preconceptions of today's "green" activists.

Until the 1950s, for over 30 years, the USSR was the world's most advanced country in the field of ecology, not only in its ability to protect the environment, but also in its choice of agricultural techniques. And this was no accident. The proponents of ecosocialism themselves concede that only socialism, triumphant over the anarchy of production and private property that characterizes the capitalist system, can properly and harmoniously manage agricultural production and environmental protection on a national scale.

While "political ecology" does everything it can to distance itself from a Marxism deemed "productivist" or even "Promethean"[4], the aim here is to demonstrate how, from a theoretical, historical, and practical point of view, socialism is the "highest stage"[5] of what has come to be called "ecology," and not a supposed political adversary.

The political foundations of ecosocialism are curiously reminiscent of the first anarchist and utopian socialist conceptions of the 19th century. Today, in contrast, it's a question of overcoming the apparent contradiction between productivism and environmentalism, because the need to develop agricultural and industrial production to meet the needs of a rapidly growing population is not necessarily opposed to "Nature." Like

---

4   Prometheus is the name of a Titan who stole the fire of knowledge from Zeus, the God of Gods in Greek mythology, and gave it to humans. The latter would then be able to know and exploit nature to satisfy their immediate interests. His punishment was death.

5   Lenin's famous *Imperialism, the Highest Stage of Capitalism* (1916) demonstrated both how the imperialist stage was a *necessary* development of capitalism, and how it was *the ultimate* one. Thus, by analogy, we use the term "highest stage." Political ecology, i.e. the struggle to protect the environment, necessarily involves the question of political power, which can only be completely resolved under and through socialism, i.e. by eliminating the domination exercised by the bourgeoisie, which is largely responsible for current environmental disasters.

the *canuts* of Lyons[6] who, in the early days of the proletariat's struggle, attacked machine-tools, accused of destroying jobs, environmentalists divert the very real contradiction between Capital and Nature in favor of a very idealistic and insurmountable contradiction between Nature and Technical Progress.

Perhaps imperfectly, and within the limits imposed by imperialist encirclement, only the Soviets came up with techniques for overcoming this contradiction without the pre-industrial, petit-bourgeois nostalgia that characterizes ecology today.

Of course, one might object to Chernobyl, the Aral Sea, DDT pollution of Moldavian soils... But it is a misunderstanding of history, encouraged by the West, that prevents communists from retorting, or confines them to a defensive, nihilistic attitude, with arguments that are more often than not ineffective.

Let's be clear: the USSR was only belatedly subjected to intensive agriculture, with its well-known setbacks in terms of environmental protection. It was under Khrushchev, and not before, that the USSR chose to compete with the "triumphant" United States of America, in spite of the Marxist-Leninist theory that had prevailed until then, by using the same methods and the same rules of the game. From then on, the socialist camp aligned itself more and more openly and resolutely with the capitalist tendencies of short-termist, soil-destroying intensive agriculture.

As for the problems linked to energy policy, of which the nuclear issue is a particularly debated outgrowth today, we'll also show how communism can overcome them without falling back into the fundamental contradiction pointed out by Marx and Engels, associated with that of Capital-Labor: the Capital-Nature contradiction.

---

6 **Translators' Note:** *Canuts* ('*cannes nues*,' bare canes, alluding to their poverty level) were silk workers in places like Lyon, France, who organized and revolted against horrid working conditions in 1831 and again in 1834, and were slaughtered in their hundreds by French armies. The uprisings were in some respects a prelude to the 1848 rebellion in Lyon that coincided with other rebellions throughout Europe.

8 Communism, The Highest Stage of Ecology

From Utopian Ecosocialism to Scientific Socialism

Ecosocialists criticize the communism they claim to surpass for deriving its excessive productivism from a skewed interpretation of Marx and Engels, which ultimately resembles that of capitalists. But this "degrowth"[7] critique of Marx is not new, and while it clearly distances itself today from the illusions of the "green capitalism" movement, the identified enemy is less the bourgeoisie than human nature, which is intrinsically irresponsible in the face of technical progress, irrespective of any class struggle. We end up glorifying the model of small, self-sufficient, inward-looking communities, a kind of fantasized return to the phalanstery[8] era, even a primitive communism. In today's ecosocialist programs, we find an emphasis on "family farming," on "small units," as opposed to "mass production," as if the latter necessarily went hand in hand with the disasters we have known since the second half of the twentieth century.

As we shall see, while this model is not absurd in absolute terms at the stage called Communism (the final disappearance of the state following the political work of the proletariat during the transitional stage of socialism), it must be remembered that achieving it without transition, starting from a capitalist system of class struggle, is by definition impossible. This is where communists fundamentally differ from anarchists or social democrats claiming to be ecosocialists, for whom the socialist stage (dictatorship of the proletariat) is clearly neither necessary nor desirable.

At the same time, it should be noted that fascist currents are opportunistically taking advantage of this new environmentalist trend with anti-communist and Malthusian overtones, mythologizing "Nature" and

---

7   **Translators' Note:** Since original publication, there has been a lively debate around the meaning and political expediency of the term 'degrowth.' In this text, it used in relation to the school of thought which argues that environmentally sustainable civilisation can only be achieved with a return to a bucolic and romanticized past. Equally, these movements also argue for an unqualified reduction in all forms of consumption (and commit the same, but inverted, error of the capitalists–that of not differentiating use-values and exchange-values.) There exists a wide body of perspectives now fighting for ownership of the appellation 'degrowth.' For further analysis of these tendencies, see Engel-Di Mauro, *Ecosocialism*, 2024, pp. 74-78.

8   **Translators' Note:** A phalanstery refers to a self-contained community living in harmony and holding property in common, as idealized by Utopian socialists like Charles Fourier (1772-1837).

its spirituality, pining for feudalism, corporatism and the supposedly unchanging social and natural balances that have now been desecrated by "stateless financial tycoons..."

So here we are, back to the old polemics of Proudhon[9] against Marx, a far cry from the supposed overcoming of Marxism. And while some are still desperately seeking a "third way" between capitalism and communism through a "gray-green"[10] temptation, others are forced to "re-examine Marxism" by trying to articulate it with considerations that Marxism would not spontaneously encompass.

Ecosocialism in fact reflects an impatient, petty-bourgeois, anti-dialectical aspiration, similar to yesterday's hypocritical calls to "synthesize" Marxism with feminism, anti-racism, anti-fascism or anti-imperialism, as if the link were not obvious... Was it not thanks to the socialist camp, directly or indirectly,[11] that civil rights were granted to struggling African-Americans in the USA, for fear of the development of Bolshevism? Wasn't it thanks to the October Revolution that the right to vote and to stand for election was granted to African Americans for fear of a rising Bolshevism?

Wasn't it thanks to the October Revolution that the rights to vote and stand for elections were granted to women? In Soviet Russia, for example, the right to vote was fully granted for the first time in 1918,[12] whereas in France, for example, it was only granted in 1944... Fascism, meanwhile, was defeated in the 1940s in Europe by communist-led Popular Fronts, and then by the Soviet Union itself against the Third Reich in the Second World War. The first successful national liberation strug-

9   Today, the French thinker Pierre-Joseph Proudhon is the claimed idol of reactionary philosophers such as Michel Onfray, fascist and chauvinist militants at Égalité et Réconciliation [**Editor's Note:** A French far right political organisation], and mainstream anarchists alike, as an antidote to Karl Marx's "totalitarian" vision.

10   **Translators' Note:** "Gray-green" is an allusion to German soldiers in WWI and WWII. In this case, the author refers to nazi-fascism.

11   On this subject, see the significant work of philosopher and historian Domenico Losurdo, in particular his book *Fuga dalla storia?* (1999) [*Flight from History?*] published as *Fuir l'Histoire?* by Éditions Delga (2007).

12   Finland was the first country to guarantee women the right to vote in 1906, but only in parliamentary elections. Municipal elections, for example, remained subject to suffrage based on tax qualification.

gles, subsequently, were hard-won in the wake of Vietnamese communist victories over French and American colonialists...

There's a certain hypocrisy in wanting to "regenerate" Marxism by associating it with some exogenous auxiliary, be it feminism, anti-racism, anti-fascism, anti-imperialism or ecology... We'll see that far from being a gap in dialectical materialist analysis and the practice of scientific socialism, ecology is, on the contrary, consubstantial with them.

This is not to say that the "partial" struggles mentioned here have no *raison d'être*. On the contrary, they are often central to the struggle. We enter the general struggle against capitalism with our own motives at the outset, for the woman oppressed by feudal mentality, as for the indigenous person squeezed by a French multinational or the African-American victim of daily police repression. But the mass nature of these struggles, such as those waged by activists against "junk food" for example, logically converge when it comes to uniting to defeat the common capitalist enemy and establish a new system that would guarantee everyone's rights with a certain degree of stability.

If the Soviet Union once strove to protect the environment and transform it while respecting its equilibrium, if Cuba still stands out today for its ability to use its soil and energy resources while winning the admiration of Western environmentalists, it is not by chance or by some tactical concession designed to please the latter, but by a theoretical and practical necessity linked to their mode of production, even if it is "productivist."

Protecting Nature: A Matter for Scientists, Not Shamans

Basically, the anti-productivist principle of the ecology (environmentalist)[13] movement stems from a philosophical presupposition about an idealized Nature, which can only be "desecrated" by human labor, contrasting human progress with technical progress. Yet the history of humanity is first and foremost that of the domestication of its environment, the founding act of which was the Neolithic revolution. Prehistory is marked

---

13 **Translators' Note:** In a European context, the "ecology movement" does not refer to a scientific field, but to a socially wider environmental movement. In the text, ecology and environmental movements are terms that are used interchangeably.

by the transition from hunter-gatherer tribes to sedentary human groups who domesticated plants and animals to meet their basic needs by attaining greater security, regularity, and quantity of necessities. They were the protagonists of the first "Great Plan for the Transformation of Nature," without which horses, cows, sheep, wheat, barley and a thousand other humanly-shaped creatures would not exist today.

For millennia, this radical transformation of the human environment spread across the planet, defying the fears of shamans terrorized by the imminence of celestial vengeance. Humanity itself has been transformed in return, particularly in eating habits and metabolic adaptations,[14] without the sky ever falling.[15]

First of all, we need to distinguish how human transformations of the environment can alter major natural balances without compromising the long-term ability to satisfy human needs for food or energy. In other words, we need to identify the extent to which the necessary modifications to our living environment are linked to the satisfaction of our needs, our vital interests, (quantity and quality of our food, renewal of the energy needed for our activities), or alternatively, to the quest for maximum profit, characteristic of the capitalist system.

Then it's a matter of demonstrating how it is the working class—the basis of material production and whose historic role is to defeat the capitalist system in order to satisfy both its own interests and, by extension, those of all humanity—that must be in the vanguard of the struggle against this parasitic bourgeois class that is leading us to our ruin, including with respect to our natural resources.

14 From the Neolithic period onwards, cattle breeding enabled humans to drink milk through adulthood, resulting in hereditary enzymatic adaptations for late lactose digestion. The production of starches and grasses during the same period led to a multiplication of the amylase gene in the genome of farmer-breeders, so that they could better digest the starch that was now abundant in their diet. Numerous examples of this type have been uncovered.

15 If we follow the reasoning of ecological fundamentalists, we can better understand the new American craze for "paleo diets." Their followers opt for an exclusively meat-based, organic diet. They take part in bizarre sporting activities designed to develop humans' original musculature, jumping from trunk to trunk or clinging to liana vines. In fact, the idea is to return to the Paleolithic practices that preceded the Neolithic revolution, which is deemed against nature and the origin of the double "original sin" of productivist agriculture and livestock farming.

It's at these two levels that we need to understand both the anti-productivism and anti-communism of the early ecology movement, right up to its ecosocialist mutation. While the latter is an objective advance in terms of the convergence of anti-capitalist struggles, it retains a dangerously divisive potential when it comes to castigating a particular strategic option of states fighting for national sovereignty against predatory imperialism, a particular struggle for the jobs of workers in today's industry, or even a particular picket line from which the black, toxic fumes of burning tires escape...

Marx exposes this with clairvoyance, intimately linking the two struggles without calling into question the famous disembodied "productivism":

> All progress in capitalistic agriculture is a progress in the art, not only of robbing the labourer, but of robbing the soil; all progress in increasing the fertility of the soil for a given time, is a progress towards ruining the lasting sources of that fertility. The more a country starts its development on the foundation of modern industry, like the United States, for example, the more rapid is this process of destruction. Capitalist production, therefore, develops technology, and the combining together of various processes into a social whole, only by sapping the original sources of all wealth—the soil and the labourer.[16]

It would therefore be possible and obviously desirable, according to Marx, to develop production techniques without increasing the ruin of such sustainable resources. Engels was even more precise in pointing out the capitalist's responsibility for the irrational destruction of the environment. One hundred and fifty years before the first ecosocialists appeared, he asserted:

> As individual capitalists are engaged in production and exchange for the sake of the immediate profit, only the nearest, most immediate results must first be taken into account. As long as the individual manufacturer or merchant sells a manufactured or purchased commodity with the usual coveted profit, he is satisfied and does not concern himself with what afterwards becomes of the commodity and its purchasers. The same thing applies to the natural effects of the same actions. What cared the Spanish planters in Cuba, who burned down forests on the slopes of the mountains and obtained from the ashes sufficient fertiliser for one generation of very highly profitable coffee trees—what cared they that the heavy tropical rainfall afterwards washed away the unprotected upper stratum of the soil, leaving behind only bare rock! In relation to nature,

---

16 Marx, *Capital*, Volume 1, 1867.

as to society, the present mode of production is predominantly concerned only about the immediate, the most tangible result; and then surprise is expressed that the more remote effects of actions directed to this end turn out to be quite different, are mostly quite the opposite in character; that the harmony of supply and demand is transformed into the very reverse opposite[...].[17]

Lenin—need we add?—was no more "productivist" than his inspirers, and shared their views, reminding us, for example, that:

> The possibility of substituting artificial fertilizers for natural ones [...] in no way refutes the irrationality of wasting natural fertilizers by polluting rivers and the air in industrial districts.[18]

While the fight to protect the environment logically follows from anticapitalist struggles, it never refers to any instinct on the part of humans to produce and pollute in a fatal headlong rush inherent to their very nature. If "productivism" is defined by a "quest for maximum profit," the foundation of capitalism, how can we label its antagonist, socialism?

On the contrary, only science, as permanent human work in the field of knowledge and techniques, enables societies to prevent the long-term degradation of resources that could be exploited spontaneously, immediately and to the end, when this degradation is not perceptible on the scale of isolated individuals. Here again, we will demonstrate how the socialist system outperforms the capitalist system not only in theory, but above all and consequently in practice, when it comes to implementing reasonable strategies that respect natural resources.

On a practical level, we know to what extent the capitalist system privileges and finances the most lucrative sectors of research, with the aim of quickly satisfying its thirst for maximum profit. On the contrary, it holds back less immediately profitable sectors, or if it wishes to develop them, it proves incapable of injecting sufficient funds... unless, for example, it wishes to compete with the Soviet pioneer in the aerospace race, so long as the latter was threatening its hegemony.

From a theoretical point of view, the brakes imposed by the bourgeois *pensée unique* are notorious among agronomists who have tried to

---

17   Engels, 'The Part played by Labour in the Transition from Ape to Man', 1876.

18   Lenin, 'The Agrarian Question and the "Critics of Marx', *Collected Works*, 1961, Vol. 5, pp. 103-222.

dissent. Claude Bourguignon, an agronomist and lecturer well known for having reintroduced biology into the debates of agricultural professionals, which had been until then conditioned by chemistry alone (artificial fertilizers and pesticides from agro-industry), testifies to the disappearance in France in the 1970s of chairs in soil microbiology at university, and the impossibility of fighting against the lobbies of "chemically" intensive agriculture within the INRA (*Institut National de la Recherche Agronomique*, the French National Agronomic Research Institute).

Clearly, as long as a state exists—that is, as long as the class struggle exists—it is never indifferent to the scientific research it funds. But it is also the dominant ideology disseminated by this state throughout society that determines, even more than funding, the work of theoretical production. In this sense, we shall see that *dialectical materialism*, the dominant paradigm under socialism, was able to move away from Western aspirations for short-termist, intensive agriculture, in favor of a much more "ecological" integrationist vision of the environment, the living world, and even the soil.[19]

BEHIND "DEGROWTH," THE REACTIONARY MALTHUS...

The neglect of historical sources is quite symptomatic of the environmentalist movement. As it was Karl Marx who first spoke of "sustainable development,"[20] there's a trace of wilful obliviousness deeply rooted in the thinking of environmentalists and even, in a way, of eco-socialists. As nature abhors a vacuum, this neglectfulness defaults into Malthusianism.

Malthus, the nineteenth-century economist, made a name for himself with his controversy over birth control. In the midst of the rise of industrial capitalism, this Anglican bourgeois transposed to human demography a typical business angst linked to the cyclical nature of economic crises of overproduction:

---

19 Soviet Russia was a pioneer in pedology (soil science) and, more. generally, in agroecology. All the major concepts currently used in ecology (biosphere, biocenosis, climax, etc.) were first introduced and developed in the Soviet Union at the beginning of the 20th century, as we shall see below.

20 "All progress in increasing the fertility of the soil for a given time is a progress towards ruining the more long-lasting sources of that fertility" (*Capital*, Volume 1).

> A man who is born into a world already possessed, if he cannot get subsistence from his parents on whom he has a just demand, and if the society do not want his labour, has no claim of right to the smallest portion of food, and, in fact, has no business to be where he is. At nature's mighty feast there is no vacant cover for him. She tells him to be gone, and will quickly execute her own orders, if he does not work upon the compassion of some of her guests. If these guests get up and make room for him, other intruders immediately appear demanding the same favour. The report of a provision for all that come, fills the hall with numerous claimants. The order and harmony of the feast is disturbed [...].[21]

In other words, against Marx and others, Malthus claimed that population was increasing exponentially, while available resources were only increasing arithmetically, i.e. much more slowly. This principle, which underpins the harshest and most inhumane voluntarist "regulations," still prevails, as we understand it, not only in the "anti-immigration" conceptions of Western reactionaries, but also—and this is more surprising—in those of environmentalists concerned with the planet's available resources, starting with those of the soil and subsoil.

While it is true that non-renewable energies are anti-environmental (we'll come back to this point), we need to start combating the caricatures that have been perpetuated for too long in this field, even if they are "common sense," knowing that they allow part of the "left" to condemn, along with capital, economic growth and an improvement in living standards to which the peoples of the South, and in particular China and India, are deemed not to be entitled: meat consumption, improved public health and lower mortality, development of means of transport, and so on.

Malnutrition worldwide is declining as a proportion of the world's population. In other words, thanks in particular to technological progress (instant, worldwide circulation of information on declared famines, leading to almost immediate food supplies, except in areas of armed conflict), nutritional deficiencies due to a real lack of local resources are diminishing. In 1990, it was estimated that 15.4% of the world's 5.3 billion people were undernourished. In 2000, the figure was 13.5% for 6.1 billion. In 2015, the figure was 9.1% for 7.3 billion, and forecasts estimate it will be at 6.7% for 8.3 billion in 2030.

---

21 Malthus, *Essay on the Principle of Population*.

The idea that explosive population growth would lead to the depletion of food resources is false, both because of scientific progress and because of spontaneous birth-rate regulation when "steady-state" is reached for different peoples. Of course, voluntary birth control is possible, but it is primarily linked to national limits, and never to global limits, since demographic growth more or less follows that of the means of production, themselves linked to technical and scientific progress.

We might even add that the increase in the "ecological footprint," i.e. the ecological "cost" or "indebtedness" of human populations on environmental resources, is much greater in the northern hemisphere, where populations are growing very slowly, than in the southern hemisphere, where populations are growing much faster. Thus, food shortages are fully linked to the degree of exploitation of peoples by imperialism, and even to the wars it provokes, and "food riots" such as the historic ones in 2008 [**Editor's Note**: in e.g. Cameroon, Egypt, and up to 30 countries in total] were linked to financial speculation on the world's agricultural resources, and in no way to the overpopulation that Malthus warned against.

Of course, in absolute terms, we could argue that the planet is not inexhaustible and could not support hundreds of billions of humans, but we're a long way from that, and we need to reason on our time scale to guarantee political effectiveness. The idea of limiting births rather than fighting the system that impoverishes us comes directly from Malthusian anxiety about this "great banquet of Nature," where newcomers would have to be denied at all costs what had been granted to the first arrivals... If environmentalists endorse the openly Malthusian conceptions of major global organizations such as WWF,[22] it is at best due to an ideological deficit. The only factor limiting food resources in relation to world population growth is not so much the world's arable land as the alteration of its fertility (linked, as we shall see in detail, to the suicidal techniques of intensive capitalist agriculture).

In many ways, capitalism's over-exploitation of the soil since the Sec-

---

22 "The Earth has its limits, and even with the best technologies imaginable, these cannot be pushed back indefinitely. To respect life within these limits, and to ensure that those who have less will soon have more, two things are necessary: to halt population growth everywhere, and to stabilize, if not reduce, the consumption of resources in the rich countries" (Report "Saving the planet: a strategy for saving the future of life" published as *Sauver la planète: stratégie pour l'avenir de la vie* (WWF, 1991).

ond World War is reminiscent of the over-exploitation of the 'invisible' colonial peoples, providing a Western labor aristocracy with the crumbs it needs to purposely nurture social peace in the heart of the metropolis. To the last degree, the barbaric pursuit of profit has, in the history of capitalism and under very specific conditions, led to a headlong rush to exploit labor without any concern for regenerating the workforce. In the Nazi labor camps, inmates were pressed to death, with human losses regularly renewed by the arrival of "fresh" recruits. In periods of adjustment of the capitalist system, it took a long period of trial and error for the blind development of capitalist exploitation to concede rights and more "liveable" conditions to workers, through workers' struggles, so that they could reconstitute their workforce over the longer term.

We sense that this blind development, still present today and also exerted on the soil's resources, is not immediately resisted this time (by nature) and is therefore difficult to regulate. Indeed, agricultural soils must regenerate in the long term, otherwise they will be permanently depleted. And this exhaustion is not immediately reflected in natural resistance: the only resistance that will enable "green capitalism" (which it is inevitably forced to be) to continue its race for profit in the long term will be that of the peasantry (greatly weakened) and environmental activists (essentially from the petty bourgeoisie).

Genuine, sustainable protection of the planet means first and foremost identifying the troublemaker: not overpopulation, or rising living standards in the South, but the global capitalist system. The alternative to this catastrophe is not agricultural "degrowth," but a technical revolution that only the socialist system can plan. We're not talking about a "return to small family units," but about the revolutionary transformation of large-scale farming techniques, based on the (deliberately) overlooked experience of socialist countries in this field.

Ecological USSR versus Productivist USA

In view of the Socialist camp's obvious lead in the field of ecology and so-called "organic" agriculture, some will claim, while conceding that the "betrayal" of the first ecological innovations and the shift to agricultural "productivism" dates not from the 1950s with Khrushchev's revisionism, but from Stalin's accession to power in the 1920s.[23] This is an aberration that we will correct, with concrete evidence to back it up. On the contrary, the thirties and forties were the heyday of agroecological concepts and practices in the USSR.[24] Not without reason, communists were already criticizing the "triumph" of capitalist intensive agriculture in the 1950s, when it was still in its infancy, and enduring the mockery of Western scientists, foremost among them the famous geneticist Jacques Monod.

Francis Cohen, for example, a French communist journalist who came to the aid of Soviet agronomy under fierce attack in the West, recalled in 1950:

> What good would agrobiology do for the American trusts?
>
> What's the point of scientific research that improves the soil from year to year, when it is more advantageous, in order to cut costs, to engage in forced cultivation that destroys and exhausts the soil, turning millions of square kilometers of arable land into deserts? What use to capitalists would genetics be in improving plant and animal species? The aim of agricultural genetics is to create pure, categorizable, standardized varieties that can be sold to farmers with guaranteed characteristics. So-called pure varieties degenerate in two or three years when grown in the field. So much the better, the country will have to buy seed again![25]

Current events provide excellent and symptomatic illustrations of this last point. For example, in recent years, farmers' trade unionists have been protesting against European legislation aimed at limiting and appropriating seed varieties used in agriculture. In 2013, José Bové, an EELV[26] member of parliament and a

---

23 Forced to acknowledge Soviet precocity in this field, Jean Batou, for example, tried in the 1990s to place the trend reversal in 1928, without ever finding evidence in the country's agronomic practices at the time (*Révolution russe et écologie, 1917-1934*—Jean Batou, 1992, *Vingtième Siècle*—a history journal), blaming Stalin for the disasters of Chernobyl and the drying up of the Aral Sea, both inherited from the Khrushchev ("Virgin Lands Campaign") and Brezhnev periods from the 1960s onwards.

24 Agroecology is the name given to agricultural principles and techniques that aim to protect the environment and satisfy basic human needs.

25 Génétique classique et biologie mitchourinienne, Éditions La Nouvelle Critique: *Science bourgeoise et science prolétarienne*, 1950.

26 **Translators' Note:** *Europe Écologie—Les Verts* (Ecology Europe—The Greens) is a French political party formed via a merger of The Greens and Ecology Europe.

Confédération Paysanne[27] trade unionist, denounced the European Parliament:

> The new proposal for a seed regulation presented today by the European Commission is counterproductive and dangerous. Numerous scientists and UN agencies such as the FAO are sounding the alarm. Biodiversity is in danger. Multinationals have focused their efforts on the creation of high-yielding plants that are fragile. They can only survive in an artificial environment dependent on chemical fertilizers and pesticides, and therefore on oil. This proposal, which reinforces the stranglehold of the world's four major seed monopolies, should instead have been put forward by the lobbyists from Monsanto, Pioneer and Bayer (to name but a few), who held the pen used to draft this text in the shadows.
>
> By reducing farmers' rights to resow their own seeds, tightening the conditions for variety recognition by small independent entrepreneurs, and restricting the circulation and exchange of seeds between associations and growers, the European Commission is sweeping away ten thousand years of agricultural history. The incredible number of plant varieties we have today is based on the selection work of four hundred generations of men and women, and on the transmission of this knowledge to the next generation. Plant biodiversity can only be maintained by creating the conditions for a genuine partnership between networks of farmers and agronomists who don't see plants as mere repositories of DNA, but as living beings that evolve over the years, adapting to the new conditions they encounter.[28]

Green MP José Bové, an anarcho-syndicalist with a reputation for anti-communism, in unison with many of the anti-globalist currents that are regulars at the World Social Forum (WSF), describes, without naming it, a "utopia" that only Cuba's socialist society is in the process of concretely realizing today. Why such an omission?

Not all that Moves is Red, Not all that is Green is Sincere

The apparent antagonisms between sincere environmentalists and communists can easily be reconciled in the short and long term, either by recalling that the very construction of socialism saw the birth and development within it of the first aspirations to protect the environment, or by pointing out that the communist stage, with the extinction of the state, for which socialism is preparing as a transitional phase, will finally bring

---

27   **Translators' Note:** Peasant Confederation.

28   Speech quoted in "EU Seed Regulation," article dated May 6, 2013, *Les Verts*—Alliance Libre Européenne website.

all progressives to agree on a form of production unaffected by the state and its local strategies, rationalized around the real stakes for humanity beyond the class struggle: the protection of the natural resources people need to flourish.

What passed for "productivism" in the post-war socialist countries in the eyes of certain environmental activists was, at least in part, a struggle for survival and against the short-term encirclement of capitalism, when the productivism of the capitalist system is clearly part of its quest for maximum profit. There is a transitional tactic in the case of the latter, and a strategic choice in the case of the former.

In the eyes of communists, on the other hand, the diagnosis of political ecology combines objective elements, such as the petty-bourgeois characterization of its militant social base, with more debatable elements of demarcation concerning this notion of "productivism." Aware that a necessary political and ideological distinction had to be made between them and social democratic environmentalists, many communists end up positively claiming what they are accused of, for want of any other argument, all the more so at a time when the ideological setbacks, relative historical self-phobia and loss of ideological bearings in the communist movement are considerable.

Such communists would defend the strategic choices of nuclear power or fossil fuels, or even intensive agriculture and its agro-industry, through an unfortunate confusion between Marxism-Leninism and its revisionist Khrushchevian avatar, forgetting that the latter was built by simply pirating the American model.

On this point, we need to distinguish between strategic and tactical choices. For what is a strategic choice and a betrayal of Marxism in a country that at one time was the world's industrial leader, like the USSR, must be distinguished from the tactical, transitional choices of peoples fighting for their political and economic independence in times of imperialist war.

What's right at one stage of the struggle, such as Lenin's establishment of a NEP[29] in Russia in the early years of the revolution, becomes

---

29 By opening up a restricted capitalist market, the New Economic Policy (NEP) was intended, from 1921 onwards, to accumulate sufficient national capital to make the transition from a still largely feudal state to the first stages of socialist construction.

wrong or even reactionary once the country is in a position to concretely build socialism at a higher phase. Similarly, while socialist Cuba had to make do with fossil fuels supplied by the socialist camp in order to build up its economy in the early years of the revolution in the immediate vicinity of the imperialist giant, the country was later able to make the most of local renewable energies to guarantee its relative energy independence, and thus its freedom to save and redevelop its social model despite the disappearance of the Soviet "big brother."

If a state has just freed itself from the colonial yoke and inherited vast oil resources and the industrial infrastructure to exploit them, and is still unable to invest in other energy resources, can it be blamed for contributing to global carbon pollution? Of what political nature would this reproach be when you think of the decisive impact of global campaigns in support of workers throughout the world, when a people realizes the conditions for its liberation from the imperialist chain of war-makers?

The hydrocarbon wealth of a semi-colonial country is the object of imperialist covetousness, often not so much for its own supply as to keep it out of the hands of competitors. The USA's oil reserves are assured in Alaska or Texas, France's energy independence is guaranteed by its nuclear industry... but for these powers to ask a semi-colonial country to stop exploiting its oil for supposedly ecological reasons hardly conceals their desire to halt all trade with emerging, competing powers such as China or India.

The aim is not, however, to idealize the oil-rich origins of the capital that has made it possible to finance the reduction of poverty and illiteracy in a country like Venezuela, for example. Even less to blame it, when no other immediate solution can be envisaged, as the country is still largely underdeveloped due to its semi-feudal nature. We have to recognize that, dialectically, the transitory and tactical use of this oil contributes, contrary to its use in imperialist countries and even if the ecological impact is the same, to the consolidation of a system which, if it leads to independence and popular emancipation, without which no alternative energy can be exploited with the necessary financial investment.

In any case, it's quite clear whether capitalism or socialism, whatever their energy options at that moment, will be better able to overcome the fossil fuel shortage predicted for the coming decades. Only socialist planning can bring about this transition with enough realism, and without playing for time, as hypocritical capitalist states do at summit after climate summit. Only the weapon of dialectics allows us to understand that a socialist state sitting on an ocean of underground oil will always be more useful in the long run to the cause of global environmental protection than any capitalist state that has invested massively in renewable energies.

Indeed, capital's tactical acumen is well known when it comes to discrediting, demonizing or paralyzing the adversary. On this condition alone, it is able to invest massively at a loss, provided this investment does not last too long. In this way, imperialism did not hesitate to make the city of West Berlin, on the doorstep of the enemy East Germany, shine with a thousand lights, in order to arouse the envy of the latter's inhabitants. Today, we know the extent of the crisis in Europe, and it's been a long time since Berlin's neon lights shone only for the local high bourgeoisie.

Nor has imperialism hesitated to pull South Korea out of its underdevelopment by infusing it with billions of dollars, to no avail, in order to discredit the North Korean model, which initially welcomed thousands of economic refugees from the South.

On a more local, day-to-day scale, we know how private competitors, as soon as a market "opens up," are capable of drastically reducing their prices to economically break the nationalized company, before dividing the spoils between two or three of them and raising prices well above those initially charged by the public sector, once the latter is out of the picture.

Such a psychological trap should no longer mislead anyone: "green capitalism" is now contested by sincere environmental activists, even if they remain critical of "polluters" in the South. Only our internationalist support will enable these countries, once fully sovereign, to emerge from such polluting activities; certainly not our Western rantings, so opportune for our imperialist bourgeoisie.

For their part, many communist activists have forgotten their sense of dialectics, and have fallen into the habit of defending energy or agronomic options independently of context, as if a hydrocarbon- or uranium-rich subsoil were essential to guarantee greater social justice. This is a serious confusion between the struggle for national independence, a fundamental condition for social change in a *pre-socialist* context, and the construction of a society without state, class struggle or capital-nature contradiction in a *post-socialist* context, which is its logical and necessary outcome (communism).

Let's make no mistake about it: the sudden realization in industrialized countries of the harmful effects of carbon dioxide on the climate, through conferences such as COP21,[30] for example, is all about one thing: wrapping itself in the angelic wings of ecology to curb as far as possible the development of emerging powers such as China, Russia, Brazil and India, as well as that of a multitude of smaller countries taking advantage of the opportunities offered by this multipolarization of the world, and the consequent weakening of the old Occidental empires. The challenge is all the less "costly" for our "eco-responsible" empires in that their massive de-industrialization can progressively remove them from the list of major greenhouse gas emitters (even as they remain the main emitters).[31]

Germany, which today prides itself on being the European leader in the development of renewable energies, is still massively dependent on French nuclear power to meet its energy needs, and remains Europe's biggest polluter with its colossal coal extractions, inherited from the socialist German Democratic Republic (GDR). In the days of the GDR, on the other hand, fossil fuel production did not clash with its "non-consumerist" image, which was paradoxically mocked in the West. As in the entire socialist camp, the scarcity of private cars was not a virtue of "degrowth," as if everyone had to be satisfied with less, since the well-known development of free public transport, a social as well as an ecological accomplishment, more than met the needs of the *Ossis*.[32]

When eco-socialist and some communist activists become aware

---

30   The *UN Climate Change Conference COP21* brought together delegations from all countries in Paris at the end of 2015 to establish a framework convention to limit greenhouse gas emissions worldwide.

31   In absolute terms, China (10 Giga tonnes of carbon) has outstripped the USA (5 GT) and the EU (4 GT) in recent years, while in terms of production per inhabitant, a more honest value, the USA (20 T/h) and the EU (10 T/h) continue to outstrip China (8 T/h).

32   **Translators' Note:** Citizens of the former GDR.

of and draw the political conclusions from this necessary distinction between energy provision tactics and strategy, between the complex intricacies of the struggle against Capital and the concrete construction of socialism at a higher stage, a major step will have been taken in the general struggle against those truly responsible for global environmental catastrophes.

1

AGROECOLOGY:
A LITTLE-KNOWN SOCIALIST ACHIEVEMENT

A Workers' Victory for the Environment is Better than a Dozen Kyoto Protocols[1]

LOCATED IN GÉMENOS NEAR MARSEILLES, *Fralib* is a packaging plant owned by the food giant *Unilever*, of the famous *Elephant* teas.[2] Following a plan to relocate to Poland, the struggle of the plant's eighty or so workers to preserve their jobs and keep the factory open had been marked by numerous episodes and twists and turns over the past five years, but finally ended in victory.

The plant was occupied despite threats and violence from employer militias, wage suppression, lay-offs and anti-union repression (the CGT[3], with a majority in the plant, had expanded to cover most of the workers during the struggle), a nationwide boycott campaign of *Unilever* brands, legal and media battles, the omnipresence of the *fralibiens* in all union actions opposing the liberal policies of Sarkozy and then Hollande... This battle between the David of Provence and the Goliath of agribusiness was a highly significant victory for the working class as a whole. It meant the recovery of production revenues and the creation of a brand of teas and infusions, the resumption of industrial activity and the current presence on commercial platforms nationwide. With the name "1336" referring

---

1 "Every step forward, every real advance, matters more than a dozen programs": Karl Marx's famous materialist formula in *Critique of the Gotha Program* (1875).

2 **Editor's Note:** A famous brand of tea in France, since 1927. It was taken over by a Unilever subsidiary in 1975. The strike described here began in 2010.

3 **Translators' Note:** *Confédération Générale du Travail*, the largest Trade Union Confederation in France by voting results for representative bodies and second largest by membership.

to the number of days this formidable workers' adventure lasted, which spread throughout France and inspired many a site of struggle where they would export their militant know-how, criss-crossing the country without respite. It was a true vanguard of the working class against the then current liberal policies pursued in the name of big business.

But there is one aspect of this struggle that is more specifically ecological. The products now packaged are certified "organic." Without the capacity to compete with the market giant *Lipton* (Unilever) on quantity, one must go to quality to stay in business. Linden tree leaves from Cooperative 1336 are harvested locally in Provence, while other teas are imported from Vietnam, where they are grown without pesticides. Such partnerships are no accident. The CGT-FNAF,[4] the CGT's agri-food branch, is renowned for its revolutionary commitments, and remains the only CGT branch to be a member of the World Federation of Trade Unions (WFTU), the historic organization of revolutionary and internationalist trade unions. Under the impetus of the FNAF, Fralib CGT leaders had traveled to Vietnam and Cuba to meet with local trade unions and learn from their know-how in managing state-owned companies.

So it is interesting to note that an emblematic struggle in the French working class in recent years has resulted in the production and distribution of "organic" products at reasonable prices. It's fair to say that the ecological "cause" has progressed faster through this struggle alone (in which the militants don't necessarily have environmental protection as their immediate priority, since they're fighting to preserve jobs), than through years of abstract propaganda by movements with a petty bourgeois composition. It's a valuable lesson.

But it's important to analyze the situation from a materialist point of view: the transformation of this union struggle into a political one—as is the nature of workers' struggles when they are offensive—was reflected in the demand for nationalization by the State, which had to be made to face up to its responsibilities and its many more or less official promises. If this was no longer possible, as the collective was committed to a takeover of the now "self-managed" factory, the fight for nationalization of the *Eléphant*

---

4   **Translators' Note:** *Fédération Nationale Agroalimentaire et Forestière*—The National Federation of Agri-Food and Forestry.

"band" continued, since Unilever obviously refused to give up the label.

Thus, even the most symptomatic of current struggles, albeit victorious like this one, has never ceased to politically demand commitments from the government or local authorities. This clearly shows that self-management is not a model that can be extrapolated to the scale of the country, even if it must be protected and strongly supported. No tactical illusions or reproducible magic formulas for future struggles, as was once the case with the "LIP watches,"[5] for example, for their former anarcho-unionist and reformist lauders.

An "organic" brand can only gain a foothold in the market—dominated, as we all know, by the giants of the polluting agro-industry—if it receives serious commitments, aid, and subsidies from the State. Without this, the balance of power is inevitably unfavorable. To raise the question of the anti-liberal, anti-capitalist struggle, as well as that of environmental protection, we must at the same time raise the political question of power on a national scale. Here's a prime example.

THE CUBAN EXAMPLE: AGROECOLOGY "IN ONE COUNTRY"

We may recall how Trotsky and his followers challenged the Bolsheviks and Lenin's assertion of the possibility of building socialism "in one country" to begin with, considering that the revolution could only be a worldwide conflagration or nothing at all. They called it the theory of permanent revolution, a combination of impatience and adventurism.

History has shown that socialism took root in the USSR for over seventy years, and that this did not prevent other peoples from following in its footsteps throughout the 20th century. Cuba was an illustrious example.

Socialist Cuba is both the survivor of the socialist camp of the 1990s, and a globally recognized beacon of agroecology at the turn of the century. In its 2006 annual report, the WWF (*World Wide Fund for Nature; World Wildlife Fund* in the US and Canada), the world's largest environmental protection organization, stated that Cuba is the only country in the world to have achieved sustainable development:

---

5   **Editor's Note:** LIP is a French watch and clock company whose turmoil became emblematic of the conflicts between workers and capital in France.

Sustainable development is a commitment to improving the quality of human life while living within the limits of the ecosystems that sustain us. The Human Development Index is used by the United Nations Development Program (UNDP) as an indicator of well-being, and the [ecological] footprint is a measure of demands on the biosphere. The progress of nations towards sustainable development can therefore be measured by cross-referencing the HDI and the footprint. The HDI is calculated on the basis of life expectancy, literacy, education and GDP per capita. The UNDP considers a country to have a high Human Development Index if its HDI value is above 0.8. For the footprint, a footprint of less than 1.8 global hectares per person, i.e. the average biocapacity available per person, is considered indicative of sustainability on a global scale. Successful sustainable development implies at least that the world as a whole meets both criteria [...]. Neither the world as a whole, nor any individual region, meets both criteria for sustainable development. Only Cuba does, according to the data it provides to the United Nations.[6]

Another major organization, the *Global Footprint Network*, which also calculates national and global trends in the human ecological footprint, produced a similar statement. In the same year, the *Energy Globe* world prize, awarded by several international institutions including the UN to reward initiatives aimed at developing and making renewable energies profitable in relation to natural resources, was awarded to the The University of Oriente—Santiago de Cuba.

Cuba's revolutionary history and socialist commitment are the main reasons why it sets an example to the world in terms of environmental protection.[7] In this respect, the large Caribbean island is no exception, since, as we shall see later, the Soviet Union had distinguished itself as a world pioneer of agroecology before the turn of the fifties, at a time when, incidentally, no one in the West was concerned about the environment.

But it should be noted that this feat was achieved, to such worldwide recognition, despite Western propaganda against anything that evokes socialism, and against a backdrop of increasingly severe economic embargoes by the USA during the "special period" of the 1990s. And it is essential for all sincere environmental activists to draw the political conclusions: only a socialist state in charge of the national economy can and must successfully implement such a sustainable and ecological ag-

---

    6   WWF, *Living Planet Report 2006*, p. 21.

    7   But it is also true, in the fields of education and health, it should be stressed, as these three sectors of the Cuban economy are intimately linked.

ricultural project, independently of the disastrous global input market. No capitalist state is in a position to achieve a tenth of this feat, because it presupposes national planning that bans intensive agriculture (which competes to the death with any desire for organic farming on its domestic market) at the same time and throughout the country, while mobilizing the indispensable human, educational, scientific and technical resources.

From the Cuban revolution in 1959 under Khrushchev, to the collapse of the Soviet bloc in 1990, the model developed on the Caribbean island followed that of the USSR—blinded by its obsession with catching up with the American model—intensive agriculture based on massive use of chemical fertilizers and pesticides, and extensive mechanization (including several thousand Russian tractors, in particular). While this model enabled rapid economic and social development, it did not call into question the monoculture system characteristic of semi-colonies,[8] based essentially on sugarcane production. Virtually all of Cuba's agricultural production was shipped to socialist countries, which in turn supplied Cuba with hydrocarbons at preferential prices (four or five times below world prices).

In essence, this kind of exchange of goodwill resembles the reciprocal services currently offered by the Latin American members of ALBA (*Bolivarian Alliance for the Americas*), to which Cuba now exports its trained doctors and organic fertilizers rather than its cane sugar. But this kind of interdependence, while it helps to avoid autarkic blockage, remains a fragile foundation for the Cuban economy, when a partner is lost to a pro-imperialist putsch...

The nineties were a time of miraculous resilience, with the "special peacetime period." When 80% of food and energy imports vanished overnight, the people experienced an unprecedented crisis: power failures lasting several days, food shortages, the virtual disappearance of public transport, widespread technical lay-offs... In a context aggravated by the tightening of economic constraints linked to the deadly embargo imposed by the United States. The U.S. had no qualms about taking ad-

---

8   In colonial times, each empire unilaterally over-exploited the resources of its colonies, with a tendency towards specialization: Algerian oil, Moroccan and Tunisian phosphates, Vietnamese or Congolese rubber, Cuban sugar cane, and so on. In many cases, the entire territory was devoted to a single product, with all the population's subsistence products being imported from metropolitan France (thus relieving its own market).

vantage of the catastrophic situation to tighten the noose even further, in the hope that the system would collapse in on itself even faster, as it had been dreaming of happening since 1959. The *Helms-Burton* Act, designed to topple Fidel Castro and install a U.S.-subordinate government in Havana, was accompanied by additional restrictions over the course of the decade to punish any surrounding vessel that had contact with the Cuban coast, as well as any state trading in any way with Cuba... But the "Castro regime" finally achieved a tour de force with a veritable "green revolution," long before the recent diplomatic victories that led to the gradual loosening of the blockade.⁹

The NGO group *AgriCulture Network*, unlikely to be suspected of Castroist sympathy, makes it clear that the island's green revolution is not the result of historical necessity alone, nor of the spontaneity or voluntarism of the peasants, but of the force of state levers and planning:

> Several components of the system were already in use [in the 1990s]: production centers for biological pest control, pilot agroecological farms, training in organic farming, organopónicos (raised garden beds) in urban areas and the development of a social movement promoting organic farming (the Cuban Association for Organic Agriculture and Organic Agriculture Group). The motivation behind the emergence of agroecological practices in Cuba in the 1990s was not, however, the result of a deliberate change of mentality on the part of the population, but rather the need to ensure self-sufficiency. [...] The absence of agrochemicals does not necessarily suppose an ecological production system; such a conversion requires a conscious decision. Arguments drawn from Cuban research and projects suggest that organic production is technically feasible and economically viable as an important part of a nation's food security strategy. Cuba's success in improving food security, and agricultural productivity more generally, has demonstrated what can be achieved when the political will is there.¹⁰

The state quickly made food a matter of national security, and encouraged agricultural production methods that were still in their infancy, or even non-existent in the West: shared mixed farming and livestock, development of "organic" urban and peri-urban agriculture, autonomous production of seed varieties with the aim of strengthening biodi-

---

9   **Editor's Note:** Since the book was written any 'loosening of the blockade' has been reversed by the subsequent American administrations.

10   Julia Wright International Programme, Henry Doubleday Research Association, Ryton Organic Gardens, Coventry—published on agriculturesnetwork.org.

versity and the country's agricultural independence from internationally patented seeds, massive reforestation and the development of a highly competitive model of agroforestry and mixed farming, without any pesticides or chemical fertilizers. At the same time, the ban on pesticides in the area explains why bees are thriving there, while elsewhere on the planet they are on the brink of extinction.[11]

Soil restoration techniques and the production of organic fertilizers and earthworms are at the cutting edge of current innovations in agroecology. It is the only country in the world to have achieved this feat, and today covers 70% of local food requirements for vegetables and fruit.

Reporter Geoffrey Couanon, author of the documentary *Si se puede!*, explains how Cuba offers far greater potential than a country like France when it comes to making ecological choices:

> In Cuba, the government can define a political choice and organize the rules of the economic game. We're in countries with a market economy, where we have rulers who say: "I'd like to be able to do that, but if I decide to go that way, we'll have capital flight; if I decide to favor local companies, I'm at odds with the World Trade Organization." [...] In France, there has been a rapid and strong concentration of land, and a decline in the number of farmers. In Cuba, there has been an extraordinary redistribution of land: in ten years, over one and a half million hectares! On a French scale, this would mean the Midi-Pyrénées and Aquitaine regions combined.
>
> In France, the prevailing view is that the two types of farming can coexist very well, that we can have peasant farming and then more intensive, more export-oriented agriculture. But it's very complicated to talk about agroecology

---

11   "Threatened almost everywhere in the world by devastating pesticides, bees may have found their little corner of paradise: Cuba. Why Cuba? Because this country abandoned pesticides in the 1990s. Given that our entire ecosystem depends to a large extent on the survival of bees, this may well be the model to follow. [...] In Cuba, some beekeepers manage to collect 45 kg of honey per hive. To give you an idea, the average production in France would be half that. These spectacular yields have even made organic honey Cuba's fourth-largest export. Production in 2014 even reached 7,200 tonnes, for a total estimated value of $23.3 million! [...] Cuba's record honey production (organic, no less) is obviously good news for the sector and for honey lovers. But beyond this simple fact, it is also, and above all, good news for humanity. The Cuban example proves that not using pesticides can save bees. Bees are the planet's main pollinating insect and, as such, are responsible for much of what we eat, and therefore for our survival on Earth!" (*In a pesticide-free country, Cuban bees are in great shape!* Axel Leclercq, January 27, 2017, PositivR).

and at the same time talk about competitiveness with all that goes with it, i.e. cheap labor on farms, industrial agriculture.

Do we want a human-scale peasant agroecology with a multitude of farmers, or an intensive supermarket agroecology with a handful of agromanagers who can choose how they want to feed us? These are two very different social projects.[12]

It is estimated that with such food independence in the hypothetical case of a total interruption of imports, in the event of war for example, Cuba would be much less at risk than France, which only has around four days' reserves in its supermarkets.[13]

These results have nothing to do with the benevolent application of the directives of some well-meaning world summit, such as COP21. On the contrary, they reflect the renunciation of a former colony fighting for its food, energy, and political independence—an independence that the depletion of the world's natural resources has made impossible. A socialist superstructure [that is, socialist governance] would enable organic farming to be implemented throughout the country, without unfair private competition based on intensive agriculture.

This exemplary result is based on material achievements stemming from the production relationships established on the island: reasoned and harmonious planning on a national scale, a well-developed education and health system capable of spreading awareness of environmental issues to the entire population at school, and large-scale training in agroecology-related techniques for agricultural and electrical engineers, and for the farming community itself.

Let's not forget that, over and above the harmful effects of the non-ecological practices that marked the period of partnership with the post-Khrushchev USSR, the significant benefits of these in terms of national development enabled such an educational system to surpass that of the whole of Latin America, thus enabling today's national agroecology to be placed on a solid footing, unlike all the countries that lived through the same period with no improvements or even net setbacks.

---

12   Interview given to *Reporterre* magazine—'Cuba, the country where agroecology is really applied,' December 2014.

13   Source CESER (*Conseil Economique Social et Environnemental Ile de France*).

While the Cuban population represents almost 2% of the total Latin American population, it includes more than 11% of the sub-continent's scientists, corresponding to an enormous human resource capable of propagating the indispensable knowledge without which organic farming could not develop, in a peasantry spontaneously attached to its habits and resistant to techniques reputed (wrongly) to be unproductive.

In the space of a decade, the country has emerged from the food crisis, doubling its agricultural production and increasing its sources of calories by 25%, while maintaining a perfectly equitable social distribution system. In France, for example, this redistribution is particularly unfair, with prices for "organic" food being prohibitive for the working classes...

In particular, the country is committed to maximizing seed biodiversity, a guarantee of food sovereignty. To a certain extent, this aspiration makes it possible to avoid the use of pesticides to combat pests and diseases. Biodiversity helps to limit losses in the event of epidemics, as certain varieties are more resistant to disease than others, and therefore have a chance of surviving if others are decimated by a parasite, a disease, or a sudden change in the environment.

But more broadly speaking, pest control requires specific skills in polycultures (some species of which protect their neighbors from pests, for example) and natural pesticides based on plant products. It therefore requires a high level of theoretical knowledge, which our "chemistry-fixated" agronomists, who swear by synthetic molecules and short-term solutions, have forgotten.

Finally, field fertilization is based on the reintroduction of soil flora and fauna, wiped out by chemical fertilizers and pesticides when agriculture is intensive. Earthworm and mushroom farms have been set up in direct collaboration with agricultural workers' cooperatives. Cuban organic fertilizers and compost are now even exported throughout Latin America.

Cutting-edge techniques include *cover cropping*,[14] whose aim is to protect the texture and life-forms of cultivated soils, in contrast to the

---

14 **Translators' Note:** Cover crops involve the sowing and growth of plants appropriate to local climate and agroecosystem to reduce water and wind erosion as well as, among other beneficial effects, replenish soil's organic matter, which contains plant nutrients.

bare soils of intensive agriculture destroyed by chemicals and plowing, but also, and perhaps above all, agroforestry. Agroforestry is based on the principle of alternating trees and crops, with significant advantages in terms of productivity.[15]

Ten thousand Cuban families have adopted this technique in the last decade. Once again, this explosion is the result of nationwide peasant coordination through the ANAP (the National Association of Cuban Small Farmers), linked to the centralization of the socialist system. Farmers are seeing tangible results. In 2008, for example, all the residential monocultures were decimated by a tornado in the provinces of Las Tunas and Alguin, while the agroforestry plots saved half their harvests, the trees protecting the market garden crops on the ground from the force of the wind and rain.

Cuba is one of the few countries in the world whose forest area is larger than it was fifty years ago, and is still growing. The island boasts 23 national parks and 6,300 protected plant species, 51% of which are endemic.

When it comes to energy independence, Cuba is not to be outdone. With a 14.5% rise in investment in this sector for the Central America/Caribbean region in 2015, the area is pulling up relative to the other continents (Asia with 12.4%, largely thanks to China, and far behind North America with 3.6% and Europe with 5.2%).

Considered a veritable energy revolution, its program launched in 2007 has cut kerosene consumption by 66%, gas consumption by 60% and oil consumption by 20%, without any of its famous social, educational, or health programs suffering as a result—a feat in itself.

This program is based first and foremost on energy savings. As President Fidel Castro put it in 2006: "We're not going to wait for oil to fall from the sky, because fortunately we've discovered something even more important: energy savings, which is like discovering a great deposit of oil." Within nine months, 100% of the country's filament bulbs, notorious for their energy losses, had been replaced free of charge by more

---

15   The present book contains an appendix ('Trees are the Masters of the Soil,' see pp. 173-176) recalling the basic scientific elements of soil functioning and the multiple interests of agroforestry. See also Appendix 4: 'Cuban Socialism and Agroecology: Mutually Reinforcing' on pp. 187-192.

environmentally-friendly fluorescent bulbs. In 1997, the Ministry of Education's National Energy Saving Program (PAEME) introduced young Cubans and workers to energy-saving measures.

But the program also concerns the development of renewable energies themselves: 2,364 rural schools have been equipped with solar panels, giving all pupils the same access to lighting, computers and televised educational programs. Countless rural clinics have been similarly equipped. As a result, Cuba was awarded the "Global 500" prize by the United Nations in 2001.

In recent years, the network of the public electricity distribution companies (the National Electric Union) has been completely renovated to limit losses due to obsolescence. With all these measures, it is estimated, for example, that Cuba saved almost a million tons of oil in 2006-2007.

One hundred wind power stations are currently being installed in eleven provinces, and two new wind farms have been built, giving a total output of 7.23 megawatts for the country as a whole. The first grid-connected solar power plant is under construction, as are three hundred biogas stations, recycling animal waste to make cooking fuel.

Last but not least, the island has developed its own unique biofuel production system. As a matter of principle, the island refuses to produce fuel at the expense of food production, which would be the most dramatic solution, on a national scale and probably on a global scale, to offset the programmed depletion of fossil fuels by multiplying famines. On the other hand, it is possible to extract a highly appropriate form of energy from the vegetable waste of mass-grown sugar cane ('bagasse'). While wind power grew by almost 16% over the period 2001-2012, it was energy from such biomass that saw the greatest growth at the end of the period (2011-2012), at +22.3%. Bagasse power plants have an annual production capacity of 478.5 megawatts. This form of energy is ecologically neutral, inexpensive unlike solar or hydroelectric plants, and does not have the disadvantage of being intermittent as is the case with wind or solar power. During the sugarcane harvest season (four to six months of the year), this production supplies 30% of the electricity grid!

Why it Works in Cuba and not Elsewhere

The Cuban "miracle" illustrates this double necessity: on the one hand, the construction of a sovereign socialist system necessarily implies the preservation of its own resources, in terms of both agriculture and energy, and thus an agroecological plan. On the other hand, environmental protection can only be achieved in a socialist system, with sufficient yield and a high technical level, without parasitism or unfair competition from short-termist agribusiness.

We know that bits and pieces of agroecological development exist in countries like France and Germany. We also know that socialist countries have historically developed without any concern for the environment, as was the case in the contemporary revolutions of the post-Khrushchev Soviet Union. But these are partial realities, which show that nothing is absolutely mechanical or linear. In fact, it is the economic and social gains accumulated by the exploitation of fossil resources themselves over an entire period which, when the time came, enabled the national investment needed to organize such a large-scale agroecological model. That's the difference with capitalist countries that continue to pollute massively and unscrupulously between various "national climate conferences" despite major solemn commitments.

It's possible to create and even defend, for a time at least, beleaguered islands of socialism on the very territory of a capitalist country, whether it's a social security system, a factory reclaimed and "self-managed" by the workers, an "organic" farm operating on a semi-autonomous exchange system, or a town whose municipality finances the strike funds of the surrounding factories... All this is perfectly possible, and desirable, because these are, to paraphrase Lenin on trade union struggles, "schools of socialism."

But the most advanced workers know that such victories are often one-offs, never guaranteed to last. One way or another, capital, conqueror by nature, will reverse its own setbacks as soon as it is stronger, or as soon as we are weaker. The only relative guarantee that these advances will have a modicum of stability is a revolutionary outcome, the overthrow of the system itself.

In other words, if the protagonists of such partial struggles, having won a particular victory or made a particular advance, theorize their local strategy as a model that can be applied simply by increasing the number of people on the ground (i.e., without any revolutionary "qualitative leap" in the long term), as was the case with the "self-management" anarcho-syndicalist currents, they'll be off to a flying start, without vigilance, and will sooner or later come up against brutal setbacks.

Conversely, the nihilism of certain leftists who seek to discredit any punctual advance as "lost in advance" and therefore "counter-revolutionary" will be no less disconcerting. Revolution is not called for by armchair readings and a mystical millenarianism that puts the "world revolution," a distant substitute for the Last Judgment, on a level that no current struggle can reach.

In this sense, the example of Cuban agroecology shows how ecological proposals can, to a certain extent, be coordinated, materialized and developed, when the superstructure is favorable to them. At the same time, it shows how a country under siege and struggling to build socialism has no choice but to impose so-called "sustainable" techniques on its soil. By extension, it can be said that all anti-colonial struggles, whether in Asia, Africa or Latin America, have at least begun this work of developing organic farming.

The full implementation of Cuban agroecology is inspired by a first historical experience in an anti-imperialist context during the 1980s: that of Burkina Faso, once governed by the Marxist Thomas Sankara. It shows once again how a revolutionary struggle, through the planned mobilization of national productive forces, can make this possible, with far greater success than the fragile experiments emerging in European capitalist countries. The education system and the capacity for popular mobilization were the two prerequisites: relations of production and productive forces.

The main aim was to protect and regenerate an environment seriously degraded by the colonial presence: massive deforestation, soil erosion and damage caused by intensive livestock farming. The political program was based on a number of emergency measures taken at the very start of the Burkinabé revolution: the "three struggles" campaign (against deforestation, against bush fires, against the roaming of livestock), an educational campaign in schools to sensitize pupils to the cause of the environment, and a broader campaign to protect the environment. These include the "one school, one grove" program, the widespread use of "improved stoves," popular harvests of forest seeds, the systematic establishment of village tree nurseries, and the creation of a Ministry of Water.

Thomas Sankara didn't want to stop there, and devoted himself to a transnational project in partnership with other Sahelian countries: the "great green belt." Its scope and proactive nature may have reminded some people of the Soviet "Great Plan for the Transformation of Nature" of the late 1940s.[16]

All these voluntarist campaigns were based, it should be noted, on forms of struggle in defense of traditional culture (undermined by imperialism), to which the peasantry was particularly sensitive. These were all abandoned after the assassination of Sankara and the overthrow of the government in 1987, with a return to the French colonial past and destructive agricultural practices. Pierre Rabhi, a Burkinabé permaculturist with a high profile in the media and influential in ecosocialist activism, witnessed this adventure for himself, and remains an admirer of the Marxist leader.

While such campaigns are to be applauded in Asia, Africa, and Latin America today, it's clear that none have been entirely satisfactory, either because the experiment was brought to a halt by a putsch and a return to destructive neo-colonialism, or because it was unable to benefit from the massive investment that only a state in transition to socialism can allocate to agroecology, as is currently the case in Cuba.

THE FIRST HISTORICAL OVERCOMING OF THE CITY-COUNTRY CONTRADICTION

These revolutionary experiences of the 20th century, more or less successful, must lead the sincere environmentalist movement to reject anti-communism, and must also lead to the communist movement's rejection of the fable of a "productivist" socialism, which is fundamentally tied to the over-publicized but deceptive model imposed by Khrushchev and his successors.

---

16   This involved planting trees over huge areas as part of an agroforestry-type project. This will be discussed in greater detail in the second part of this study.

The most successful environmental protection projects in Cuba, in particular urban and peri-urban organic subsistence farming, are geared towards overcoming one of the most famous contradictions identified by Marx and Engels, and later Lenin, namely the urban-rural contradiction. And it is in the resolution of this non-antagonistic opposition that most modern environmentalist projects reside. For Engels:

> Only a society which makes it possible for its productive forces to dovetail harmoniously into each other on the basis of one single vast plan can allow industry to be distributed over the whole country in the way best adapted to its own development, and to the maintenance and development of the other elements of production.
>
> Accordingly, abolition of the antithesis between town and country is not merely possible. It has become a direct necessity of industrial production itself, just as it has become a necessity of agricultural production and, besides, of public health. The present poisoning of the air, water and land can be put an end to only by the fusion of town and country; and only such fusion will change the situation of the masses now languishing in the towns, and enable their excrement to be used for the production of plants instead of for the production of disease. [...]
>
> The abolition of the separation of town and country is therefore not utopian, also, in so far as it is conditioned on the most equal distribution possible of modern industry over the whole country. It is true that in the huge towns civilisation has bequeathed us a heritage which it will take much time and trouble to get rid of. But it must and will be got rid of, however, protracted a process it may be.[17]

While some may have seen in this aspiration of the first communist theorists an absorption of the countryside by the industrial cities, we shall see below how it reveals, on the contrary, the need to combine the development of the productive forces—indispensable to the building of socialism and then communism—with the need to protect the environment. It should also be noted that the rural exodus has been halted in Cuba thanks to the development of its agroecology and the indisputable improvement in living conditions for the island's farmers.

We're not talking here about the "sharing of misery" that would be imposed by a return to an agropastoral Middle Ages, or even to the Neolithic communism preceding the class struggle, but about a "sharing of wealth," to which both rural and urban workers should be entitled, once

17 Engels, F. *Anti-Dühring*, 1878.

the capitalist exploitation they've all had to endure has been overcome.

Today's agroecologists know that the widespread adoption of environmentally-friendly farming techniques cannot be compared to a "return to the Middle Ages," nor can it consist of the overnight cessation of intensive farming techniques. With the current world population, the only feudal trait we could find there, if such were the case, is not a romantic "return to Nature" but a very real return to famine.

To take full advantage of a country's agroecological potential, a society's productive forces must be developed, not "reduced." A good example of this is the story told in 1934 by a Soviet *kolkhoz* (cooperative farm) manager during collectivization. It talks of polyculture, which regenerates cultivated soils in contrast to monoculture, which tends to exhaust them, while avoiding the use of pesticides (indispensable in intensive monoculture) thanks to the mutual protection of certain plants grown together against pests:

> We could very well introduce other crops, but they would require the use of other machines, or even more capital. During the period when these machines are inactive, they would also weigh on the farm without producing anything. They would therefore reduce income. The same would be true if we introduced the cultivation of fodder in rotation with wheat and other cereals, in short if we adopted the ordinary and accustomed system of poly-culture. [...] The introduction of crop variety on the large mechanized farm brings with it the need not only for new installations and new machines, but also for new technical frameworks. The more machines the workers will have to use, the less they will know about them and the less they will like them.[18]

It's obvious that polyculture, among other alternative techniques, requires capital to buy more agricultural equipment, and specific training for peasants in the use of this equipment and agronomic knowledge of the strategies to be implemented. In other words, it requires a high level of training for the entire peasantry, and, as Marxism predicts under communism, reduces the virtual frontier between manual and intellectual labor.

Large-scale agroecology can only result from an economic and civilizational leap forward, as only socialism can guarantee in the long term.

---

18   Reported in *La collectivisation des campagnes soviétiques*, Guido Miglioli, 1934.

Hydrocarbons: An Energy "NEP" for Certain Anti-Imperialist States

From a historical angle, and without forgetting the sense of dialectic that many analysts lack, we need to understand the energy strategy of certain countries in the South, including Cuba, in the particularly complex context of anti-imperialist liberation. Countries such as Venezuela, Bolivia, Angola, Algeria, Libya, Nigeria and many others are renowned for the hydrocarbon wealth of their subsoil. Depending on the nature of the state that holds this wealth, it is either a windfall for the people or for imperialism and the local bourgeoisie who sell themselves to it. And it is this distinction that must prevail in any political analysis of the country.

When the subsoil is exploited by imperialism, it's for the sole benefit of a global oligarchy linked to degenerating, warmongering finance capital, blocking the productive forces on a massive scale. The wealth produced is therefore, at best, at an economic loss for those countries. At worst, the wealth produced leads to throwing people into situations of war and chaos, a return to the Middle Ages.

When it is nationalized by an anti-imperialist popular government, such as that of Venezuela or Bolivia, the redistribution of the wealth produced enables spectacular advances in health and education, and a genuine reduction in poverty. In fact, this is what guarantees popular support for the leaders of such countries to a certain extent, as the people have never before been able to benefit from oil rents.

Even Cuba's exemplary agroecology survives largely thanks to oil imports from ALBA countries, in exchange for exports of medical and alternative energy know-how. Although Cuba is gradually developing the means to achieve energy sovereignty, it is still largely dependent on fossil fuels, and does not have the means to switch overnight to so-called clean energies, unlike the world's richest countries, which, with political will, could provide themselves with the means for a genuine energy transition.[19]

---

19   Moreover, a relative shift away from fossil fuels seems much simpler when it comes to switching to nuclear power, as has been done in France (where nuclear power accounts for 74% of the country's electricity production), than when it comes to switching to clean energy sources. Germany, which is presented as a model of transitioning away from nuclear power and to clean energy, still largely depends on coal mining, which, it

But even under such conditions, this energy policy—which is certainly reprehensible in absolute terms if we consider only the environmental issue in isolation—enables the accumulation of wealth and the development of productive forces capable of financing and organizing, through a high-performance education system, the training of local agronomists and farmers in agroecology and alternative energies. Productive forces also need to be built up to modernize energy supply and distribution infrastructures. And we mustn't forget that, in the long term, the extraction of hydrocarbons will be limited and will have to be abandoned in favor of other solutions, which must be planned and financed now. Only planning and state intervention can ensure the feasibility of such a policy.

It is therefore absurd to condemn the vital hydrocarbon extraction in Bolivia or Venezuela as "a negative aspect" of the system. It is positively the only solution based on national resources for building a country-wide ecological alternative, even if the predatory imperialist powers will understandably be quick to exploit this apparent contradiction for their own political interests.

To ask a country with an oil resource today to stop exploiting it immediately, in the name of environmental protection, suggesting that we can develop another anti-imperialist model, even if it's slower and more fragile... is to ask the impossible. No poor country can build an independent, ecological alternative without the support of its own resources, even temporarily, and it takes time and investment for this country to be able to implement an independent, concrete and solidly grounded agroecological project. It's not enough to decide to stop everything and tell farmers they're going back to the age of the plow for production that feeds—barely—only themselves. On the contrary, agroecology requires a high level of technical expertise, a high level of training in biology for agronomists and farmers to know how to grow crops with a sufficient yield, and modern infrastructures, including energy supplies for farms.

In a way, we can say that countries fighting for their sovereignty against imperialism can only build such a system in return for a polluting initial investment, unlike rich countries which, if the state were not bourgeois, could achieve the same result without this unfortunate transition stage.

---

should be noted, is far more polluting than hydrocarbons extraction itself.

It's a process reminiscent of the famous *New Economic Policy* (NEP) in the early years of revolutionary Russia. Coming out of a devastating war, in a country still largely dominated by feudalism and the peasantry, the soviets instigated a transitional policy during which the market economy would once again be authorized, under supervision. This made it possible to rapidly accumulate the wealth needed for collectivization, the foundation of socialist construction.

Lenin once said: "We are not yet civilized enough to move directly to socialism, although we have the political premises."[20]

We can state without hesitation that the implementation of a project such as Cuban agroecology requires not the negation of the local context and an adventurous voluntarism, but on the contrary a "civilizational" leap, a renewal of modernity, both in the relations of production and in the productive forces. From this point of view, "tactical retreat" is the only option for a pragmatic anti-imperialist leader concerned with the interests of his people. Every militant who has ever led a struggle on his own scale knows this.

However, in the infinite diversity of anti-imperialist struggles, opportunist tendencies have developed within the world communist movement itself, born of the apparent blockage of the contradiction between the necessary development of productive forces and the equally necessary protection of environmental resources. The worldwide revolutionary ebb triggered by the collapse of the socialist camp can partly explain these drifts, which are currently fermenting in the "ecosocialist" movement. It tries to resolve this contradiction by turning one's back on the teachings of socialist Cuba. One exists in the imperialist centers where the Trotskyist movement may have had some harmful influence in the post-Soviet period, while another exists in the periphery, with the highly significant example of the former Kurdish Communist Party (PKK).

THE INCONSEQUENTIALITY OF GREEN TROTSKYISM

The Trotskyist movement, reputed to be a "workers' movement" and little inclined towards considering peasant issues from the outset, had no theoretical affinity with the struggle to protect the environment. From

---

20   Lenin, 'Better Fewer, but Better,' 1923.

the very first years of the Russian Revolution, Trotsky believed that the countryside had to be collectivized immediately, regardless of the state of the peasantry's level of development at the time, and before the "NEP" had delivered on expected results. He had nothing but contempt and suspicion for the peasants, considering them to be by nature a reactionary, feudal social stratum.

On the contrary, Lenin wanted a revolutionary state for the proletariat *and* peasantry. Driven from within by intense class struggles between the poor peasantry and feudal landowners, the aim was of course not to leave this ultra-majority class in the country at the mercy of "white" counter-revolutionaries, but to rally it to the revolutionary prospects opened up by the working class *by* satisfying its immediate needs. The many polemics and political conflicts between Lenin and Trotsky between 1902 and 1920 essentially revolved around the peasant question and its revolutionary potential in the perspective of socialism, with Trotsky holding working-class and Eurocentric positions on the subject.

Moreover, of all the intellectuals who claimed to be Marxists, Trotsky was the one who spoke least, if at all, about the environmental question, and ultimately took a very dim view of what, beyond *historical materialism* (allowing the analysis of the history of class struggles), constituted *dialectical materialism* for Marxist-Leninists (allowing the analysis of matter in general and in all its extent, including human history but also natural history). For many Trotskyists, this "dialectical materialist" broadening undoubtedly constitutes a risk of ontological "dogmatism" in Marxism and of potential for "totalitarianism."

For all these reasons, we can explain why the Trotskyist movement has never really taken root in semi-colonies and national liberation struggles, whereas it has been able to flourish relatively well in imperialist centers where the working class is quantitatively more developed, when traditional organizations (parties, unions) have tended to weaken. It denies any progressive or revolutionary potential to national independence struggles that do not immediately translate into socialist revolution, believing that the working class should not ally itself with other social strata during the struggle, and that national liberation has no anti-imperialist character (weakening imperialism by depriving it of its capital-exporting zones on the periphery) independent of an immediate, worldwide socialist revolution.

We know that the Trotskyists distinguished themselves from Leninism with their theory of "permanent revolution" (revolution must spread throughout the world at once, starting from a revolutionary focus, otherwise it is doomed to failure), as opposed to "socialism in one country" (the theory that it is possible to build socialism in one country or a group of countries, despite capitalist encirclement). It's easy to understand why revolutionaries in the colonies had little interest in this particularly defeatist and counter-productive version of Marxism, for whom it would be a replica of the great October Revolution (followed by an immediate worldwide wave of conquest of power) or nothing...

So, when we see Trotskyist organizations today criticizing the "Stalinist productivist model" of "post-Soviet" communist parties, for the sole reason that the rise of the environmental movement can add an extra charge to the anti-communist indictment, we recognize a double error on their part: a historical one, which, as we've said, attributes the model of intensive, polluting agriculture to Stalin, whereas it didn't come into its own until the 1960s; the other, a theoretical one, since the Trotskyist literature has never addressed the issue of the environment, unlike anarchist or anarcho-syndicalist prose, for example, and despite the fact that the very practice of Marxist-Leninist leaders took it into account, even at a time when no one was predicting imminent environmental catastrophes.

But none of this has stopped some of these Trotskyist organizations[21] from joining opportunistically the current ecosocialist movement, in contrast to joining any Marxist-Leninist parties, where *democratic centralism* forbids the formation of internal tendencies. This is why Trotskyist organisations, based as they are on the principle of the "right of tendency," gravitate towards any non-communist "left" movements (without democratic centralism, and therefore open to tendencies), be it a twentieth-century traditional social-democratic party or the environmentalist currents of today.

Basically, after pledging allegiance to ecosocialism, why don't these organizations claim Cuban agroecology as their natural model, as would

---

21   In France, for example, the *Nouveau Parti anticapitaliste* (NPA) and the *Gauche anticapitaliste* (GA) have adopted the "founding principles" of ecosocialism, following in the footsteps of their international organization (Fourth International—unified secretariat).

be logical? Firstly, because Cuban socialism was forged in spite of, or even against, Trotskyists,[22] and, secondly, because Trotskyism, even beyond the island's pro-Soviet past, challenges the very legitimacy of national struggles and the validity of the concepts of nation and national sovereignty.[23]

Yet it is precisely the question of anti-imperialist struggle and national sovereignty that has committed Burkina Faso and Cuba to agroecological safeguard programs, as the state of their socialist production relations, built up to a certain point, promised them success in this field.

From the point of view of serious politics, you can't raise the ecological question in a country without first raising the question of national sovereignty, and this is precisely what the Trotskyists and their single-focused "world revolution" are incapable of doing. If communists opt for internationalism, it's first and foremost because the independence of anti-imperialist nations, by multiplying of its economic and political interrelations (as was the case in the socialist camp, or to a lesser extent in today's ALBA), paves the way for concrete socialist revolution, without one people ever setting out to make socialist revolution on other people's territory and in their place...

But, there's something even more serious concerning "eco-Trotskyism": for the NPA, for example, which has officially signed up to the "Ecosocialism Charter" like the rest of the Fourth International (unified secretariat), political criticism is not lacking against an anti-imperialist government renowned for its ecological commitment: that of Evo Morales in Bolivia.

---

22   "Trotskyists? [...] We decided it wasn't wise for Trotskyism to continue calling for subversion. [...] We took certain measures to ensure that these people, who represent nothing and from whom we do not know where they got their money, continue, on extreme left-wing positions, to hinder the development of our Revolution," E. Che Guevara, interview given at the University of Montevideo (Uruguay, 1961), reported in *Révolution Internationale* N° 388 (2008).

23   Trotskyists usually quote Marx's "*Working men have no country.*" This is a well-known misunderstanding, easily deconstructed by giving the full quotation from the *Communist Manifesto*: "The Communists are further reproached with desiring to abolish countries and nationality. The working men have no country. We cannot take from them what they have not got. Since the proletariat must first of all acquire political supremacy, must rise to be the leading class of the nation, must constitute itself the nation, it is so far, itself national, though not in the bourgeois sense of the word."

Evo Morales' party, the *Movement Towards Socialism* (MAS), which is part of the "Bolivarian revolution" in Latin America in the wake of Venezuelan Chavismo, combines its program for the nationalization of the State's main resources (in particular fossil fuels) with agrarian reform and a project for a plurinational "indigenous" State, combined with a return to traditional values of defending the Earth and its resources against imperialist pillaging: the cult of *"Pachamama"* (Mother Earth). But the impossibility of giving up hydrocarbons for the time being—the only means of satisfying popular demands—is being used as a pretext for all kinds of petty-bourgeois and Trotskyist movements, for which the NPA in France is one of the mouthpieces. However, these movements have been denounced by President Morales as attempts at intimidation fomented by the landowners of the oil-producing regions of the east, who are more or less secessionists, and instrumentalized by the CIA under the table.[24]

The Trotskyist denial of Cuba's agroecological experience is neither coincidental nor ideologically negligent: it must be relativized, hidden, even denied, because it is not based on any "ecosocialist" prophecy, on the one hand, and because it is the result of the sovereign forces of the Cuban people, against all the presuppositions of the theory of permanent revolution, on the other. Every effort must be made to prevent a socialist state that emerged from the "bureaucratic," "degenerate" Soviet camp from becoming the example to follow in environmental protection, as it undoubtedly already is in education and health throughout the world.

THE "ECO-ANARCHIST" MUTATION OF PART OF THE KURDISH NATIONAL MOVEMENT

Perhaps even more worrisome is the ideological turn taken by certain national liberation struggles following the demise of the socialist bloc and the new, particularly predatory and aggressive impetus of imperialist ambitions.

---

24   **Editor's Note:** Subsequent history has shown the shameful continuation of such 'left' attacks on the popular leadership of Bolivia, even at times of extreme danger, such as when the right temporarily succeeded in overthrowing the people's government in Bolivia in 2019, supported and immediately propped up by US imperialism. Intense popular mobilization and resistance returned the MAS to power again in 2020.

The Kurds are today's largest stateless people. They occupy a territory straddling four countries, the largest part of which is the south-eastern region of Turkey. The most influential political movement for independence since the 1970s has emerged in Turkey, where more than half the Kurds live. It is the Kurdish Workers' Party (PKK) of the famous political prisoner Abdullah Ocalan. Initially a Marxist-Leninist party, it advocated a nationwide guerrilla struggle for national liberation, based on the Cuban model. It benefited from internationalist support, particularly from the Soviets against the American potentate Turkey, a NATO forward base on the doorstep of the socialist camp.

The Gulf War saw the first major reversal of the Kurdish cause, when the imperialist coalition invading Iraq used the claims of the Iraqi Kurds in the north, who populated the country's second richest territory in hydrocarbons. With Western "help," this invasion transformed Iraqi Kurdistan into a vast autonomous region vis-à-vis Baghdad, destabilizing or inspiring the claims of other Kurds, notably in Turkey.

For this quasi-Kurdish state in the new Iraqi "federation" will suggest to PKK militants that the watchword of national independence has become obsolete, and that it would be more accurate to demand relative autonomy in all the states concerned. Such a suggestion will be all the more effective given that the Soviet ally is no more, that the influential Kurdish Republic of Iraq is forging diplomatic and economic ties with its long-standing enemy, the Turkish government, thanks to its coveted oil, and that the Western imperialist powers are supporting it politically in the face of an Iraqi regime that is potentially insubordinate to their roadmap, or not very "reliable" over the long term.

The contradiction between the two possible avenues of struggle was complicated when the Kurdish fighters in Syria, with the help of neighboring PKK fighters, began fighting the barbaric Islamic State in the Kobane region without any military aid from NATO, on the hypocritical pretext that their movement has been officially registered as "terrorist" since the 1970s.

While the national question cannot be avoided in Marxist analyses, as Trotskyists, for example, would have us believe, it is not intrinsically linked to the class struggle on an international scale, and imperialism has understood perfectly well for several decades that it can be instrumentalized to weaken troublesome or rebellious states, themselves fighting for their sovereignty. The bourgeoisie's campaigns of "humanitarian interference," often accompanied by Western military intervention, for the "freedom" of minorities in oil-rich Biafra, gold-rich Katanga in Lumumba's Congo, Serbian Kosovo, and Chinese Tibet, are typical examples, and Iraqi Kurdistan can easily be placed in this category.

Thus, the PKK, which has become the "Kurdish People's Congress," has officially abandoned Marxism-Leninism for a better way of thinking. Since 2005, it has adopted the "ecological libertarian municipalism" theorized by Murray Bookchin, an American ex-Trotskyist and essayist appreciated within the anti-communist movements of the American "New Left."

While this "new ecosocialist thinking" has taken many forms since the 1970s, it sees, at minimum, the need to "overcome" the main contradiction that Marxists recognise, the "Capital-Labour" contradiction, in favor of other contradictions such as that between Capital and Nature. As for "Municipalism," it is an old political correlate of anarchist origin, opposing itself to the national question or responding to it with a decentralizing struggle in favor of autonomous village communes.

Armed struggle was officially abandoned by the PKK in the 2000s, while the defense of Kurdish culture and language was left to the now-legal parliamentarians of a pro-Kurdish social-democratic wing of the Turkish oppressor's political tribunes. Of course, anti-Kurdish cultural, political, and economic repression has not ceased, and the famous political prisoner Ocalan remains behind bars to this day...

Paradoxically, the resource that has strategically enabled the Kurdish republic of Iraq to become autonomous—oil—has become something that the Kurds of Turkey and Syria (whose subsoil is far less rich!) must absolutely ban, along with urbanization and intensive agriculture. Environmental protection thus functions as a negation or substitute for the class struggle itself, as a centrifugal force that distances Kurdish national minorities from one another. At the same time, it may constitute the only possible ideological demarcation remaining for the former PKK, once the question of national emancipation and class struggle has been sidestepped, vis-à-vis its competitor in Iraqi Kurdistan, now a major oil supplier.

This opportunistic exploitation of ecological issues (in rural areas that are in fact little concerned by these issues), like that of decentralized village communes included in this same centrifugal movement, is the sign of a clear ideological retreat from Marxism-Leninism. Without a Marxist compass, there is no effective guide to action. If bits and pieces of a state within a state are being built in Northern Kurdistan, without any class analysis, how can we prepare for the inevitable reactions of the Turkish state? How can we anticipate the manipulation of the wealthiest strata of the Kurdish people by the Turkish state to divide and weaken the emancipatory movement? How can we act when certain communes vote democratically for the return of intensive agriculture or massive oil exploitation? How can massive urbanization be halted if Kurdistan begins to develop its own productive forces? We see here all the aspects of a dangerous political idealism, which rejects any idea of national planning and the social composition of power.

The Kurdish example, despite the complexity linked to the multiple borders crossing the territory of this nation in prolonged gestation, shows the extent to which imperialism can look after a national minority in Iraq when its demands coincide with their interests, while continuing to blame it on neighboring countries, even when their demands have been softened. It is a tragic *double standard* that also reveals how the question of the environment can be disguised as a sterile substitute for the struggle of classes and peoples against Capital.

Marxism recognizes the existence of a contradiction between Capital and Nature, but gives it a relative place, emanating from and therefore dependent on the Capital-Labour contradiction. It's the Soviet example itself that lends it the most weight, given that at the time, up until the 1950s, there could be no question of opportunism when it came to defending the environment, since the "ecology" movement didn't exist politically. What's more, until quite recently, Soviet ecology was the subject of ridicule from Western intellectuals who swore by the "scientific" exploitation of natural resources and intensive monocultures, based on the American-European model.

2
THE SOVIET UNION:
THE STORY OF A GREEN REVOLUTION!

Was the USSR really Productivist?

UNTIL RECENT YEARS, Western critics of agriculture in the USSR, at the time the world's second-largest economic power, scoffed at the alleged inadequacy of its productivity. In retrospect, this was rather strange propaganda, given the extent to which any economic power seeking a certain degree of self-sufficiency in food and energy in the face of imperialist dependency systems is more readily accused of destroying the environment. It's even "productivism" that Trotskyists and other "left" anti-communists now blame on the "nostalgics" of the USSR!

"For the past ten years, the Soviet Union has been importing massive and ever-increasing quantities of cereals," wrote the *Lutte Ouvrière* newspaper in 1982.

> As far as wheat is concerned, it has now become the world's leading importer. These imports, which might have seemed exceptional a few years ago, have become a permanent phenomenon. [...] The USSR is the only country in the world to experience the contradictory situation of having both a relatively well-developed industry, since it is the world's second-largest power, and an agricultural deficit, despite being the world's largest country.1 [...] It appears that the USA produces at least a third more agricultural products than the Soviet Union. But the big difference is that there are only 3.9 million American farmers, compared with some 30 million Soviet farmers, counting only

---

1   The article goes on to concede that "In the world's largest country, three quarters of the land is uncultivable due to cold climates in the north and east, and deserts in the south. Barely 27% of the country is used as agricultural land, of which only one-third is cropland. This is barely larger than the USA, which is three times smaller than the USSR. What's more, the climate affecting arable land is often dry and capricious. To be fair to Brezhnev, drought is a very real scourge for Soviet agriculture."

the working population. And even then, at harvest time in the Soviet Union, urban workers, young people and soldiers have to be mobilized to supplement the workforce. US agriculture is therefore at least ten times more productive per worker than Soviet agriculture.[2]

For the Trotskyists and their anti-Soviet followers of the time, the inadequacy of agricultural exploitation and mechanization was criticized, using as an example... the United States and its ultra-productivist model of intensive agriculture! Indeed, the USSR was the world's leading wheat producer, but this production, which was sufficient to feed its people, was not enough to feed the livestock that produced meat and dairy products. So wheat had to be imported, even if it meant undermining the country's food independence.

But what's perhaps most interesting for our purposes is the persistence of Soviet "backwardness" in the development of intensive agriculture, normally modeled, as we said, on the catastrophic US model of the time. For the post-Khrushchev USSR, based on the abandonment of dialectical materialism and the desire to "catch up" with its American adversary, could not reform so quickly an agricultural model built up over almost half a century on other, much more interactionist and ecological principles, as we shall see. This is what our *Lutte Ouvrière* Trotskysts unwittingly confirm, by visibly attributing all the evils to "Stalinism" and the "advances" to the post-Khrushchev revisionism of recent years:

> There are half as many tractors as in the USA (but in 1960 there were four times as many). [...] Despite great progress, fertilizer production is still very inadequate. [...] When you look at agriculture in the USSR, the first thing you notice is that it is one of the most backward sectors of the Soviet economy. Despite undeniable progress, it is still very under-equipped compared with Western countries or the USA in terms of agricultural machinery and, above all, equipment and infrastructure [...] It should be noted [...] that importing foodstuffs does not in itself mean that a country is malnourished [...] since a number of rich industrial countries import large quantities of food. Yet their situation is infinitely better than that of Brazil, for example, which in just a few years has become the world's second-largest producer and exporter of soya, but whose population suffers from hunger and even famine. [...] Under these conditions, the Soviet Union's cereal imports not only mean that the regime is in an international situation that allows it to engage in such imports, but also that

---

2   'Les difficultés de l'agriculture soviétique,' *Lutte des Classes* N° 98, 1982. French monthly magazine of *Lutte Ouvrière*.

it finds sufficient cereals on the market, which would not have been the case twenty years ago, and that, in the event of insufficient harvests, it has chosen not to reduce consumption and, in particular, to feed livestock in an attempt to maintain milk and meat consumption at a certain, albeit low, level. [...] In reality, far from deteriorating, the food situation in the Soviet Union actually improved. Between 1965 and 1977, per capita consumption of meat rose by 39%, milk and dairy products by 28%, and that of fruit by 46%. On the other hand, potato consumption fell by 14% and flour and starch consumption by 10%, indicating an improvement in food quality.[3]

The USSR was, of course, "productivist," since it had to massively produce food for populations whose demographics and quality of life were steadily increasing.[4] It was also all the more true in later decades, when the country opted for the massive use of pesticides and chemical fertilizers in agriculture, as well as for much more intensive mechanization. But even in this context, elements reminiscent of the above-described Cuban agroecology remained in the form of "individual plots" left to cooperative farm members, who depended on the cooperative farm economy (the so-called "auxiliary" market of private plots combined with cooperative farming). It is this type of market, strangely enough, still excluded from the grip of intensive agriculture, that our anti-Soviet Trotskyists most ironize about:

> [Peasants] were free to cultivate individual plots for their own subsistence, selling any surplus to cooperative farms or on the open market. The degree of freedom granted to individual plot owners has varied over the last fifty years.[5] Generally speaking, the more difficult the agricultural situation, during the

---

3   Ibid.

4   From outside, it's difficult to judge whether there is an increase in quality of life, given that in a capitalist country, the most visible changes—in cities, for example, the apparent signs of opulence—are only the consequence of the ever more ostentatious rise in the standard of living of the richest. In capitalist countries, the decline in living standards for the poorest is always much more discreet and hidden. The general standard of living in a country is therefore not measured by the degree of development of the city centers of wealthy cities. Rather, average values give a real indication of the rising standard of living of a population where social disparities are far less pronounced than in capitalist countries. Hence the need to calculate the HDI (Human Development Index), discussed with respect to Cuba, for example.

5   This implies, notably, that such plots have existed since the early days of the USSR, including and in particular, under Stalin.

last war for example, the more rights the authorities granted to plot owners.[6] These individual plots [...] still provide a quarter of agricultural production on 3% of cultivated land! Moreover, this share of production is declining very slowly: it was 33% in 1965. We've reached the paradox that the most archaic[7] sector of agriculture is the most productive, while the most mechanized, most modern sector, the kolkhozes [cooperative farms] and sovkhozes [state farms], are much less so! [...] The plot has now become a factor of social progress. The latest Soviet constitution recognizes that every citizen is entitled to a plot of land of up to half a hectare. And the authorities now ask the public sector to support the private sector, helping it with fertilizers, equipment, etc., sometimes free of charge. In January 1981, a decree was issued to boost production on private farms. Today there are thirty-seven million individual plots, twenty-two million belonging to peasants (fourteen million to kolkhozians, 8 million to sovkhozians) but also 15 million belonging to workers living in rural areas. [...] In the same vein, we should mention the company farms. As their name suggests, these are farms set up and dependent on industrial enterprises. Their role is to feed the staff of the companies in question. It is hoped that, as the workers have a direct interest in their canteen being properly supplied, the farms in question will be the object of attentive care. Indeed, this is often the case. Some large companies own very modern, very large farms, for which they make all the necessary equipment themselves. For example, there are 80,000 company farms, whose surface area, which has increased considerably in recent years, reached 7.5 million hectares in 1981, which is relatively large—one seventh of the surface area of France. [...] The inter-company unions that the scheme is currently promoting are more or less along the same lines, but on a different scale. The aim is to create complementary agro-industrial groupings, so that coherent decisions can be taken at least at the level of the group as a whole. On the other hand, it's a question of facilitating the industrialization of the countryside, while at the same time involving workers in the production of agricultural products and providing peasants with industrial goods.[8]

So, despite the USSR's decision to intensify agricultural production by any means, the state of production relations in the socialist regime still allowed for many productive innovations that closely resembled today's agroecological ideas, notably "local production, without pesticides or

---

6   So it was precisely under Stalin that maximum freedom was given to the cultivation of individual plots, in parallel with collectivized agriculture, which of course never ceased.

7   "Archaic" according to the criteria of capitalists and Trotskyists who were once in favor of intensive agriculture! But this fairly high productivity already suggested that the agribusiness model was probably not the best, even in terms of long-term returns.

8   Ibid.

chemical fertilizers."

This salutary "backwardness" with regard to polluting intensive agriculture gives Russia a considerable advantage on the agricultural market, as this American analyst points out:

> Russia today has some of the richest and most fertile agricultural soils in the world. Because the economic constraints of the Cold War dictated that the products of the chemical industry be devoted to the needs of national defense, fertile Russian soil has not been subjected to decades of destruction by fertilizers or chemical sprays, as has happened on much of western soil. Now it's becoming an involuntary blessing, as European and North American farmers struggle with the destructive effects of chemicals in their soils that have largely destroyed essential microorganisms. It takes years to obtain rich agricultural soils that can be destroyed in a short time.[9]

The author also sheds particular light on the period commented by our Trotskyists above:

> During the Soviet era, especially after 1972, when poor Soviet harvests caused shortages, the USSR used its oil dollars to become a major importer of American grain. U.S. grain cartel companies like Cargill and Continental Grain worked with U.S. Secretary of State Henry Kissinger to negotiate astronomical tariffs from Russia, in what was known as the Great Grain Robbery.[10]

We're talking here about the worst period in the history of the USSR in terms of intensive agriculture, some elements of which point to setbacks compared to an earlier situation that was more advantageous for the environment. We'll look at this in more detail later. But we can already note that where the damage was most obvious, corrections were made, even in this period, based on techniques that are now well known in agroecology. Thus, under Khrushchev's impetus for a vast "virgin land campaign," an ecological disaster had already been programmed, neglecting so-called "sustainable" techniques (cessation of plowing, moderation of irrigation which can leach the soil, formation of windbreak hedges, etc.). As agroecologist Rabah Lahmar asserts:

> Regardless of the nature of the soil, forty million hectares of "virgin land"

---

9   Article 'Russia seeks to dominate the biological food market' by the American economist and geopolitician W. Engdhal, published on the website *New Eastern Outlook* (NEO), 2016.

10   Ibid.

in the steppes of northern Kazakhstan have been cleared by slash-and-burn. Marshes were drained and desalinated. Deep dry-farming was applied. The sovkhozes [...] founded on this land were intended to produce spring wheat. After several years of good harvests, yields fell [...]. Moreover, the steppe soils, to which the same techniques as those used on the black earth from Ukraine were applied, began to degrade. Dust storms then developed. Wind erosion locally destroyed the entire topsoil.

After the loss of thousands of hectares of soil, corrections were made to adapt techniques to the natural environment: choice of short-cycle wheat varieties, very shallow tillage with specially designed machines, planting of windbreaks [...].[11]

Although the mechanization of agriculture had been strongly developed since the thirties with collectivization, to make people's work easier, this kind of nihilistic plan, neglecting a science—pedology—which had in fact been born on Soviet soil, had never yet been implemented. It inaugurated a policy of extremely dangerous competition with the USA, in this field as in many others. It should be noted that, on the American side, environmental disasters were just as important, without of course generating as much controversy in the West. We are not questioning the indispensable technical and economic development of the USSR, the only guarantee of stability in the face of the predatory American giant, but the rules of the game chosen for this struggle which became an unnatural "geostrategic competition." From the thirties to the eighties, the Soviet Union sought to make its agricultural production profitable by any means possible, including, for the period inaugurated by Khrushchev and closed with Gorbachev, by polluting intensive agriculture based on pesticides and chemical fertilizers.[12] This desire is entirely logical, given that the ultimate goal, far from any capitalist tendency towards agribusiness, was to satisfy and raise the food needs of the Soviet peoples. There was never any question, even in the last few decades, of "production for production's sake."

11   *L'opération des Terres vierges du Kazakhstan*, Lahmar, Rabah 1997.

12   The use of chemical fertilizers began with collectivization in the 1930s, but never reached the heights of the post-war period under Khrushchev or the USA. In this case, we cannot speak of intensive agriculture as criticized by today's environmentalists, simply because the financial resources of the young USSR did not allow it, even if it had wanted to, to produce enough chemical fertilizers, pesticides, and agricultural machinery to alter the environment.

Yet it's this desire to "produce for the sake of producing" which, in the minds of environmentalists, characterizes the famous problem of "productivism." This is not simply a matter of increasing agricultural productivity. Otherwise, it would be enough to blame any overpopulated country refusing to return to the days of chronic famine. Irrational production not only exploits a soil incapable of regenerating quickly enough, but also unleashes unfair and deadly competition between the rich countries, which dominate the market with colossal subsidies, and the poor countries, which themselves produce excessively without being able to stem famines or nutritional deficiencies, and are dependent on food imports even though they are agricultural countries. Even after becoming the world's second-largest economic power, the USSR never fell into this first category.

At the same time, discussions about respect for the environment that predate today's West were already taking place in the USSR in the 1970s, at the height of East-West economic rivalry. There was talk of respecting wild environments, reforestation and even limiting the use of pesticides such as DDT (an insecticide whose health and ecological damaging effects are well known today), which caused havoc in both the West and the East. In the Soviet press of the time, we could read arguments of the utmost interest in view of today's unhelpful "agricultural productivity versus ecology" debate: "Of two things: cars or pine trees, preserving nature's riches or squandering them for the sake of progress and civilization... But is this really a dilemma? Isn't there a third solution?" said a Soviet journalist in 1972.

> In Estonia, the forest area is growing year by year, the natural landscape is being reconstituted on the huge areas where mineral deposits have been exploited, and lakes, ponds and rivers are becoming increasingly well-stocked with fish. In Estonia, the use of DDT is prohibited... But perhaps industry is developing more slowly than elsewhere? Perhaps cities are not growing? The proportion of urban population is the highest in the USSR. [...] Growth in industrial production is higher than the USSR average.
>
> Perhaps something else: aren't we sacrificing something for the sake of the environment? For example, if we had given up DDT, the most effective insecticide of all, wouldn't we have reduced crop yields, with the sole aim of protecting soil, vegetation, birds and animals from toxic contamination? Wrong again; the crops were growing! Over the past three years, the potato prices in Estonia have risen by 50% [...] Yet Estonia is not the Kuban or the Ukraine,

with their fertile black soil! [...] Is it a false dilemma, then, to [...] justify humans' unbridled, irresponsible and, all in all, suicidal violence against nature? [...] No doubt we need the means, competent specialists. But you have to start somewhere! [...] To plant more and cut down fewer trees, we don't need "cosmic" technology or billions of rubles. You just have to be aware of the situation and want to do something about it. This is just as necessary for the appearance of the truly gigantic resources required for "global" projects.[13]

With regard to DDT, the discussion reported in this article is no less interesting. An Estonian agricultural engineer testified that:

> Of course, we are looking for biological means of plant defense. We have already developed certain methods and are applying them in practice. So far, however, chemical processes are much more effective. In fact, all chemicals are harmful. Chlorophos is even more toxic than DDT, but we don't intend to give it up [...] It's how you use it that counts.[14]

In the 1970s, natural pesticides were developed under certain conditions, but above all, restrictions on chemical pesticides were gradually reintroduced. This is what is known in the West today as "rational agriculture," the maximum that can be generated in our part of the world to protect the environment and consumer health. In other words, a restriction capable of balancing crop yields and health protection as far as possible. The only solution proposed today in capitalist countries is to pretend to protect the environment with pretty words, this being what the Soviets were accused of in the seventies and eighties... For the record, in France, we continued to spray the worst known carcinogen, an insecticide called chlordecone, whose high toxicity has been known since the seventies, on the banana plantations of Guadeloupe until the nineties, for strictly financial reasons and with the scandalous backing of the Ministry of Agriculture:

> The power acquired by Soviet environmentalism, led by scholars, some of whom were members of the CPSU [Communist Party of the Soviet Union], constituted an important phenomenon, and the debates were not merely formal. In the 1970s and 1980s, when Marxist philosophy began to revive in the Soviet Union under the leadership of Ivan Frolov, it highlighted a number of the essential ecological presuppositions inherent in Marx's thought, starting

---

13 "Nature and Humanity," Pavel Volinem from the Soviet magazine *Works and Opinions*, N° 165, September 1972.

14 Ibid.

with the concept of metabolism between man and nature, and it did so before Western Marxists.[15]

It's easy to see how, even after a period of particularly unbridled intensive agriculture in the 1960s, pesticide consumption remained very limited in the socialist countries compared to the capitalist countries of the time [Figure 1]. Even when it came to chemical fertilizers, Eastern European countries were poor consumers compared with European countries [Figure 2], although they rivaled the USA in the latter period. While they were on a par with the colonial and semi-feudal Maghreb in the early 1960s in terms of chemical fertilizer consumption, they had already made up for their post-war lag with the USA in terms of agricultural production, without yet copying the latter in their technical options, as shown in Figure 13—see page 136. There's a "mystery" here that we'll unravel later.

Figure 1: Pesticide consumption in 1990 just before the end of the USSR.

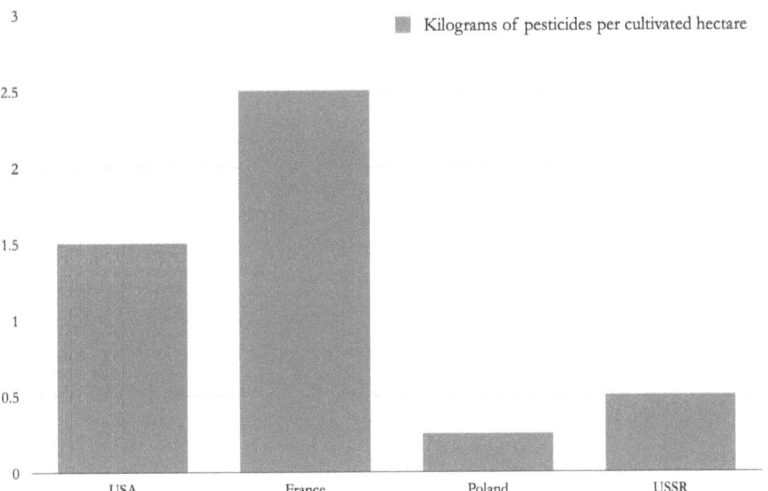

Source: Institut Français de l'Éducation (IFE) website, Pesticides and Health Theme (Conso Pesticides).

---

15 'Marxism and the Environment,' interview with John Bellamy Foster, *Médiapart*, May 19, 2016.

60   Communism, The Highest Stage of Ecology

Figure 2: Chemical fertilizer consumption in four regions from the Khrushchev period onwards.

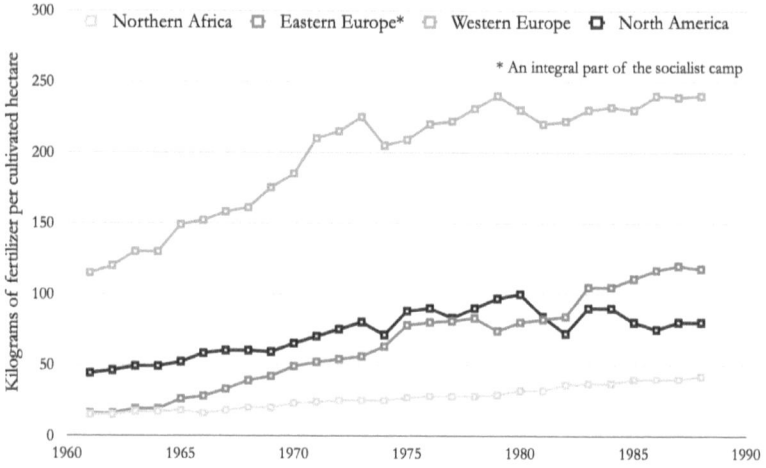

Source: Institut Français de l'Éducation (IFE) website, Nitrates and Health Theme (Conso Pays).

Despite a general intensification of collectivized agriculture from the Khrushchev period onwards, the Soviet Union still lagged far behind the agri-cultures of the major imperialist powers in terms of pesticides in 1990. If, for decades, the Soviet Union lagged behind these same powers in terms of chemical fertilizer consumption, this was undoubtedly not the result of "economic backwardness" alone, as the Soviet Union was still the world's second-largest industrial power after the United States of America. It's undoubtedly an effect of local history, which few bourgeois historians have found interesting or useful to mention, and not without reason.

Soviet Agriculture Before Khrushchev's "Chemicalization"

All the history books attest to a voluntarist period of "chemicalization" of Soviet agro-industry, especially around the production of chemical fertilizers and pesticides. But the precise dates of this transition are surprisingly vague: so the big bad polluter of Russian and Ukrainian soils wasn't Stalin?

Obviously, the main concern of those in charge of Soviet agriculture since Lenin has always been to produce more to satisfy the needs of a huge population emerging from the feudal age, both quantitatively and qualitatively. However, in agronomy, there are in fact two antagonistic strategies for increasing agricultural production: *intensive agriculture*, which, when arable land is limited, consists in "doping" the soil and cultivated plants with pesticides, hormones and chemical fertilizers, and *extensive agriculture*, which consists in producing the same yield per hectare, but with ever larger cultivated areas.

Soviet geography is obviously more conducive to the latter. On the one hand, its surface is gigantic, and marked by a world-renowned diversity of soil types and flora; on the other hand, soil fertility is extremely variable, between the famous "black soils" of Western Russia and the Ukraine, being the richest, and the very poor and impracticable "podzols" of Siberia. It is estimated that less than a third of the total surface area of the USSR is arable. The challenge for the Soviets was clearly to take advantage of this soil richness and to do everything in their power to fertilize the easternmost parts of the territory.

A year after Stalin's death, in 1954, the aim of the famous "virgin lands" project was still to fertilize the poor soils of the steppes of Kazakhstan and Siberia, even if the adventurism and amateurism of the project were severely criticized by the last "Stalinists" in the Central Committee, Vyacheslav Molotov and Lazare Kaganovich. The campaign produced results in the first two years, but eventually reached an impasse. Between 1954 and 1958, the number of hectares under cultivation rose from 10 to 28 million. Annual harvests rose from 332 to 1343 million pounds. Agricultural strategies, on the other hand, were catastrophic, already borrowing from intensive capitalist agriculture, with the application of chemical weaponry and the elimination of protective hedges, etc. Soils immediately suffered the consequences, so that within a few years the plan was abandoned due to profitability losses, despite the late corrections in terms of agronomic choices (resumption of sowing under plant cover and no-till techniques on the most fragile soils), as mentioned above.

In the same way, the famous drying-up of the Aral Sea was the result of this short-termist policy from the 1960s onwards. To intensify irrigation of the cotton-growing regions of Kazakhstan and Uzbekistan, reputed to be dry, the diversion of the Amu Darya and Syr Darya rivers began to lower the level of the sea, leading to the gradual disappearance of many local ecosystems and the local fishing economy. This notorious ecological catastrophe was also the result of Khrushchevian policy, as shown below in Figure 3.

Figure 3: Evolution of the Aral Sea surface during the Soviet period

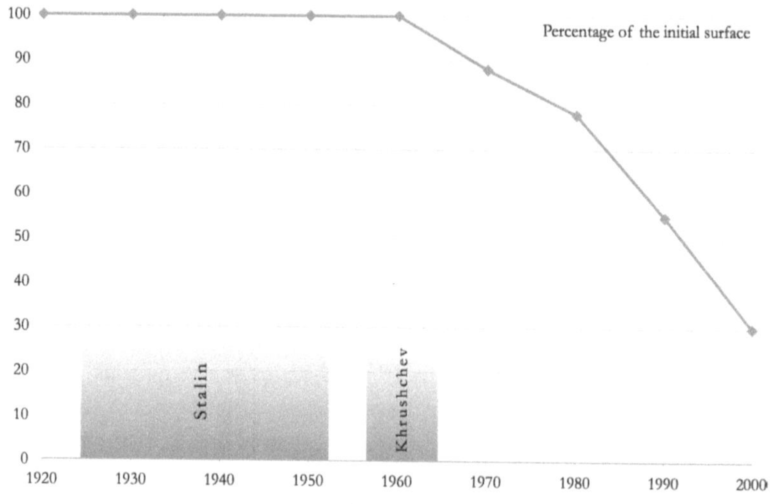

Source: Surface measurements from chronological maps on Wikipedia—Aral Sea.

The great turning point in Soviet agriculture was Khrushchev's work, as numerous sources attest. If he decided to "chemicalize" Soviet industry and agriculture, in other words, to deliberately switch to the intensive use of chemical fertilizers and pesticides, it was because agriculture under Lenin and Stalin was based on other principles, oriented towards extensive rather than intensive farming.

"Khrushchev resolved [...] to move from extensive cultivation (of which the clearing of virgin land was the most spectacular application) to intensive cultivation, which required a tight irrigation network, increased equipment and, above all, what was known in the U.S.S.R. as the 'chemicalization' of industry," says Russian specialist Bernard Féron.[16]

Another Russologist, Jean Radvanyi, gives more details:

Neglected under Stalin, chemistry was a weak sector of Russian industry until N. Khrushchev took steps to accelerate the development of synthetic chemistry in May 1958. Spurred on by direct and indirect investment programmes (e.g., campaigns to chemicalize agriculture and support pharmaceutical equipment), the sector as a whole underwent spectacular development, boosted by the presence of rich sources of raw materials (oil and gas, mineral salt and sulfur deposits) and low energy prices.[17]

The figures speak for themselves:

In 1959, the USSR was still lagging far behind, since its share of global production represented only 4.3-5.3% of total industrial production, compared with 8.8% in the USA and 8.5% in the countries of the European Community.[18]

Lenin's well-known definition of Russian socialism—*Soviet power plus the electrification of the whole country*—had undergone an eloquent modification: "If Lenin were alive today, he would certainly have said: communism is the power of the soviets, plus the electrification of the whole country, plus the chemicalization of the national economy," Khrushchev hammered home.[19] This turning point in the fertilizer and pesticide industry can be verified with the figures available [Figure 4, next page].

16 Casterman 1966, *L'URSS sans idole* [*The USSR without Idols*].

17 Armand Colin, 2007, *La nouvelle Russie* [*The New Russia*].

18 M. G. Sokolov, 1968, 'L'industrie chimique en URSS [Chemical industry in the USSR],' Compte rendu par Pierre George in *Annales de Géographie* N° 423.

19 Remarks reported in *L'industrie chimique en URSS* [*Chemical industry in the USSR*], *op. cit.*

Figure 4: Chemical fertilizer production from Stalin's USSR to Khrushchev's.

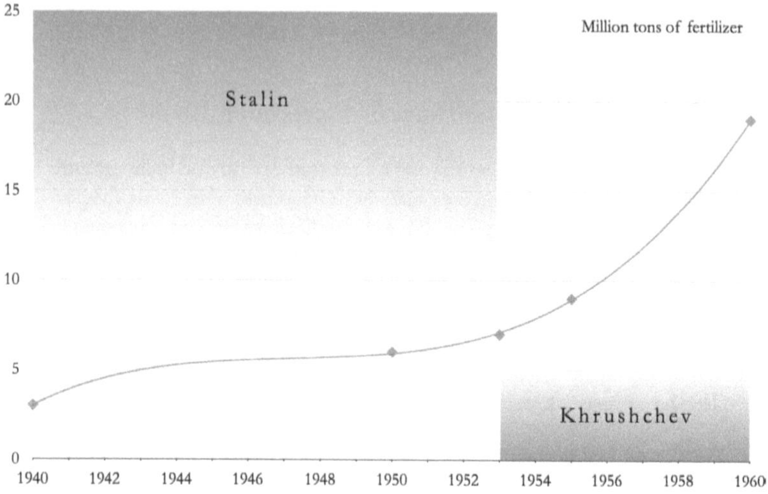

Source: The agricultural situation in the Soviet Union, Inna Kniazeff (1957, Études et conjectures N° 7).

The final component of this paradigm shift was regarding ecological preserves or natural reserves. In the Soviet Union, huge nature reserves were protected by the state against all intrusions, apart from those of specially authorized scientists, in order to guarantee the conservation of natural biodiversity over this vast territory. Among the six categories of the IUCN classification (1994), the *zapovedniki* correspond to the first category, that of "protected nature reserves."[20]

These reserves were born and developed throughout the so-called "Stalinist" period before being scoffed at by Khrushchev's cadres from the 1960s onward, coinciding with the above-described turnaround in agriculture. The USSR had nineteen *zapovedniki* in 1937, twenty-seven in 1940, and thirty-one in 1948. "De-Stalinization," on the other hand, saw a drastic drop in these natural reserves, as can be seen in the graph in

---

20   Stéphane Héritier & Lionel Laslaz, 2008, *Les parcs nationaux dans le monde: Protection, gestion et développement durable* [*National Parks across the World: Protection, Management, and Sustainable Development*], Ellipses.

Figure 5. This fall was momentary, but significant of the paradigm shift concerning the environment when it was openly envisaged to "catch up" with the American productivist model. Khrushchev had this to say about this pillar of national culture: "What is a *zapovednik*? It's national wealth in need of protection. But it turns out that our *zapovedniki* are worthless. What would happen if *zapovedniki* didn't exist? Nothing at all [...]."

It was largely due to his adventurism in agricultural and environmental matters that Khrushchev was removed from office in 1964, when the USSR became dependent on US grain imports in this area. Despite his dismissal, the countryside remained under the yoke of intensive agriculture until the system imploded in 1991.

Figure 5: Change in total *zapovedniki* area (protected nature reserves) during the Soviet period.

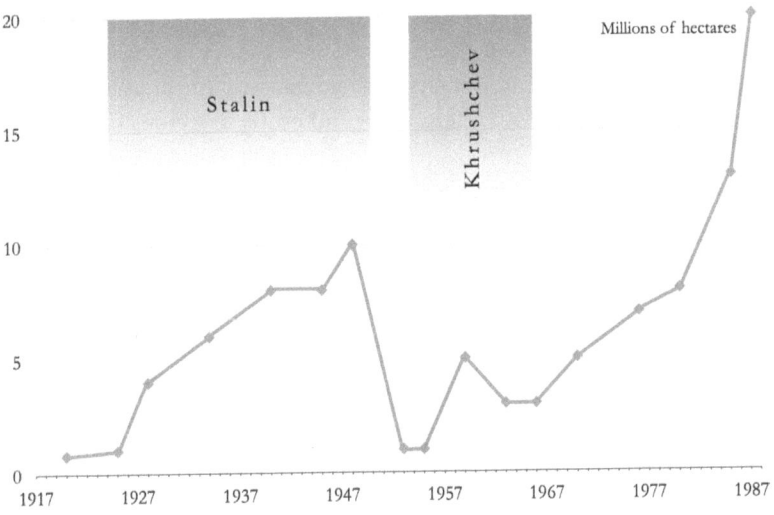

Source: *Lesmatérialistes* website article "The *Zapovedniki* question" (Ecology section, April 2016).

Alongside these decisions concerning nature reserves, Khrushchev put an end to Stalin's "Great Plan for the Transformation of Nature" (henceforth "Great Plan") as soon as he came to power. The *Minleskhoz*, the Ministry of Forest Management responsible for reforestation and forest protection, was also liquidated and integrated into the new Ministry of Agriculture. All the projects of the "Great Plan" drawn up in 1948, which essentially consisted in extending woodland areas throughout the country, were canceled by Khrushchev as soon as he was installed in the Kremlin. To put it in today's terms, the "chemicalization" of agriculture at that time was logically accompanied by a brutal end to Soviet agroforestry, with the aim of massively increasing the cost of the timber industry, without any concern for the environment.

The "Great Plan" was of a completely different nature. Adopted by the Soviet Council of Ministers in 1948, it was intended to increase agricultural production through the development of extensive farming and to limit soil erosion, in particular by multiplying the number of forest windbreaks; to develop irrigation through the creation of surface waters capable of stemming drought; and to introduce crop rotation enabling the soil regeneration that intensive farming by definition prohibits.

Forest strips averaging two hundred meters in width were to surround cultivated areas in huge farming regions, with the dual aim of improving the soil's ability to retain water and protecting crops from wind and rain damage.

Finally, the aim was to put into practice on a large scale the methods of the soil scientist Williams and his famous inspiration, Dokuchaev.[21] These included the use of polyculture to avoid the use of chemical pesticides, and the use of straw and fallen leaves from trees to develop *cover cropping* (a fundamental element in the protection of soil structure and life, more information on which can be found in the Appendix—see pp. 173-176).

The goal was clear to the USSR as early as 1948: to ensure food self-sufficiency for Soviet citizens, and to begin with the development of the vast forest belts not only ensured soil and crop protection, but also stimulated an increase in animal and plant biodiversity in Soviet ecosystems. In addition

---

21   These Russian scientists are the founding fathers of soil science. Williams rethought soil science using the principles of dialectical materialism in an interactionist model very similar to the principles currently in vogue in agroecology. [**Editor's Note:** Vasily Robertovich Williams (1863-1939) and Vasily Vasilyevich Dokuchaev (1846-1903).]

to protecting soils and crops, the development of vast forest belts was also intended to stimulate the increase in animal and plant biodiversity in Soviet ecosystems, themselves as varied as the country's landscapes and climates.

The full name of the plan was: "*Plan for protective forest plantations, introduction of variable grass seedlings, construction of dykes and artificial ponds to achieve high and stable yields in the steppe and woodland steppe regions of the European part of the USSR.*" It's worth noting that, in the face of its Khrushchevian antithesis of "virgin lands" a few years later, this plan, with the words "high and stable yields," provides the very first formulation of today's "sustainable development."

The agronomists of the time understood very early on that the "stable" or "sustainable" fertility of soils depended less on mechanical amendments of mineral salts (fertilizers) than on their structure, capable of conserving the water and mineral salts that plants need in nature, on the model of the forest floor, the most fertile of all, yet receiving no human additions. So, according to them, plant cover regenerates the soil in exactly the same way as today's environmentalists advocate, based on the *in situ* production capacity of clay-humus complexes. At the time, the magazine *Études Soviétiques* explained:

> This method is based on the following observation [...]: abundant, ever-increasing harvests [...] are only possible on soil with a solid, finely granular structure. The most effective way of ensuring a finely granular soil structure is to periodically introduce a mixture of perennial grasses, legumes and cereals into the crop rotation. As they degrade, the roots of perennial grasses do a tremendous job of improving and enriching the soil's physical qualities. The soil acquires a fine, solid structure with a remarkable capacity to accumulate and conserve the moisture that appears at the time of rainfall and snowmelt. Nor does the water from summer thunderstorms manage to ravage the land; it is retained and subsequently used by plants.[22]

To give an idea of the immensity of the reforestation planned over the next fifteen years, the idea was to cover with trees an area larger than France, Great Britain, Belgium, Luxemburg, and The Netherlands combined, integrating the country's three agroecological resources. To this end, 3.6 million hectares were to be reforested by the *kolkhozes*, 580,000 by the *sovkhozes* and 1.5 million by the Ministry of Forest Economy (*Minleskhoz*), while 570 forest protection stations were to be built

22 Etudes Soviétiques [*Soviet Studies*], December 1948.

throughout the Union.

From the point of view of production relations, the plan was also intended to help stimulate the integration of the kolkhozes, the collective farms that still operated autonomously, into the major state projects. Involving them in these plans was tantamount to boosting national capacities to respond collectively to the major problems of independent development in the context of capitalist encirclement. The context was thus similar in form to that currently experienced by Cuba under embargo, albeit on an immeasurable scale.

For the first time, a huge plan to protect nature and, in turn, provide people with the means for a sustainable livelihood, based on organic farming and agroforestry, was being implemented on a country-wide scale, under the impetus of its state, thanks to its centralized socialist structure.

The dissolution of the plan a few years later with the arrival of Khrushchev has a dual significance. The first, in terms of superstructure, is due to the fact that, everything being linked, the abandonment of dialectical materialism effaces any "ecological" vision of the environment, just as capitalism has always done in the West. The second, in terms of infrastructure, reminds us that any large-scale project, profitable not in the short term but in the long term, requires considerable, centralized investment from the outset, such as only a socialist state can make, provided its accumulated resources allow it to do so.

Here again, investment was particularly important, and it may have seemed to Khrushchev that a greater reliance on non-renewable energy and chemical resources would pay off in the short term, at the expense of long-term, sustainable development.

That said, the project did not date back to 1948. As early as 1935, Joseph Stalin declared at the 14th Congress of the CPSU, before the tragic interruption caused by the World War:

> As far as drought control in the regions beyond the Volga is concerned, the planting of forests and the establishment of forest defense zones in the eastern regions beyond the Volga are of enormous importance [...] As far as their irrigation is concerned [...] this matter cannot be allowed to drag on. It is true that it has been somewhat delayed by certain contingencies, which have absorbed a great deal of strength and resources, but today there is no longer any reason

to postpone it.²³

By this time, one hundred and twenty-nine forest strips had already been planted between the Don and Volga rivers, based on the groundbreaking work of the great Russian ecologist Dokuchaev, with a very satisfactory productivity record. The aim was to protect the soil from erosion and drought, thus preventing natural disasters and stabilizing crop yields despite the vagaries of the climate, a real calamitous danger in Russia. Thanks to the efforts of numerous *kolkhozes* and *sovkhozes*, the Rostov region had also been reforested by this time, with equally positive results.

We were already aware of the scale of the material investments required for this kind of plan: mass training of agronomists capable of directing the implementation of the plan in all the regions concerned[24]; production of machinery adapted to the agricultural techniques planned on the scale of an immense territory; and the creation of innumerable nurseries to prepare tree plantations.[25]

Figure 6 [next full spread]: The irrigation, afforestation and hydroelectric production networks envisaged by the "Great Plan for the Transformation of Nature" in 1948.

---

23   Stalin, quoted in 'Les grands travaux et la lutte pour la transformation de la nature en URSS [Major works and the struggle for the transformation of nature],' Jean Baby, article in *L'information géographique* N° 2, 1952.

24   Twenty higher education establishments were founded to train the forest engineers needed for this project.

25   Every season, three hundred million tree seedlings were prepared by such nurseries. In all, the project involved several tens of billions of trees.

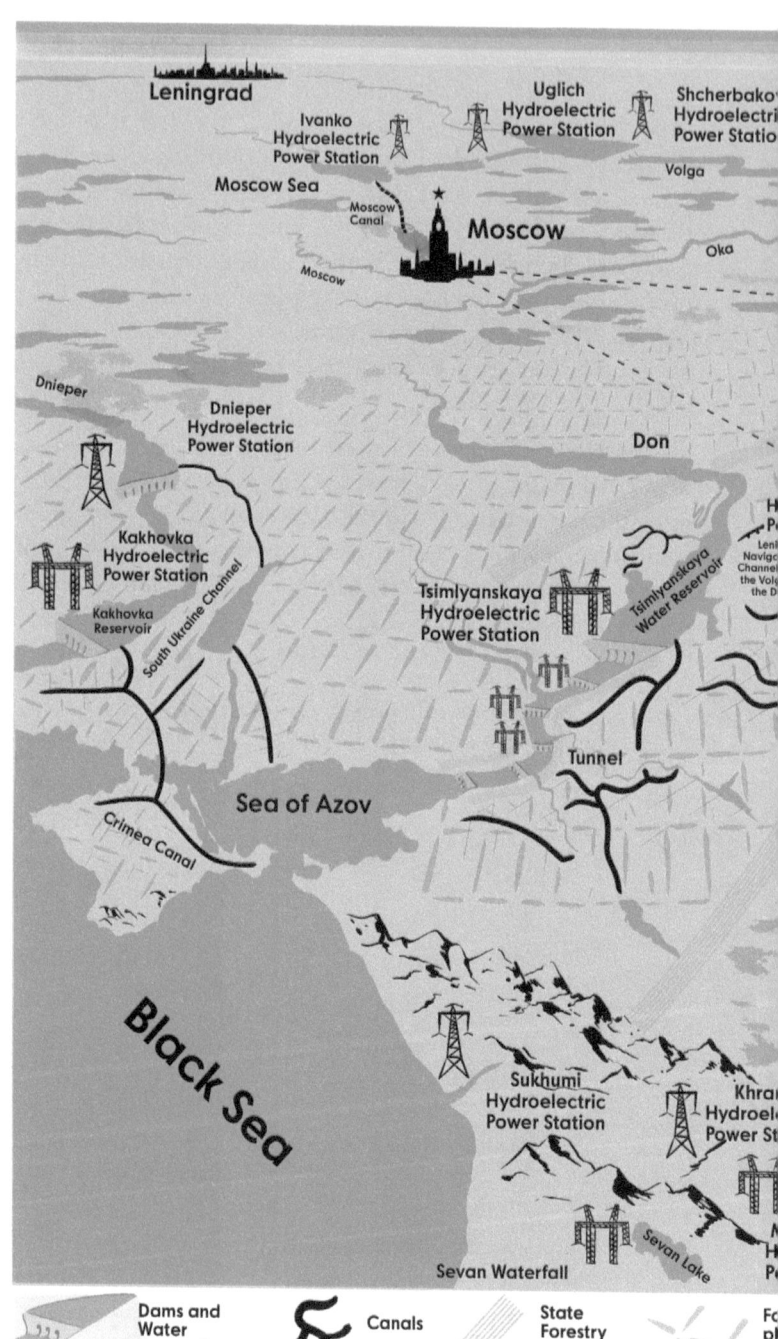

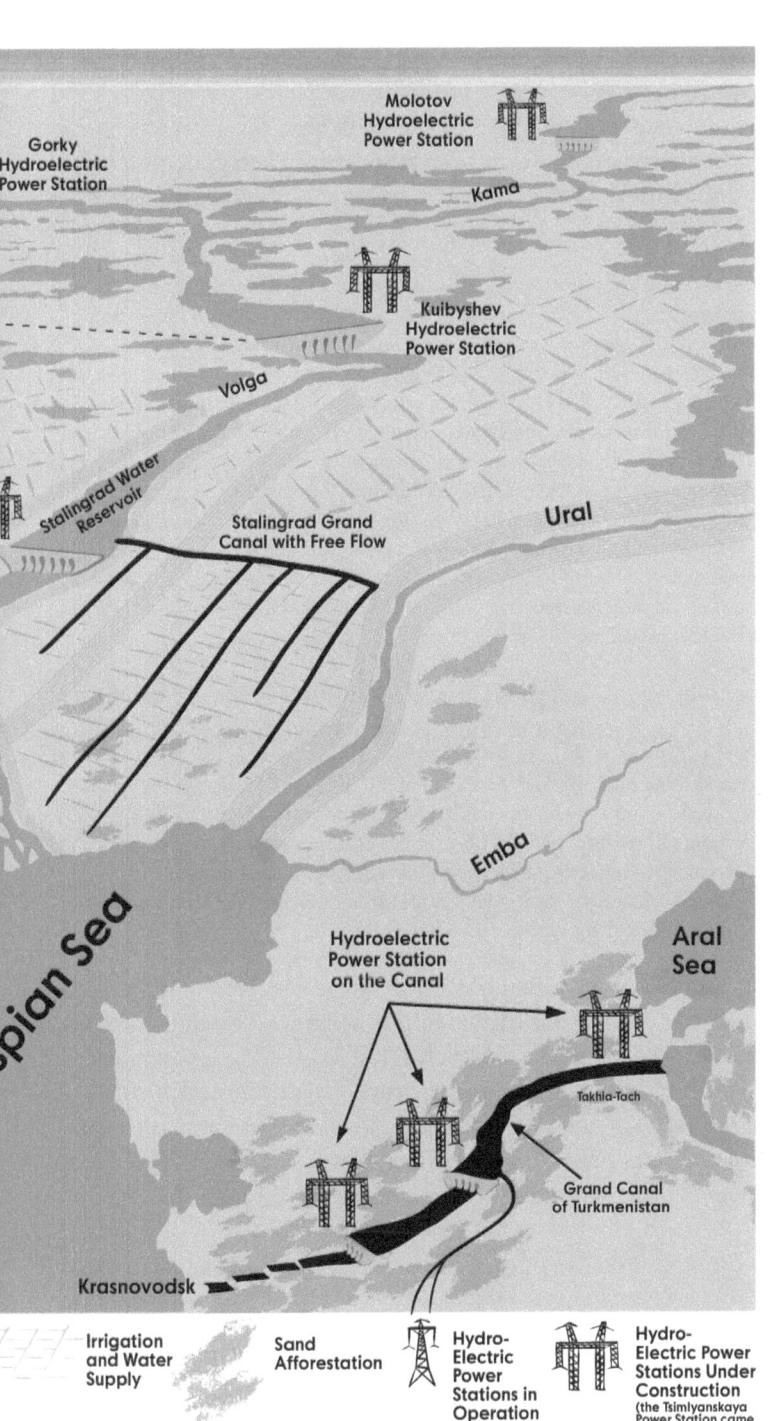

Unlike its inverted double, Khrushchev's adventurist and ecologically disastrous "virgin lands" policy a few years later, this plan was based on tried and tested experiments, from forest strips to crop rotation techniques. For example, the agronomist J. Baby reports in the same issue of *L'Information géographique*:

> The question of soil growth and fertility is one of the fundamental theories of agronomic research in the USSR, combined with research based on the work of Michurin. In Satarov, I visited the Institute of Agriculture for the entire South-East region. [...] It directs the activities of twenty-eight attached scientific organizations, has seventeen laboratories staffed by dozens of professors and research fellows, and two hundred workers cultivate the Institute's experimental fields. Furthermore, a sovkhoz and forty-eight kolkhozes are also experimental fields controlled by the Institute. [...] Work is directed in six different directions: 1) cereal and forage crop rotation; 2) forest plantations; 3) methods of using organic fertilizers; 4) how to work the soil; 5) water and snow retention; 6) coordination of all these problems in the field. [...] A sandy, sterile soil had thus been rapidly transformed into black soil (Chernoziom) by the simple, rational use of microorganisms and appropriate sowing.[26]

The author adds, and this is crucial in the comparison we are trying to make between socialist and capitalist agronomy:

> The theory, confirmed by experience [...] of increasing soil fertility [...] is opposed to the pessimistic theories widespread in America [...] on the "law" of decreasing soil fertility, which is nothing but an admission of powerlessness and an attempt at justification in the face of the disastrous consequences of soil erosion and exhaustion, resulting not from natural data but from cultivation conditions linked to a given economic system.[27]

We can see that the voluntarist agroecological techniques advocated throughout this period until Stalin's death were not chosen by default. They were not the result of a lack of chemical fertilizers and pesticides, as one might think, since intensive agriculture (capitalist, and Khrushchevian in its wake) had only begun to take hold everywhere from the 1950s onwards. On the contrary, it was a deliberate political choice, linked to a fundamental, materialist critique of the bourgeois agronomic science of

---

26 'Les grands travaux et la lutte pour la transformation de la nature en URSS' [Major works and the struggle for the transformation of nature], J. Baby, article in *L'information géographique* N° 2, 1952.

27 Ibid.

the time. The latter was based (as it is today, albeit with a few restrictions and concessions to the ecology movement) on the supposed exhaustion of the soil, with no other strategy than its chemical exploitation, like a non-renewable fossil fuel... Indeed, while the reintroduction of life into the soil—the only way to bring in organic matter (through plant cover, for example)—is the only solution to increasing soil fertility, Western agronomy on the contrary implied that cultivated soil is doomed to certain exhaustion, since harvesting removes from the system the organic matter that would enable it to regenerate. Intensive farming, which substitutes permanent chemical fertilization for the necessary restoration of soil life, is a perfect illustration of this fundamentally reactionary way of thinking.

In the USSR, on the other hand, it was thought that maintenance and scientific work on the soil would regenerate its capacity to retain mineral salts and water, as opposed to the "chemical" exhaustion caused by unlimited inputs that pollute and ultimately sterilize the soil. These are the pillars of current ecological thinking on agriculture. What's more, such agroecological projects presupposed huge initial investment to enable the production of the appropriate specific equipment (remember, for example, that polyculture implies an increase in the number of different working tools, and therefore additional material resources) and an education system to train engineers and disseminate knowledge to the peasantry in *kolkhozes* and *sovkhozes*.

This resembles the context that exists today, on a smaller scale, in Cuba, and presupposes the same primitive accumulation of resources, all things considered. Lenin's NEP, which in the early years of the Russian Revolution was supposed to accumulate enough wealth to begin the actual construction of socialism, could therefore in a way be extended into the 1940s by an environmental "NEP," a period of accumulation of wealth and scientific knowledge, before beginning the development of real socialist agroecology on a union-wide scale. Planting trees implies a fairly long wait before harvesting the fruits... and it's certainly not a serious option for the capitalist in search of maximum and immediate profit... By contrast, in the pre-war USSR threatened by a world war, and even in the seriously weakened USSR of the immediate post-war period, afforestation remained the preferred option! All the more so in a country which, during the tsarist era, had regarded forests as a traditional pillar of its national extraction industry. Seen from this angle, the abrupt cancellation of the "Great Plan" in favor of a "virgin lands campaign" based, as we've seen, on antagonistic agronomic principles, constitutes yet another anti-ecological revision in Soviet policy, the initial principles of which were set by Lenin and Stalin, adding to the ideological, economic, and political revisionism of Khrushchev and his successors. This was not an "intensive" solution to an earlier problem caused by "Stalinist" agroecology, but a choice linked to the impatience and adventurous voluntarism of a Soviet leadership destabilized by the American adversary during the "cold war."

From the 1950s onwards, under the impetus of Khrushchev, the decision to halt afforestation, as can be seen in Figure 7, for example, was not linked to the unproductiveness of this technique until then. On the contrary, the forest strip technique was almost proportional to yield increases, largely due to the limitation of losses due to climate disturbances, as can be seen in Figure 8. The thesis that unproductive agriculture in Stalin's time was the result of overly "archaic" approach falls apart and is all the more obvious today, when modern agronomists are almost forced to make the opposite observation about intensive agriculture, which destroys soils over the long term.

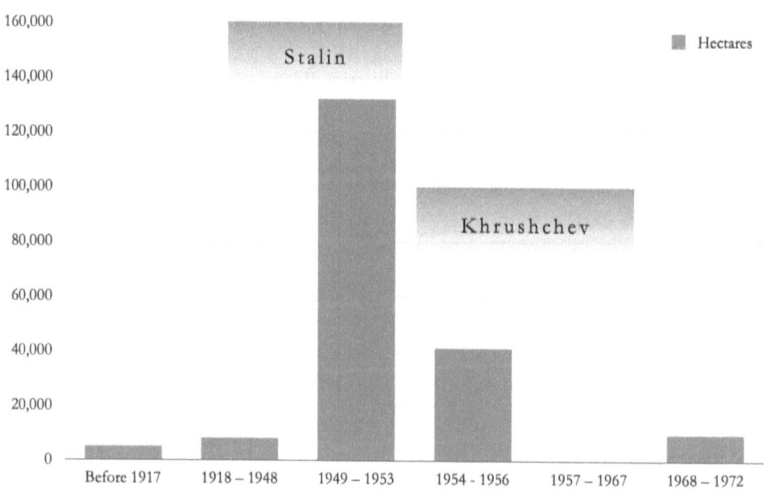

Figure 7: Annual surface area of tree plantations at different periods in Soviet history.

Source [previous page]: Jean Radvanyi, 1975, Les bandes forestières de protection dans les steppes soviétiques[Forest protection belts in the Soviet steppes]," *Bulletin de l'Association des Géographes Français* N° 429.

Figure 8: Trends in afforestation and agricultural yield in the south-east of the Rostov region (USSR).

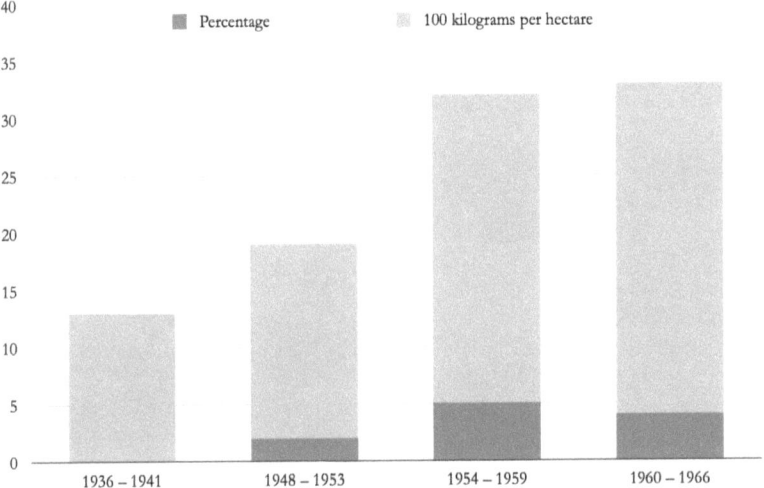

Source: Jean Radvanyi, 1975, Les bandes forestières de protection dans les steppes soviétiques[Forest protection belts in the Soviet steppes]," *Bulletin de l'Association des Géographes Français* N° 429.

Pedology, i.e., the science of soils, was born in Russia, with its founder Vasily Dokuchaev, and its eminent Soviet followers: Vernadsky[28] and Williams. The impressive diversity of soils covering Russia and the USSR in general, across eleven time zones and twenty-two million square kilometers, no doubt partly explains this focus on the natural sciences related to soils, climates and natural ecosystems. This vast territory is home to a whole range of soils, from the richest in organic matter, the chernozems (or black earths) of Ukraine and Kazakhstan, to the poorest and most sterile, the Siberian podzols. In reality, only a modest proportion of this Soviet land was arable, with climatic disturbances that have always hampered agricultural yields [Figure 9].

---

28 **Editor's Note:** Vladimir Ivanovich Vernadsky (1863-1945).

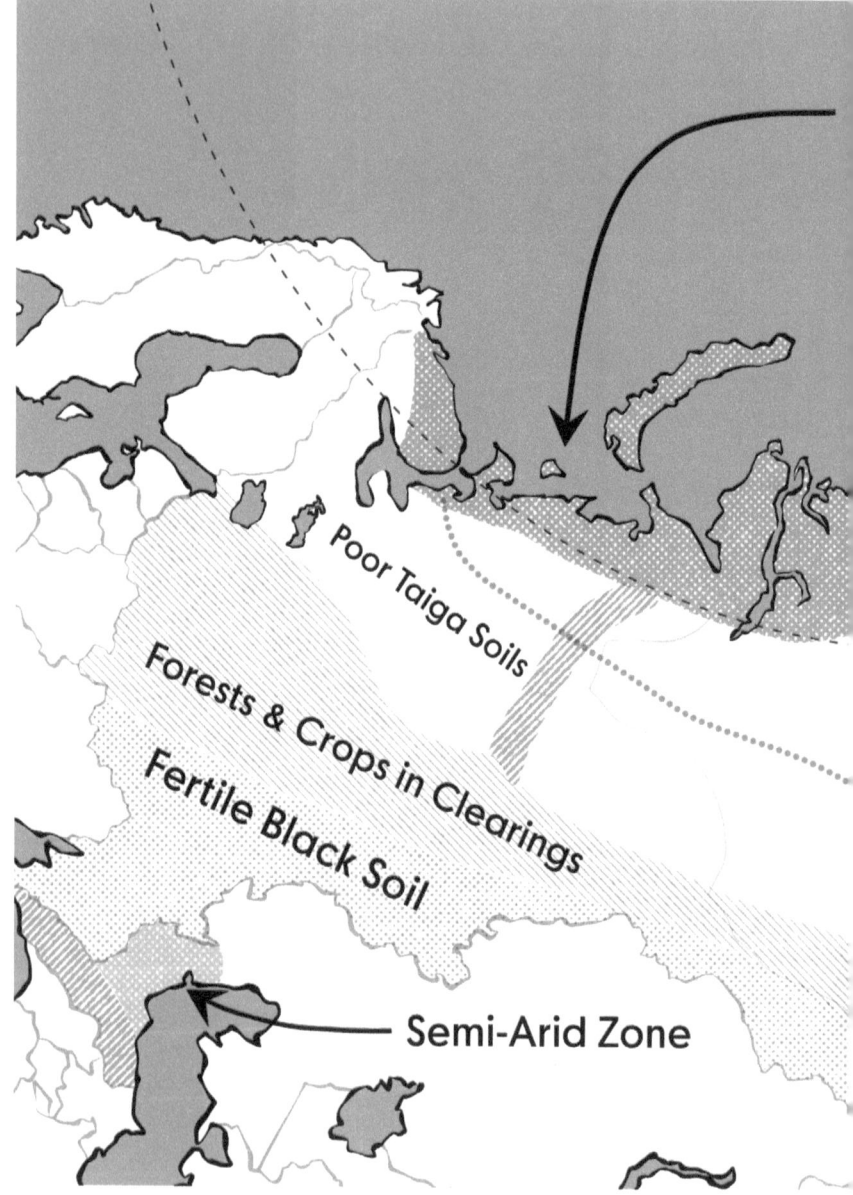

Figure 9: A huge but relatively infertile area in the USSR.

The Soviet Union: The Story of a Green Revolution! 77

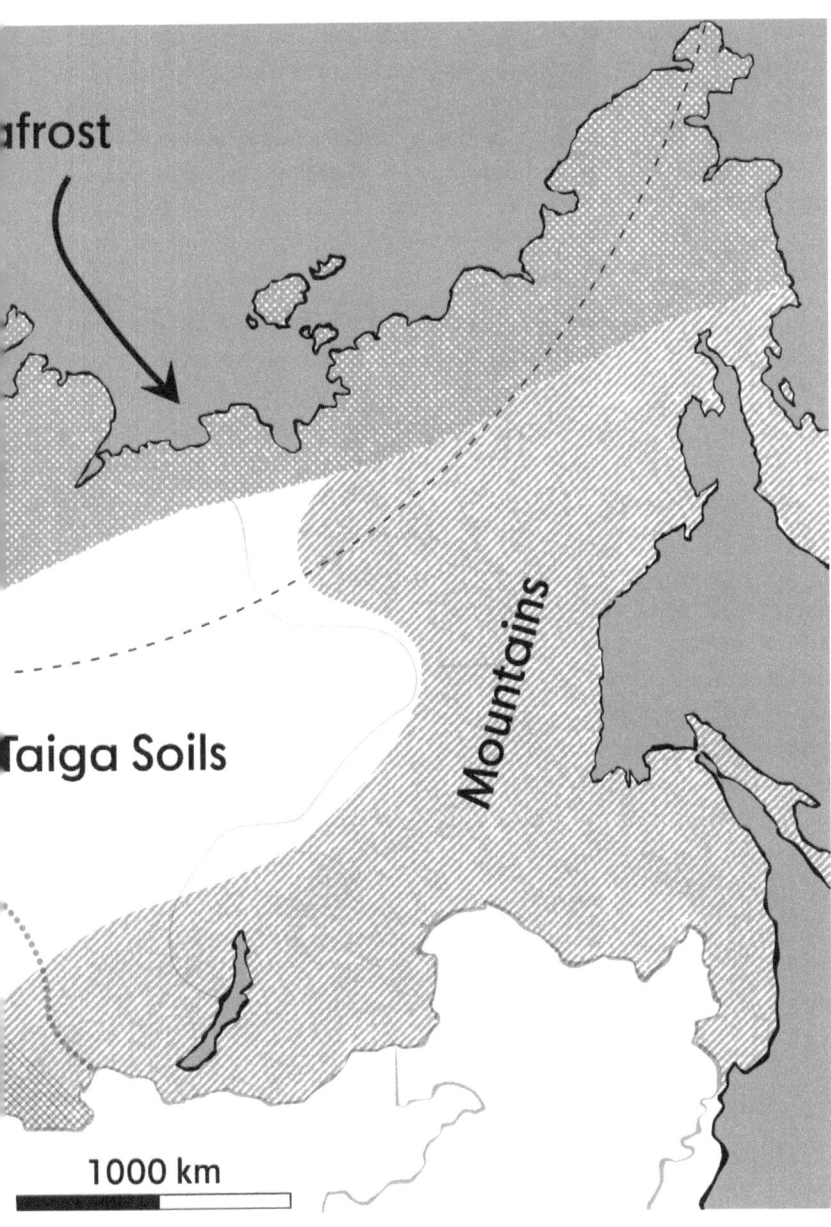

But it was precisely this national, almost cultural or traditional interest in understanding the history and formation of such soils that fertilized pedology from the 19th century onwards and led the Soviet Union to develop extensive rather than intensive agricultural practices. Agricultural profitability was not limited by immutable national borders, but by the fertility deficit of immense Soviet territories left uncultivated. The aim was naturally to remedy this situation by understanding how to fertilize poor soil (and not how to "boost" fertile soil of limited surface area, as advocated by intensive agriculture); first and foremost, by understanding how soil is formed, how it evolves naturally and without human intervention.

This terrain was a necessity for the development of such a science, but it was not enough in itself. What was also needed was a practical guide, a way of thinking capable of integrating knowledge not in a descriptive, formalistic way, but by connecting it dynamically with one another. A world in which all parts are linked, interconnected and set in motion by internal contradictions, transforming quantity into quality and vice versa—that's what dialectical materialism is all about.

While people in the West were still satisfied with a soil classification of soils based strictly and uniquely on underlying parent material, Russian geologists, on the other hand, argued that a soil is born from the dynamic interaction of the mineral subsoil with atmospheric activity and biological activity (the production of humus by bacteria, fungi and microscopic and macroscopic fauna). The players involved in soil formation are therefore numerous and interdependent, and one type of soil can change into another, because everything is dynamic, even if the subsoil remains the same.

In his characterization of Russian soils at the end of the 19th century, Dokuchaev recognized a latitudinal zonation corresponding to climatic zonations. It was his pupil Vladimir Vernadsky, the Soviet "father of science" at the Academy of Sciences, who first formulated the notion of the 'biosphere.' This refers to the thin living envelope formed at the interface between the mineral lithosphere, the hydrosphere (oceans and rivers) and the atmosphere, on the Earth's surface.

The biosphere, a dialectical materialist concept formulated by Vernadsky in 1926, still forms the basis of all ecological considerations, whether concerning soil, climate or human pollution. It emphasizes all the interactions organizing the Earth's different envelopes, and suggests that we should never consider modifying one of its elements while neglecting the others. It's an avant-garde holistic vision that predicts everything that environmentalists are denouncing today in terms of the capitalist system's excesses with regard to the environment.

Why, then, does capitalism overproduce pigs in Brittany with no *a priori* concern for the excess manure to be spread, and therefore toxic nitrates above a certain concentration threshold, in the region's cultivated soils? Why has industrialization produced so much carbon dioxide without considering its impact on the greenhouse effect? Why has overfishing been practiced to such an extent without any thought for the impact of fish disappearance on the trophic balance of the oceans? All these impacts are anticipated in the dialectical materialist approach of Vernadsky, who in this respect is undoubtedly the true father of modern ecology.

When it comes to the issues that have become central to many ecologists today, it's Vernadsky again, as a geochemist, who studied the carbon cycle in particular (between the different terrestrial envelopes where it circulates essentially in the form of carbon dioxide) and the impact of human activities on these geochemical cycles.

During the same period, botanist Vladimir Sukachev[29] developed an even more precise theory of the necessary and dynamic interactions governing living matter and its mineral and organic environment, under the term biogeocenosis (geobiological community). Soviet scientists were undoubtedly at the origin of ecology as a multidisciplinary integration (and not as a purely descriptive and systematizing approach), and remained in the vanguard at least until the 1950s.

Serious historians readily attest to the fact that ecology was born with these Soviet scientists, but refuse to correlate their scientific work with the concrete productions of the Soviet *system*, as if presuming the latter's inability, in its well-known "productivist" *a priori*, to implement genuine environmental protection. But it's not enough to think, we have to act. And in this area, the evidence that ecology was born in the USSR becomes even more dangerous for the West, especially as it did not concern the Leninist period but the so-called "Stalinist" period, before being profoundly called into question with Khrushchev!

29   **Editor's Note:** Vladimir Nikolayevich Sukachev (1880-1967).

As far as the soil is concerned, there are three areas in which a real commitment to environmental protection was evident throughout this period, echoing current Cuban strategies but on a much greater scale. The protection and development of forests, agricultural techniques similar to today's permaculture and agroecology, and the development of the famous *zapovedniki*.

These protected nature reserves, for which Russia is still famous today, were developed in Soviet Russia following the nationalization of land after the Bolshevik revolution. Lenin thought it would be a good idea to generalize to the whole territory the unique experience of the famous Dokuchaev on a first *zapovednik* created in a very limited Russian steppe.

Only a revolution could expropriate the feudal lords in order to manage and integrate the Russian soil, now a recognized and protected national asset. The multiplication of such *zapovedniki* was then easily achieved, since the State owned them on the legal basis of the law "On Natural Monuments, Gardens and Parks" conceived by Lenin in 1921, inspired by the agronomist Podiapolski. While hunting and fishing were strictly limited and controlled on all territories, access to the reserves was banned outright (except for accredited scientists). The aim was to create wilderness reserves throughout the country, both to protect the great diversity of the Soviet environment and its biodiversity, and to enable agronomists to draw inspiration from nature and its natural cycles, adapting the most appropriate agricultural techniques to local conditions.

These *zapovedniki* were places of science, protection of natural resources and instruction for farmers, who were more interested in nature's complex biological responses to permanent environmental disturbances than in formalist, purely "chemical" responses that could be used everywhere, all the time.

Following the recommendations of Vernadsky and his disciple Kojevnikov, each *zapovednik* was to function as an association of autonomous ecosystems, presenting all trophic levels and resembling an ideal fragment of the biosphere. It's easy to see how valuable *zapovedniki* would be today for understanding the impact of man on the environment and climate, at a time when these issues have been pressing for several decades.

There's no romanticism in this political will to develop wilderness reserves. On the contrary, it's a fundamental scientific need to gain a better understanding of the environments (in which man must flourish) and their own history, dynamics, relationships and so on. Soviet ecologist[30] Vladimir Stantchinski, for example, was the first to establish the existence of "biomass pyramids" in the ecosystems observed in these reserves: solar energy is the fundamental "economic" basis of food chains, consumed by primary vegetable producers, which in turn are consumed by animals, with increasing energy losses at each link due to energetic metabolism and digestive efficiency. The stacking of biomass, taking into account losses at each stage of the food chain, thus takes on the characteristic shape of a pyramid.

The wilderness reserves' status rarely changed during the Soviet period. The first temporary change came in 1951, with a decree issued by Alexander Malinovsky, who had been appointed head of the national *zapovedniki* administration a year earlier. His intention was to extend the legal status of the *zapovedniki* with a view to their partial exploitation in connection with the forest plantations of the "Great Plan." The second, much more drastic change, came during Khrushchev's term in office, when he scorned the very concept of *zapovednik* and significantly marginalized them (as shown in Figure 5 on p. 65). Malinovsky's decree concluded a lively and rather complex debate within agricultural decision-making processes, but objectively paved the way for Khrushchev's policy of the almost total dissolution of the *zapovedniki* system.

Feliks Shtilmark, a scientist who was a first-hand witness to the period, even though he was a Khrushchevian, considers Malinovsky to be a precursor to the questioning of the *zapovedniki*, having taken advantage of the massive need for resources that the "Great Plan" implied at the same time:

> We cannot accept the version of events that attributes the instructions for the dissolution of the *zapovedniki* system directly to Stalin or Beria. This story was imposed by Malinovsky himself, and was supported by his successor at the Hunting Journal, Gusev [...] Stalin would have wanted the reform of the

---

30   The term "ecologist" is of course used in its scientific and not "political" sense. [**Translators' Note**: In French there is more non-technical usage of the word 'ecologist' to mean a lay person concerned with environmental issues in general, in this translation those uses have been rendered as 'environmentalist' in English, whereas a scientist who studies ecological systems retains 'ecologist.']

zapovedniki to drag on for centuries, and to be carefully discussed and accepted. No one took the process seriously. It was quite different from ordinary Stalinist repression. [...] In this situation, the setting up of a government commission on the *zapovedniki* was in practice under Malinovsky's control [...].

So, who was the real culprit behind the events of 1951? Some might name Lysenko, others Beria, and still others Stalin—who for us, as everyone knows, was Lenin resurrected. I'm concentrating, however, on the profile of four particularly memorable figures. The most immediate candidates are Boreïko-Malenkov, Merkoulov, Kalachnikov and others, and in particular Minister A. I. Bovin, who had a personal interest in dissolving the *zapovedniki*; and finally, of course, the author of the action himself—Alexander Malinovsky.[31]

This belated legal breakthrough in 1951 was not at all in keeping with the major principles that had prevailed until then. The great afforestation plan did not encroach on the *zapovedniki*, which were considered at that stage only as resources of seedlings, acorns and tree seeds, and not as cultivable areas. Rather, it heralded the fundamental questioning of the Khrushchev period, which would be marked by "productivism" in the sense that environmentalists use the term today.

Soviet Soil: A National Treasure to be Protected

It's obvious: the agronomic techniques of the thirties and forties were inspired for the most part by scientific observations made in these wild reserves where nature evolves freely without human interference. Those who credit postwar Americans with the invention of permaculture, for example, are mistaken. This "permanent culture," based on the linkage of all the components of a rationally and dynamically evolving agrosystem, was originally a pre-war Soviet innovation, which others have subsequently perfected.

In agrobiology, this period saw the confrontation of a science presented as "patriotic" and "dialectical materialist" (led by Lysenko for biology and Williams for pedology) with a science largely inspired by Western scientific theories, often formalist and mechanistic, or even

---

31 Feliks Shtilmark, 2003, *History of the Russian Zapovedniki*, Russian Nature Press.

"chemicalist" (led by Vavilov[32] for genetics and Prianitchnikov[33] for pedology). The latter, like their Western counterparts, relied on the thesis of "decreasing fertility of cultivated soils," the corollary of which was the palliative and therefore necessarily massive use of chemical inputs (chemical fertilizers and pesticides). This theory of diminishing fertility was at the heart of polemics in the USSR at the time, but we can of course add that it remains highly topical in the fight against the abuses of intensive agriculture and for environmental protection.

We know to what extent Trofim Lysenko personally became the subject of controversy well beyond the borders of the Soviet Union, and of unparalleled demonization in the West during the 20th century. We'll come back to this in detail, as we need to formulate a dialectical and scientifically argued critique of the issue. That said, his opponent Vavilov himself recognized certain abilities in this self-taught agronomist and son of Ukrainian peasants. These abilities are linked to a form of "permaculture before its time," as the serious scientific press (rarely, it must be said) acknowledges:

> Nowadays, Lysenko is generally regarded as a pseudo-scientist, but a closer look at his research reveals that his early work on plant improvement was in the mainstream of biology at the time, which opened the doors to recognized scientific conference centers. In 1927, the *Pravda* newspaper dubbed him the Barefoot Scientist, reporting that he had demonstrated that fields usually left fallow during the winter could be used to grow peas and oats for animal fodder. Vavilov sent an emissary to investigate Lysenko's work. He described Lysenko as a fearless and obviously talented experimenter, but added that he was extremely egotistical, believing himself to be the new messiah of biology.[34]

These proposals for a more autonomous and rational form of agriculture are in line with modern permaculturists, who criticize monoculture

---

32 **Editor's Note:** Nikolai Ivanovich Vavilov (1887-1943).

33 A chemist by training, Dmitri Prianchnikov was the Soviet agronomist who most vigorously defended the model of intensive agriculture in the USSR, wishing to develop the country's capacity to produce chemical fertilizers (superphosphates and nitrogen fertilizers) to the maximum. Since the First World War, fertilizer factories have been used collaterally to supply the arms industry with explosive materials, making them doubly useful in wartime.

34 Daniel J. Kevles, 2009, 'Vavilov, Russian martyr of genetics,' *La Recherche* N° 428, March 2009.

and the absurd specialization of entire regions for one type of agricultural production or breeding.

Lysenko and Williams, in their respective fields, focused their research on biology and not just on soil "chemistry," and from this point of view, the *zapovedniki* could represent an important observation terrain. This vision is resurfacing today, precisely in the ecology movement, against the promoters of immediately profitable intensive agriculture, which means exhausting the soil and robbing it of all life except for cultivated plants.

Basically, agronomy is a far-reaching science, as it lies at the crossroads of the history of humanity (which needs to be fed) and the broader history of living organisms (fauna and flora evolving themselves, on different timescales). It is therefore at the heart of political and ideological games, which have not failed to manifest themselves in the Soviet Union, a country which was perpetually encircled and threatened.

Attempting to increase agricultural yields without impacting environmental resources means, above all, increasing the quality of cultivated soils (pedology, mainly under the direction of Williams) and the optimized capacities of cultivated varieties themselves (biology, mainly under the direction of Lysenko). We have deliberately left aside the purely biological aspect of Lysenko's work, certain polemical aspects of which we will return to in the third part of this book. Soviet pedology, on the other hand, offers several aspects that will be of interest to today's environmental activists, and which we present here.

For W. R. Williams, soil is built up slowly, in stages, following a well-known cycle. In the Russian model, which covers all the climates of the northern hemisphere, the soil is born with the tundra and its lichens ("protosol"), and develops into podzol, a taiga soil poor in humus but rich in accumulated organic matter, in the process of being digested by bacteria. This podzol gradually becomes richer and more organized, acquiring a structure that increases its capacity to retain water and mineral salts (thanks to the high production of clay-humus complexes). This is "black earth" or "chernozem," the ideal type of fertile forest soil. But the gradual agglomeration of the natural clods of chernozem eventually makes it impermeable and less fertile. It evolves naturally into steppe soil or even a totally barren desert. It's the end of a natural cycle.[35]

But human intervention, according to Williams' theory, would enable any soil to regain its potential, whatever its stage of development, when the diagnostic is properly carried out, i.e. when we understand the geological or climatic reasons why a given soil has stopped developing below its capacity. All that is needed is for the soil to regain a favorable "structure." This quality alone, according to Williams and Lysenko, defines the fertility of a soil far more than its simple mineral content.[36]

And Even with all the faults and limitations of Williams and Lysenko's view of soils and vegetation, this is the discourse of all the agronomists who are supporters of modern agroecology, whose job is most often to "restore" or "regenerate" a soil worn down by agricultural or industrial pollution, based on a diagnosis of its physico-chemical and biological state. Williams' avant-garde analysis bears a striking resemblance to those of today's dissident agronomists, with the same concern to consider first and foremost the life of the soil, rather than its purely physical relationship with the environment.

Williams already said:

> Soil sterility is often linked [...] to a lack of moisture and, in most cases, to poor soil physical properties. These two [...] factors interact, so that any qualitative or quantitative change in one cannot fail to have repercussions on the other. [...] The physics of the soil is determined by its biology, by the vital activity of plants and microorganisms.[37]

We have every reason to suppose that it is in fine silt that we find all the soil

---

35   **Editor's Note:** This understanding of soil formation and development cycle has been superseded since the 1940s by a more open-ended approach that sees changes in soil type as variable and contingent, as a function of changes over time in regional climate and ecosystem type, as well as human impact, relative to underlying parent materials, influx of variable substances, and landscape position.

36   **Editor's Note:** This sanguine and simplistic take on human impact on soil does not take into account of the fact that soil potentials change over time and that soil properties, of which structure is only one among many, can be much less flexible, especially after negative impacts like topsoil disappearance through erosion or heavy metal pollution.

37   W. R. Williams, 1951, 'Description of land mechanical analytical procedures,' Article cited in, Stolétov, 1951, *Principes élémentaires de biologie mitchourinienne* [*Basic principles of Michurian Biology*].

nutrients accessible to plants, as well as all the decomposing organic matter they contain. Thanks to [its] physical properties [...] the decomposition of the latter exerts a very great influence on the cohesion of the soil, and the fact that it contains all the organic combinations contained in the soil places under the dependence of the quality and quantity of the silt what is called the structure of the soil and the stability of this structure.[38]

To this end, Williams proposed what he called a "herbal system," on the basis of which the most bitter critics were particularly vocal in the 1970s in the West, at the height of the golden age of intensive agriculture. Jaurès Medvedev[39], for example, sought to ridicule the herbal systems theory by comparing it to the "highly competitive" model of chemical fertilizers and pesticides in terms of immediate profitability alone:

> At the start of the war, the grassland system was temporarily buried. The country needed bread, not a specific structure of the soil that suggested phenomenal yields within eight or ten years. The country needed explosives, gunpowder and acids, and the chemical industry—the development of which Williams had opposed—was the only way to provide them. For Williams, the chemical industry was simply "the immobilization of the people's billions" [...]. At the start of the war, we had a significant number of fertilizer factories. They were quickly converted for national defense [...].[40]

For Williams, "it was only a temporary eclipse. After the war, the project was brought back into the spotlight and forcibly imposed throughout the Soviet Union. Once again, Williams' reputation was inflated to fabulous propor-

---

38 W. R. Williams, *Œuvres*, Tome 1, p. 44. We'll see that what Williams calls "fine silt" today actually corresponds to the "clay-humus complexes" (CHCs) at the heart of all fertile soil qualities. For more details on these qualities, and to note the similarities between recent analysis and that of Williams, please refer to Appendix 1, 'Trees are the Masters of the Soil' on pp. 173-176..

39 Jaurès Medvedev was a "Soviet dissident" who wrote a systematic pamphlet in France in 1971, which remains a benchmark for critics of Lysenko and Williams. The book is prefaced by the famous Jacques Monod, a Nobel Prize winner well known at the time for his molecular biology bestseller, *Chance and Necessity* (1970, Éditions du Seuil). Monod, who was also director of the Pasteur Institute, abolished the chair of "soil biology," which testifies to the influence, including ideological, of the chemical fertilizer and pesticide industry on all alternative forms of agronomy at the time (testimonial by agronomist Claude Bourguignon).

40 Jaurès Medvedev, 1971, *Grandeur et chute de Lysenko* [The Rise and Fall of Lysenko].

tions, and once again the Prianitchnikov school was declared reactionary."[41]

One can only imagine the astonishment of environmental activists fed on anti-Soviet propaganda when they read this astonishing praise for chemical fertilizers. If, as a tactical retreat in wartime, the USSR temporarily reintroduced intensive agriculture, taking into account its collateral interest, why did it immediately after the war embarrass itself with an agroecology presumed ineffective since the thirties? Hadn't it been able to see for itself the results of the pre-war grassland system compared with those of intensive agriculture during the Second World War? In a country in ruins in 1948, how could we explain this return to the grassland system as the basis for the "Great Plan," other than as a form of suicidal headlong rush? If grassland systems hadn't worked as part of the "Great Plan," wouldn't Stalin have been quick to condemn Williams, Lysenko, and all their colleagues for "anti-Soviet sabotage" or "undermining national security"?

Does not ironizing about "late" results, as opposed to those of intensive agriculture, which are so rapid but so costly for the farmer and the environment, completely discredit the point? Indeed, it was not until Khrushchev that Williams' grassland systems and Lysenko's "plant education" disappeared, to be replaced by intensive agriculture and heterosis[42], that the USSR, with its "virgin land" campaign, returned to an agriculture similar to that of today's capitalist countries.

The grassland system doesn't mean copying the same model everywhere in the USSR, but diagnosing a suitable soil restructuring plan for each region, based on a principle linked to the optimal characteristics of chernozems. For Medvedev, this is a fanciful model compared to that of the "mineral agrochemists":

> [Pryanitchnikov] emphasized the use of mineral fertilizers [...] and the intensification of agriculture by introducing high-yielding varieties into the planting cycle, as is done in Western Europe [...]. Williams, for his part, advocated not developing the fertilizer industry [...] and renouncing the use of certain machines (harrows, tractors) which, according to him, destroy the texture of the

---

41 Ibid.

42 Heterosis consists in producing new varieties by multiplying the number of chromosomes (polyploidy) in seeds. It's a technique derived from genetics, which Lysenko opposed because environmental conditions had no place in it.

soil. [...] Williams claimed, without putting forward any positive facts, that only heavy, fine-textured soil can be fertile, and that soil texture is the most important factor in obtaining good harvests.[43]

This kind of thinking is taken for granted by today's permaculturists. It's preferable to re-enrich the soil with organic matter (cellulose and lignin in particular), a source of humus, than to apply chemical fertilizers that will leach out or attract weeds, which are highly nitrophilic (which implies or even imposes the use of herbicides, which are normally superfluous). Moreover, the idea of covering soils and stopping plowing to respect their structure and thus their fertility is now commonplace, even if many people are unaware that it was put into practice in the USSR. That doesn't stop Medvedev from mocking these "far-fetched" ideas:

> Lysenko proposed his famous method of planting southern winter varieties on unplowed stubble in Siberia. This, as always, without the slightest experimental support. The theoretical underpinnings of his plan were simple: by dispensing with plowing, he was undoubtedly preserving the integrity of the soil's texture, which, according to Williams' doctrine, would ensure fertility.[44]

All current soil restoration techniques are based on stopping plowing, respecting soil structure and, more often than not, plant cover (in this case "thatch," i.e. mulching) to protect the soil from bad weather and drying out, while stimulating the work of microfauna and microflora by providing a natural supply of degradable organic matter.

Another interesting method at the time was to manufacture compost for soil restoration in natural reactors, using a new formula. The idea was to enable humification from soil and organic fertilizers (animal manures), instead of administering chemical fertilizers directly to the soil. This would avoid the often harmful excesses of nitrogen fertilizers, which would in any case be compensated for by the natural nitrogen enrichment provided by previous crops of leguminous plants[45] (crop rotation), and would add to the soil the lignin and cellulose needed to form clay-humus complexes, thanks to the constant work of soil bacteria and fungi. The

---

43   Ibid.

44   Ibid.

45   Some plants, such as legumes, are able, thanks to root nodules working in symbiosis with nitrifying bacteria, to release into the soil an unabsorbed supplement of nitrates needed to supply nitrogen to other plants in the soil.

idea of inverting the proportions of manure and straw in compost (80% straw and 20% manure, rather than vice versa) may seem far-fetched, but the contribution of lignin and cellulose (straw) in particular took precedence over the contribution of mineral salts[46] which are often too rich in manure. The often serious consequences of excessive nitrate[47] inputs into cultivated soils are well known using manure alone (a nitrogen fertilizer often richer than the chemical fertilizers themselves).

Why emphasize the return of organic matter and life to the soil, rather than chemical fertilizers? Because intensive farming with its pesticides kills the microfauna at the root of humus formation, and without humus the soil progressively loses all fertility, leaving cultivated plants with nothing more than a "dead" soil.

This inert "support," with nutritional requirements supplied exclusively by chemical inputs, does not prevent Medvedev from ironizing once again:

> One of Lysenko's [...] most typical ideas was that manure should only be spread once it had transformed into humus—it was Williams' favorite dream. The disadvantage of this system was that the most precious element in manure, nitrogen, was lost and evaporated into the air. But according to Williams, organic matter was all that mattered. Agrochemists strongly criticized Lysenko's use of [such] small doses.[48]

In fact, Williams had understood before all the Western "agrochemists" that organic compost does not feed plants directly, but rather the soil and its micro-organisms, which digests this material to make humus. Excess compost is always useless. On the other hand, developing the micro-organisms to better digest this compost and turn it into natural humus is a priority for those who want to restore their soil.

---

46   The current effects of excessive slurry application to cultivated soils are well known, as in Brittany, an intensive pig farming region: excess nitrates attract weeds, forcing the use of pesticides in parallel, and seriously contaminate water tables and rivers (green tides, etc.).

47   The example of Brittany is symptomatic. Local pig farmers feed their fields with huge quantities of liquid manure, which they don't know what to do with. The result is that groundwater is no longer fit for human consumption, since the water is so rich in nitrates that it is carcinogenic.

48   Ibid.

Lysenko and Williams still took a radically different line from Western agronomists when it came to plant protection treatments designed to reduce losses: pesticides were heavily criticized as a means of protecting soils, whose fertility depended to a large extent on the work of their microfauna. They preferred to experiment on a large scale with ladybugs, predators of aphids, or even the free-range rearing of poultry, known to feed on weevils in beet fields.[49] In the 1940s, coastal areas benefited indirectly from these fertilizers through run-off, to the detriment of the local ecosystem. As most weeds are nitrophilic, excessive fertilization also requires the use of pesticides, which could have been avoided with less rich compost. In the 1940s, a station was set aside specifically for the breeding of "natural enemies of harmful insects." What environmentalist today could disavow such a policy?

With regard to the forest strips that complete the picture of the grassland system applied to the "Great Plan," Lysenko recommended "nesting plantations." He argued that the majority of seedlings would sacrifice themselves for the benefit of one survivor per nest, strengthened and thus protected from parasitic weeds by its peers. In a kind of effectively madcap romanticism, he asserted that these seedlings "sacrificed" themselves for one of their number, in a kind of intra-specific "altruistic" collaboration.

In reality, this somewhat absurd anthropocentric explanation, which drew hilarity from Medvedev, Monod, their peers and their successors, in no way detracts from the reality of the phenomenon. The self-thinning of tree seedlings in forests when their density is high (nesting of closely spaced seeds), also known as *self-thinning*, is a process well known to silviculturists. In fact, they define a logarithmic law relating the decrease in the number of sprouts to the total biomass of the growing group [Figure 10]. According to this law, there is an optimum seed density for which the survivor(s) will grow more readily.

This property of seedlings seems worthy of note—like other agricultural methods mentioned above—for keeping weeds at bay, which can hinder the fragile growth of a tree plant in its early stages (thus opportunely avoiding the use of pesticides), and boosting growth speed from

---

49 See Nikolai Ovchinnikov's book *L'Académicien Trofim Lysenko* (Éditions Faisceau 2010)

germination onwards, when the initial density is well chosen (thus also avoiding the use of supplementary chemical fertilizers). Medvedev mocks this technique with the following:

> Here's how Lysenko recommended acting: in a small pit, thirty to forty acorns were planted, giving rise to thirty shoots, twenty-nine of which, according to Lysenko, would, without choking each other, nobly sacrifice themselves, to prevent—like valiant soldiers—weeds from choking out the thirtieth. This new "law of the life of the species," called by Lysenko "self-clearing," did not deny the death of the majority of shoots in the nests. However, this death did not occur as a result of overpopulation, but for the glory of the species. "It must be emphasized," he wrote, "that self-enlightenment [...] occurs not because there are too many plants, but precisely to prevent them from becoming too many in the future."[50]

How can such a physiological property not exist in the living world, when we know today the multitude of collective and individual adaptations, each more precise and complex than the last, against variations in the environment?

While many today accuse this technique of having devastated Soviet agriculture, confusing all eras and all experiences, "Stalinist" and "Khrushchevian" alike, (see Figure 13 on p. 136) shows, for example, that this is not the case. Agricultural production in the immediate post-war period, including the techniques presented here, not only did not cause famines, but even rapidly caught up with American productivity at the time. Incidentally, the self-thinning technique was not invented, but only developed by Lysenko, and is referred to by today's silviculturists, who know that it was used in Germany, the Congo, and many other latitudes at the end of the 20th century:

> In 1937, Piotr Hahn, a forester in Kyrgyzstan, experimented with the method on over 50,000 hectares, with Scots pine plots containing 6 plants spaced 5 meters apart from center to center. The first results were published in 1980. [...] As early as 1911, Oguievski was experimenting with the nesting method, sowing bundles of oak acorns over a square meter in spaced plots. In 1948, and again in 1949 and 1950, Trofim Lysenko and other authors showed that the method was worthy of interest, particularly in the reforestation of steppes by creating shelterbelts. In 1938, Scots pine was planted in strips five meters apart, eight and a half meters apart, in the vicinity of Kiev. The intermediate spaces were occupied by oak nests. The experiments were very conclusive.[51]

---

50   Jaurès Medvedev, 1971, *Grandeur et chute de Lysenko*.
51   R. Pierlot, 2007, 'Reforestation in the tropics,' *Tropicultura* N° 25.

Figure 10: Nest planting, a reality. In this example, the arrows show the evolution of self-thinning for five nests with different initial densities, over time. It can be seen that there is a relationship between the initial density and the mass of material in the surviving plants.

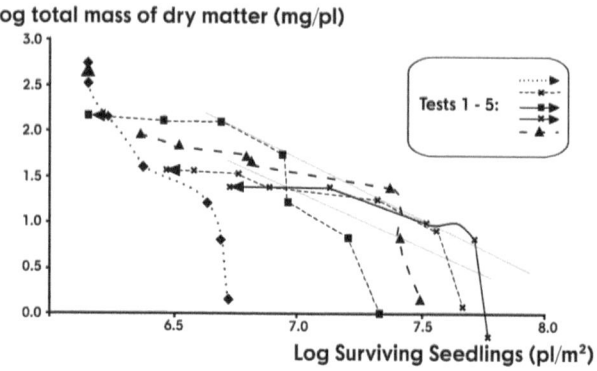

Source: M. Faravani and B.B. Baki, 2009. Population structure and its influence on self-thinning of *Melastoma malabathricum*. *Research Journal of Environmental Sciences*, 3:52-61.

The very idea of planting strips of forest between cultivated fields seems to be a recent rediscovery by the scientific lobby that is inextricably linked with agribusiness (INRA),[52] after more than half a century of destruction of protective hedges and intensive agriculture. We must avoid the ridiculous comparison with the Cuban agroforestry model mentioned above. But it's a risk we have to take: comparisons with an even older and much more controversial model could easily resurface today. So we need to anticipate this.

In a baccalauréat subject for the 2016 semester (Série ES, enseigne-

---

52   **Editor's Note:** The *Institut National de la Recherche Agronomique* (INRA) was a French public research institute dedicated to agricultural science. On January 1, 2020, it became INRAE, France's National Research Institute for Agriculture, Food and Environment, formed by the merger of INRA, the National Institute for Agricultural Research, and IRSTEA, the National Research Institute of Science and Technology for the Environment and Agriculture.

ment scientifique/Métropole), for example, INRA is presented to future students as a modern, quasi-environmentalist organization, providing information worthy of the best agroecologists, but which is particularly eloquent on the recent setbacks of agribusiness. As just one example of these formal "self-criticisms" aimed at the general public, it states in part:

> Until the middle of the twentieth century [...] the rise of mechanization and the chemical industry [...] led to a massive uprooting of trees in order to be able to work larger plots. Today, however, yields are stagnating, biodiversity is declining, pests and weeds are becoming increasingly resistant, and groundwater is sometimes polluted with NO3 nitrate ions. [...] Researchers at INRA have conducted several experiments on agroforestry systems [...] and have shown that for plots of the same size, the yield of an agroforestry plot is globally superior to that of a single crop and an isolated forest.[53]

We add that, while trees have the advantage of providing crops with a natural, permanent source of leaves and twigs containing organic matter and mineral salts returning to the soil, their roots covering large surfaces absorb excess nitrates, provide deep horizons with dead rootlets that are a source of lignin and useful for humification, and penetrate deep enough into the subsoil to accelerate mineralization of the parent rock, a source of additional clays and mineral salts. The accompanying photographs [Figures 11a and 11b, next page] might border dangerously on plagiarism, were it not for the fact that nobody remembers the Stalinist "Great Plan" just before the "middle of the 20th century"!

---

53   *Subject de Métropole, Baccalauréat enseignement scientifique Série ES session,* 2016.

Figure 11a [above]: INRA reinvents the butter knife? (1)
Figure 11b [below]: INRA reinvents the butter knife? (2)

Source, preceding two images: Photos by Christian Dupraz (INRA, 2016) to illustrate the 2016 baccalauréat subject on agroforestry. Agroforestry, an alternative technique to intensive agriculture, was at the heart of Soviet agricultural policy until the Khrushchev era and is still at the heart of Cuba's, before being promoted in a "measured" way by INRA, after the ravages of pesticides and chemical fertilizers.

The struggle between the advocates of organic, sustainable agriculture and the advocates of intensive, polluting agriculture, now more kindly referred to as "conventional agriculture," is therefore a long-standing one. But we know that this battle is far from won by the former, contrary to what agribusiness' belated "self-criticism" might lead us to believe. In 2014, a major report by INRA,[54] commissioned by the French Ministry of Agriculture, dealt blows to organic farming with rare violence and hypocrisy, given the global ravages of fertilizers and pesticides.

A slew of a hundred French agronomists from INSERM, CNRS and INRA itself, protested against the conclusions of this biased report, whose aim was clearly to discredit organic farming in all its aspects in the face of the omnipotence of "conventional" agriculture. One of the authors of the protest letter stated, among other things:

> This report proposes to approach organic farming in the same way as conventional farming, by breaking down performance by area (productivity, environment, social, etc.). But organic and conventional farming have very different logics. It's as if you were comparing the performance of a bicycle and a car solely from the point of view of speed! The aim of organic farming is not to produce as much or more than conventional agriculture, it's to produce differently, while respecting the ecological and social environment. An honest report should have presented the aims of organic farming and its holistic approach: it can only be studied by considering the system as a whole.[55]

One might at first note that such a retort might be appropriate in retrospect to Jaurès Medvedev and Jacques Monod's violent attacks on Soviet agriculture in the thirties and forties, which were basically of the same nature.

This controversy between researchers may therefore help us to understand more widely how the heterodox practices of Soviet agronomists aroused the "conventional" scientific community's violent reaction of rejection. During the golden age of intensive agriculture in the 1970s,

---

54 The report is entitled '*Vers des agricultures à hautes performances / Analyse des performances de l'agriculture biologique*' (Towards high-performance agriculture / Analysis of the performance of organic farming), under the direction of Hervé Guyomard, Director of INRA (Institut National des Recherches en Agronomie), France's biggest lobby for intensive agriculture

55 Remarks reported by *ReporTerre* magazine, *Tempête à l'INRA autour d'un rapport sur l'agriculture biologique*, Marie Astier, February 2014.

it was much easier to vilify the proponents of sustainable agriculture, given that in the USSR they had taken a rare offensive, dominant position, rather than a defensive, marginal one.

Self-proclaimed "dissidents from INRA" such as Claude and Lydia Bourguignon, well-known lecturers and proponents of agroecology, are particularly harsh on the deplorable methods encouraged and subsidized by the French state and, more broadly, the European Union and the US. Their remedy: restore destroyed or exhausted soils by reinjecting life and organic matter, the only things capable of restoring their structure and ensuring the satisfaction of plant needs. Drawing inspiration from natural environments, they put forward the ancient idea of "agro-sylvo-pastoralism," i.e. the rational and autonomous articulation of cultivation under plant cover, the use of trees (shelter from the elements, but also sources of lignin) and the use of livestock pastures (animals fed on cultivated grasses and producing slurry that can be reused for natural composts).

You will recognize here the principles that once underpinned the "Great Plan" and its pre-war beginnings in the USSR, always in favor of biology, that is, of life (Lysenko and Williams purposely declared themselves to be "agrobiologists"), against mineral, formalist, mechanistic and polluting agrochemicals, destroying the soil in the long term, from which they nonetheless made enormous immediate profits.

Energy Policy: The Premium on Renewables

As we have seen, the energy issue is not only closely linked to modern, highly mechanized agricultural production, but goes far beyond it, since it forms the basis of our industrial production and our daily lives, in both capitalist and socialist systems. The energy we consume today pollutes, depletes, and destabilizes our environment to such an extent that its complex effects are often unpredictable.

Alongside the agricultural question, this is one of the two main areas of struggle for modern environmentalists, with one constant: whatever a country's energy choices, they are always visibly marked by as many advantages as unsolvable disadvantages, which means that the overall solution is not to develop scientific research into economically and ecologically more advantageous choices, but rather to reduce energy consumption, or "degrowth."

As we have seen, up to this last proposal, Cuba is still in the vanguard, albeit largely for reasons of immediate material constraints (scarce local energy resources and the continuing blockade). "Degrowth" itself can only be implemented under a planned social regime. But then again, this is not an end in itself, but a tactical choice in difficult times, while we wait for better days. If "degrowth" were conceived as a strategic choice rather than a tactical one, it could only serve a pessimistic and defeatist policy, disarmed in the face of capitalism in the final analysis.

In the case of the USSR, the context was very different: from the outset, reserves of coal, oil and natural gas were immense and immediately available. Its growing energy needs naturally led it to exploit these resources as a matter of priority in order to "electrify the country" and lay the groundwork for true socialist modernization in both town and country, according to Lenin's well-known formula.[56]

However, even at this level, before Khrushchev, the choice of energy resources could vary according to context and geography. The five-year plans of the pre-war and immediate post-war periods, for example, combined the irrigation potential of the great Siberian rivers with the construction of large hydroelectric dams.[57] These choices were complementary, since the dams were to create countless water reservoirs capable of supplying agricultural regions disrupted by chronic drought. The Great Plan for the Transformation of Nature involved the construction of numerous dams in the region between the Dnieper and the Urals, in addition to the Uglitch, Shcherbakov, Gorky, Molotov and Kuibyshev dams in the north of the country (see Figure 6 on pp. 70-71).

These choices are not insignificant: hydroelectric generation combines a number of advantages. As a renewable energy, it is not intermittent like wind or solar power, which is important because electricity cannot be stored. What's more, it's a huge and immediately available potential energy source, with high profitability and low human investment over the long term. Finally, from an environmental

---

56   "Communism is Soviet power plus the electrification of the whole country," said Lenin in *Our Foreign and Domestic Position and Party Tasks*. He added: "since industry cannot be developed without electrification."

57   For example, the Dnieper dam built in 1932 was the largest in the world at the time.

point of view, we can say that this energy, which is totally mechanical, produces no pollution, and on the contrary contributes to the irrigation of certain agricultural regions, and even to microclimatic modifications favorable to cultivation.

The only obstacle to this kind of technology is, of course, the upfront cost, both material and human, involved in building the dam. That's why this kind of major project is more likely to be carried out in a country capable of national planning and massive state investment, with no immediate economic counterpart, than in a capitalist country that responds to demand as quickly as possible, and without considering the human and ecological costs (hydrocarbons are the most typical example).

It should be noted that the vast size of the Soviet landmass may at first seem in some ways an advantage for agriculture. However, it covers so many latitudes that agriculture remains highly weather-contingent, and is particularly susceptible to drought. When it comes to hydroelectric production, the immensity of the landmass becomes an even greater disadvantage in that the long-distance, country-wide transmission of electricity leads to the potential for substantial energy dissipation, with serious repercussions on energy efficiency.

It was no doubt these kinds of considerations that led the post-Stalinist USSR to opt for hydrocarbons on a massive scale. Indeed, in addition to satisfying the needs of the Soviets themselves, the surplus, given the immensity of underground reserves, could be sold on the international market without any problem, and to a very large number of customers. This choice, already not very ecological as we know, also heralded the beginning of a real Soviet dependence on the USA, as we have already mentioned. With the dollars provided in exchange for oil, the USSR began to buy an ever-increasing complement of cereals to feed local livestock, when agriculture became deficient. Successive plans during this period constantly pointed to the "backwardness" of the USSR in the thirties and forties with regard to oil extraction, and set themselves the goal of catching up as quickly as possible.

In the 1960s, the eminent work of Soviet climatologists on climate change was logically dissociated from national energy choices.

In the thirties and forties, the USSR Academy of Sciences produced groundbreaking work on climate change.[58]

In this context, it is important to bear in mind the importance of solar radiation and the greenhouse effect of cloud cover, as well as the aggravating effects of climate change on terrestrial albedo, particularly in the polar ice caps. While Western climatology was confined to a descriptive, formalist approach, Russian climatology had long been based on geography-climatology interactions, in other words, on much more dynamic and fruitful "physico-geographical relationships" underpinned by a materialist, dialectic reading grid. Evgraf Fedorov Jr. theorized a "climatology of complexes," criticizing the formalism of climatologists who isolated climatic conditions from one another in their studies. And contrary to this same formalism, which saw in climatic variations a constant cyclicity, he included in it a "dynamic climatology" better able to detect and understand long-term global climatic upheavals, beyond these great astronomical cycles.

A French geographer commented very positively on this work in 1967, remarking that the Soviets were the only ones to concern themselves with the Earth's radiation balance—or including albedo—from one environment to another or globally, and with the fundamental calculations for analyzing global climate change today:

> We know that the genesis of the climates of different geographic regions is determined above all by the local conditions of the radiation regime. In our country, however, we do not pay much attention to measuring the different terms of this radiation balance [...] The Jordan heliograph used for our measurements is an obsolete instrument compared with the actinometers in use at the main meteorological stations in the USSR. These [...] accurately measure the radiation flux received per unit of horizontal surface, the reflected radiation flux and the radiation balance of this surface. [...] The contents of this Atlas bear witness to the activity of Soviet climatologists and meteorologists.

---

58   Soviet climatologist Evgraf Fedorov Jr. (1880-1965) was renowned at the time for his study of these different effects. We now know that, in addition to the greenhouse effect directly linked to anthropogenic CO_2 emissions, the interrelationships between variations in solar radiation and variations in cloud cover undoubtedly explain a a non-negligible part of current global warming/climate change (see the recent work of geologist Vincent Courtillot in particular). [**Editor's Note:** this is actually not the case; greenhouse gas emissions, along with human-induced land cover change are the main factor.]

The knowledge acquired is put to good use by cartographers who rank among the most qualified in the world.[59]

Clearly, all these Soviet theoretical and technical tools, derived from a materialist and dynamic conception, as opposed to a fixist formalism, would potentially contribute to global climate change assessments. At that time, however, the average global climate in the post-war period was undergoing a slight decline, similar to but more marked than the current "climate pause."[60] Global warming and its supposed origins were not yet on the agenda. In the forties and fifties, no one could have suspected that a massive release of carbon dioxide could have global climatic consequences [Figure 12]. Unfortunately, today's global warming cannot be blamed on the cruel Stalin...

An American ecologist[61] and famous academic like John Bellamy Foster paid tribute to Soviet science, which continued more or less into the last years of the USSR:

> The Soviets developed the world's most advanced climatology and were the first to warn of the dangers of global warming, with Budenko's demonstration of the positive shrinkage of ice albedo. As early as 1961, he was the first to draw attention to what he called the inevitable anthropogenic warming created by human activities.[62]

---

59   'Atlas soviétique relatif à la climatologie du globe terrestre,' in *Annales de Géographie*, Pierre Carrière, N° 417, 1967.

60   The Earth's average temperature has in fact stopped rising since 1998, which means that climatologists analyzing global warming over the course of the 20th century have observed a climatic "pause." Some, perceiving a synchronization between this pause and that of the increase in the solar regime itself, have even tended to think that global warming has more to do with solar radiation than with the human-made greenhouse effect. [**Editor's Note:** Average global temperatures have actually increased since then and, regardless, the scientific consensus has been even in the late 1990s that the current global average temperature increases are due mainly to human causes.]

61   **Editor's Note:** Sociologist, not ecologist.

62   'Marxism and the Environment,' interview with J. B. Foster, *Médiapart*, May 19, 2016.

Figure 12: Global temperature variations over the 20th century.

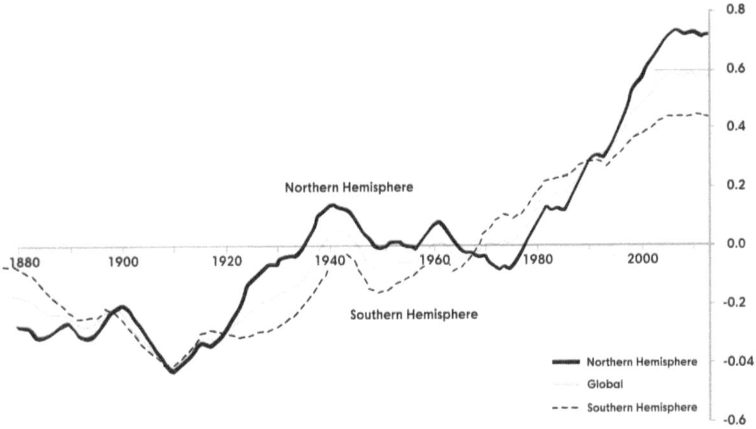

Source: Olivier Berruyer (www.les-crises.fr).

In the USSR, energy options, whether or not they were linked to contemporary climate risks, were therefore the result of two equally valid precautions: achieving complete energy independence and protecting environmental resources, which are part of the national heritage and therefore of national security. The renewable nature of the energies extracted was logically a priority; the example of the impressive development of hydroelectric dams bears witness to this, even if oil extraction also existed (although this was drastically accelerated in the sixties and seventies). At present, however, we can't say that there is a truly ideal form of energy for satisfying both powerful renewable yields and total environmental protection. In 1948, under the pen of academic geochemist A. Fersman, the magazine Études soviétiques was already predicting futuristic solutions made possible by the development of science and technology, always revealing a very cutting edge concern for renewable energies, starting with geothermal energy, a source so little talked about even today:

> The ocean of magma bubbling under our feet with immense quantities of heat will become accessible to man. Through large conduits [...] man will reach these layers where temperatures range from five to seven hundred degrees. He will heat the Earth's surface using thermal power stations buried deep under-

ground, and stop destroying forests, no longer burning coal so necessary for the chemical industry, and no longer using oil for heating. Millions of calories will spread across the Earth's surface.[63]

Geothermal energy is still a long way from replacing the polluting energies of the 20th century, even if the Soviets were once again the first to drill deep into the earth's crust with this in mind.[64]

But there is a very real project for producing energy that is at once renewable and clean (like solar and wind power), non-intermittent (like hydroelectric power), powerful and highly profitable (like oil), and incapable of "going haywire" (unlike nuclear fission): this is magnetic nuclear fusion, a scientific promise that even today seems as ideal as it is inaccessible. Here too, it has to be said, the USSR of the 1950s was in the vanguard of its implementation.

Such energy has never been produced before, and remains a major focus of physics research in laboratories around the world. But it was in the USSR that the first models were developed, and it's from them that all current research is still based: a *toroidal particle plasma generator* ("tokamak") in which the aim is to reproduce the nuclear fusion reactions of our sun. In a way, it's a matter of "canning the sun," which is the first of all energies available on Earth.[65, 66] The reaction consists of isotopes of hy-

---

63   A. Fersman, 'L'an 2000 vu par un chimiste,' *Études soviétiques* N° 2, June 1948.

64   The famous SG-3 borehole (or Kola borehole) started in 1970 in Russia and interrupted in 1990 with the demise of the USSR is still unrivaled in the world: it is by far the deepest borehole in the world, and was designed to reach the base of the earth's crust. It reached a depth of over twelve kilometers.

65   Such nuclear fusion is the source of the solar energy received by the Earth, used by plants to produce biofuels (or fossil fuels, storing very ancient plant fossils), and which drives atmospheric currents (wind), hydrospheric currents (water vapor) and ocean evaporation, thus the water cycle, turning hydroelectric dams mounted on rivers... With the exception of nuclear fission and geothermal energy, all recoverable energy is directly or indirectly solar-generated.

66   The USSR was the first country to send satellites, and then a man into space: Yuri Gagarin. Only the deadly competition between the two powers drove the USA to spend lavishly to program ambitious space programs of their own, to "humiliate" the USSR and "save their honor." Years later, they succeeded in sending men to the Moon. This was achieved, moreover, on the basis of a state-run NASA, operating without private competition, and with massive funding—just like in a socialist regime, where the enemy's weapons are always the best! It's worth noting that, once the Soviet rival began to decline

drogen, a resource present in the hydrosphere and therefore everywhere on Earth, with no possibility of commercialization or geostrategic neighborhood conflicts, to create atoms of helium, a very light inert gas notably present in the solar wind and in the upper atmosphere. Neither the raw material nor the products pose any ecological or economic problems.

The only problem with this energy source—and it's a big one—is getting the reactor up and running in the first place. The initial energy input to the system is so considerable that it has not yet been possible to produce it. Beyond an initial threshold of injected energy, conventionally referred to as "Q," the reactor is self-powered and produces unlimited energy, i.e. several times "Q," without depleting any resources and without producing stable nuclear waste or the technical risks of a runaway, for example. At present, the maximum energy produced by a nuclear fusion reactor is 20% of the energy initially injected (Q/5). The common goal of research laboratories is to one day exceed this famous "Q" threshold...

It's no coincidence that the first "tokamaks" (Russian for "toroidal magnetic chambers") were built by Soviet physicists in the early 1950s. Even if, for Western observers, this may have seemed like a "luxury" in a country seeking to recover rapidly from a particularly destructive war, and with dizzying reserves of hydrocarbons to ensure its recovery.

But it's above all the colossal investment this energy requires that makes the centrally planned socialist system, once again, the best candidate for its implementation. We know that a capitalist system, based on the desire for immediate and maximum profit, as well as on private ownership of resources and means of production, cannot by definition invest sufficiently, either financially or over time, in any "sustainable" strategy.

Only a socialist system, such as the USSR in the past (or Cuba to a lesser extent today, but with much more modest resources at its core), can afford such investments "without immediate return on investment," whether it's the implementation of colossal worksites over several years (hydroelectric dams), afforestation involving years of work, resulting in the creation of a new forest. It's a similar situation for nuclear fusion, which was born as a major project in the USSR, and developed most

---

economically and finally disintegrate, the USA rapidly abandoned all the space projects planned by scientists—because the cost was too high, of course, for an imperialism in crisis and now on the verge of collapse

extensively there, yet still failed to produce results more than sixty years later under capitalist conditions. It's obvious, then, that a communist who is currently a "productivist," rather than promoting the dangerous nuclear fission in a decontextualized way to an environmental activist, should instead promote the energy of tomorrow for its virtues that are both ecological and economic: fusion!

On the other hand, it would be appropriate for an environmental activist to take a serious, non-dogmatic look at nuclear alternatives to uranium, while awaiting the advent of this long-term solution.

Uranium has a number of major drawbacks: the risk of runaway production and lasting pollution of the environment;[67] the production of long-lasting nuclear waste, the plutonium that feeds into the lucrative military-industrial atomic weapons lobby; the scarcity of resources on the planet, leading to imperialist conflicts of interest that are the source of wars in Africa and Asia.

In the West, research programs on "molten salts" nuclear power based on thorium were deliberately blocked on the pretext that they could be used in the production of atomic bombs.[68] However, the molten-salt principle avoids any risk of runaway or overheating: it contains within itself the process of immediate shutdown by dilution, with a plug melting under the effect of overheating to trigger dilution and hence reactor shutdown. It produces waste with a lifespan a thousand times shorter than that of uranium waste, for a much smaller quantity.

The only country in the vanguard of such programs today, injecting colossal sums for results planned at the highest levels of government, under the watchful eye of the Americans and Europeans: China. China... Here again, even under a "state capitalist" form with disparate elements of socialism, whose key sectors have remained public, it's probably no coincidence.

Anti-communism generally denounces anything that, in the name of human progress, derogates from the fundamental laws of nature, wheth-

---

67   Accidents at Three Miles Island (USA, 1979), Chernobyl (USSR, 1986), Fukushima (Japan, 2011).

68   Thorium is much more common in the earth's subsurface than uranium, whose distribution is very specific and limited. It is therefore not subject to conflicts of interest.

er it's our energy production or our agricultural production. However, the Soviet experience in practice, and Marx's doctrine in theory, foresees something quite different:

> The full development of human mastery over the forces of nature, those of so-called nature as well as of humanity's own nature.[69]

For Marx and his successors, "dominating" natural forces does not mean destroying or exhausting them. If you think about it, the opposite is true. It is precisely capitalism's inability to "dominate" these forces that explains their current destruction, its inability to dominate man's "inclination" to exploit his environment without a long-term vision. Whether it's a question of the most efficient and eco-compatible energy production, or agricultural production that doesn't pit quality against quantity,[70] the Soviet Union has shown what a socialist system is capable of, the only one able to invest massively over the long term in scientific research and the best (rather than the most immediately profitable) techniques in energy and agronomy.

In retrospect, the search for a "third way" that looks back to an idealized but little-known past, by activists who see capitalism and communism as two sides of the same "productivist" coin, is understandable. But it is based on a fatal confusion: true productivism, the boom in oil extraction and agribusiness, the race for profitability, the triumph of abundance in defiance of "natural laws," are an innovation of the USA in the immediate post-war period. In the USSR, alignment with these methods was deferred until the 1960s, when Khrushchevian revisionism, the first economic and even theoretical retreat in the face of American imperialism, decided to abandon what made the USSR unique, including in the agricultural and environmental fields.

This current confusion between the pre- and post-Khrushchev Soviet Union, maintained if not organized by the dominant bourgeois ideology, operates not only in the field of technology and economics, but perhaps even more so in the realm of theory. It is in this way, however,

---

69 Marx, *Grundrisse*, Penguin, 1993, p. 488.

70 What the advocates of "organic" agriculture do on the one hand, polarized on medieval and "family" techniques) and the advocates of productivist agriculture on the other, generating food that is very abundant but lacking in nutrients.

that the Soviet specter could well begin to haunt Europe and the West again... through what is undoubtedly the most demonized paradigm: dialectical materialism.

3

DIALECTICAL MATERIALISM: BRAKE OR BOOST FOR AGROBIOLOGY?

A Handful of Crypto-Lysenkoists Shake up Conventional Agriculture

AGROECOLOGY WALKS ON TWO LEGS: one is pedology, the science of soils, which enables us to optimize or re-fertilize a field by finding ecological alternatives to agribusiness inputs. The other is just as important, but we've deliberately left it aside because it relates to a moment in the history of science that is still controversial, even if from a Western point of view, the matter seems to have been settled. It concerns the selection of plant varieties optimized for agriculture. To develop agriculture, we use the most desirable, best-adapted varieties, and give them a soil conducive to their optimal development. As far as the soil is concerned, we have seen the gulf between the Western, mechanistic viewpoint, which separates it absolutely from its natural environment, and the Soviet viewpoint, which is much more dialectical and takes account of all the natural parameters that determine it. With regard to plants themselves, the distinction is similar, between a highly mechanistic genetic point of view, we would call "above-ground soil" today, and another, Soviet, point of view, that is much more dialectical, based on the evolution of species described by Charles Darwin. To shed some light on this long-running controversy, we'll have to take a look at the history of science.

It is obvious that from the point of view of profitability and the difficulty of farming in the face of climatic hazards and losses caused by various pests, the selection of varieties that are resistant or better adapted to local conditions is a central issue in agronomy. In this respect, two "schools" of thought emerged from the 1930s onwards. The first, born in the West, is the "Mendelo-Morganist"[1] genetics approach, which asserts that species evolve *randomly* on the basis of rare, accidental mutations in genetic determinants that are hereditarily fixed ("written" or "coded") from generation to generation. On this basis, Western breeders look for plants that already carry hereditary advantages, and seek to "purify the [genetic] line" in order to exploit it in the field. This is the aim of classical genetics, founded by Mendel and Morgan, which assumes that mutations are accidental and cannot be "controlled"—a seemingly materialistic viewpoint.

In the USSR, on the other hand, Ivan Michurin,[2] at the turn of the century, then Trofim Lysenko from the 1930s onwards, developed a whole series of techniques for obtaining new varieties on the basis of what they called "plant education." These positions are irreconcilable with those of commonly-accepted genetics, although they clearly stem from practical experience and "common sense." While the former assert that hereditary variations can only occur accidentally, the latter hereditary traits: an "apprenticeship" (an "acquired trait") capable of making plants (and their seeds, since we're talking about heredity) desirable for this or that local growing condition.

For more than twenty years, these currents battled it out in Soviet laboratories, clashing over a theoretical contradiction that was clearly unsurpassable, until the "Michurinian" current became dominant, from 1948 to the 1960s. We'll see in detail the conditions under which this conflict took place, but to set the context right now, it's worth pointing out that genetics, after a long period of theoretical stagnation in the thirties and forties, didn't become the "science in vogue" until the sixties, with reproducible, indisputable results all over the world, which ensures the success of today's transgenesis (production of GMO plants and animals for agriculture and livestock).[3] Lysenko, the critic of idealistic genetics, became, quite simply, indefensible.

---

1   In 1866, Gregor Mendel was the discoverer of "genes," eòements that can be separated from one another and transmitted without distortion from generation to generation, carrying information about the characters expressed. In 1933, Thomas H. Morgan discovered that these elements are carried by the famous chromosomes that can be observed in the nucleus of dividing cells under the microscope.

2   **Editor's Note:** Ivan Vladimirovich Michurin, 1855-1935.

3   GMOs, or *genetically modified organisms*, are concrete proof that heritable and

The most memorable aspect of this period is undoubtedly the harsh polemic that the Lysenkoists aroused in the West. Accused of charlatanism, they were denounced for their dogmatism, placing "politics before science" and for silencing any sympathy for the "reactionary Mendelo-Morganist" theses.

It was too good an opportunity to condemn "Marxism-Leninism" where it had clearly sinned against its very principles. Some Marxist biologists have unscrupulously asserted theoretical untruths, radically questioning the "soma-germen" separation postulated by the scholar Weismann[4] at the end of the 19th century, and reaffirming the famous "heredity of acquired traits," the "heresy" against which genetics was founded and built throughout the 20th century.

However, the "heredity of acquired traits" did not have the same theoretical content in the idealist Lamarck as in Lysenko.[5] Lysenko claimed to be a Darwinian against Lamarck. For Lysenko, this was nothing more than a very specific form of heredity, which enabled a plant that had been "educated" by previously defined environmental stresses to produce seeds with the same resistance capacities as those of its parents, *provided that these seeds were grown*—and it's

---

isolable determinants (genes) can indeed control this or that characteristic of an organism, since we are able to transfer them selectively from one individual to another. We'll leave aside for the moment the controversy surrounding the consequences of this type of manipulation, and focus solely on the purely scientific aspect.

4   Weismann asserted the total impermeability between an individual's reproductive cells (germen) and all its other cells (soma), so that no modification acquired by the organism at somatic level could ever be transmitted to descendants via the reproductive cells.

5   The formula was coined by Jean-Baptiste de Lamarck, an eighteenth-century French naturalist: before Darwin, he considered that characters acquired during an individual's lifetime could be passed onto offspring. Thus the well-known pattern of the giraffe stretching its neck to reach higher and higher foliage, transmitting this stretching progressively from generation to generation, until giraffes are born spontaneously with a longer neck. Weisman demonstrated, in an experiment almost as caricatural as Lamarck's proposal itself, that this was not the case: mice whose tails are cut off over many, many generations never give birth to tailless mice. 'Neo-Darwinians' would synthesize genetics, asserting the random *mutation of genes*, and Darwinian *natural selection*, acting as an after-the-fact filter on these rare variations, leaving only those forms that are advantaged in a given environment to survive and reproduce. The "chance-selection couple" will act as a definitive denial of all heredity-acquired characteristics.

essential to remember this—*under the same environmental conditions as the parents*. He therefore spoke of a "heredity of characters acquired *by habit*" or "metabolic heredity" (i.e. based on "innate capacities to be acquired" when necessary). In the eyes of modern geneticists, this was just as impossible as the Lamarckian caricature, but it differed profoundly from it in its very definition and its consequences for agronomy, and at the same time ruled out any caricature.[6]

Fantasy? Charlatanry? Scientific fact? For decades, we've been talking about "pseudoscience" or "invention" designed to forcibly twist reality in a direction more in line with the principles of dialectical materialism, as a fundamentalist would have done under the filter of his sacred scriptures. But whatever we think of these results, we can feel today how alternatives to the use of toxic pesticides are gradually becoming the obsession of agronomists, especially at a time when soil fertility is becoming increasingly difficult to maintain in agrochemicals-dependent farming. During the golden age of intensive, unscrupulous agriculture, cultivated varieties were selected on the basis of criteria imposed by capital: size, profitability, inability to survive without certain inputs sold separately, etc. Today, we realize that these criteria are not always met. Today, we realize that true selection should have produced intrinsically resistant varieties, able to do without pesticides and other chemical crutches to live in variable or exposed environments.

It's against this backdrop of urgency that we're rediscovering certain independent, "eccentric," self-taught, empiricist growers capable of producing such "educated" seeds, which are obviously far from appearing in the official catalogs of the GNIS.[7]

---

6   Let's not forget that Darwin was a proponent of an equally "naïve" theory of heredity, for which he had no complaints. According to him, "gemmules" could pass from somatic cells (those that interact with the environment and can "acquire") to the germinal cells (cells that can transmit the characteristics to offspring via sperm and egg cells). "Emitted by all parts of the system, [the] gemmules come together to form the sexual elements, and their development in the next generation constitutes a new being; but they may also be transmitted in a latent state to future generations and then develop," said Darwin in 'On the Variation of Animals and Plants in the Domestic State.' This theory of "gemmules," which was soundly defeated by the first geneticists, is coming back with a vengeance with the latest generation of geneticists, in the form of "retrotransposons."

7   *Groupement Interprofessionnel des Semences et Plants*: one of agribusiness' biggest lobbies.

Take the example of independent seed grower Pascal Poot, a permaculturist who is beginning to attract media interest in France. He has made a name for himself with his tomato crops, which grow at high yields without inputs or watering. It's a prodigy that INRA agronomists are now seriously and covetously studying... How much profit can we make with such resistant varieties, without having to resort to pesticides? Jacques Monod, the famous Nobel Prize winner and co-founder of molecular genetics in the 1960s, who saw in what we can call "the Lysenko affair" the episode that was "the strangest and most distressing in the history of modern science," you would fall off your chair when you read one of his current fellow students and INRA researchers describing the work of our "sorcerer's apprentice":

> Its principle is to put the plant in the conditions in which we want it to grow. [...] Today, we call this the heredity of acquired traits: to put it plainly, stress and positive plant traits are transmitted over several generations. You have to understand that DNA is a highly plastic medium of information. It's not just genetic mutation that brings about change. There is also adaptation, with genes, for example, that are extinct but can reawaken. The plant produces its seeds after going through its cycle, retaining certain acquired aspects. Pascal Poot exploits this very well: his plants are not very different from others from a genetic point of view, but they have an impressive capacity for adaptation. [...] Seed selection work shows that plants can be pushed to impressive conditions. But modern agriculture has lost sight of this, and is not at all based on adaptability.[8]

The "epigenetic revolution"—as this radical paradigm shift concerning heredity is now called—is paving the way for a real upheaval in thinking on a broader level in biology. But it also proof that Lysenko's contention, before it would be supported by observations of geneticists themselves (and on the basis of the very concepts that Lysenko was criticizing!), had come out of serious experimental results and not out of "lies" and "charlatanism," something that explains in retrospect the mystery of Soviet Michurinism. This "false science" that was supposed to be necessarily catastrophic for agriculture according to the Western geneticists of the time, did not prevent the Lysenkoists from receiving the hon-

---

8   Véronique Chable, INRA-Sad de Rennes, interviewed by Thibaut Schepman for *Rue89/Nouvel Observateur*: "*Tomates sans arrosage ni pesticides: Cette méthode fascine les biologistes*" [Tomatoes without watering or pesticides: This method fascinates biologists], March 4, 2015.

ors of the "Red Tyrant..." instead of being "purged" to the last person for anti-Soviet sabotage!

All the classic Western criticisms[9] of the Lysenko "case," written in the seventies, i.e. at the height of molecular genetics' momentary triumph over Lysenko, have now been refuted by the practitioners of the very science they sought to honor against the Soviet charlatans, even if Lysenko's ideas were only partially correct. Epigenetics asserts that there is a heredity of *habitually* acquired traits, which is limited but reinforced in the event of stress (i.e. when it is opportune to vary because the environment is always changing), similarly to the ways indicated by Lysenko, but with the important aspects of gene-regulating factors under environmental influence. This does not replace the fundamental heredity of genes (which Lysenko had too hastily denied), but epigenetics adds to it in a relative way, as one metabolic strategy among others enabling life to maintain itself *despite* environmental variations.

Mathematician Dominique Méeus, who is clearly unfamiliar with these new developments in genetics, recently reaffirmed the clichés that it's time to reiterate, even in this somewhat outdated and caricatured form:

> Lysenko was an agricultural technician who popularized an artificial hibernation technique (known as vernalization) in the Soviet Union to prepare winter cereal seeds for sowing in spring. This produced certain results. [...] Lysenko then stated that he had thus induced a heritable modification in these cereals, i.e. that he could create new varieties simply by "educating" the plants by appropriate means. Needless to say, this was not the case. His so-called experimental results stemmed from his ignorance of scientific methods, and no doubt also from a tendency to "improve" observed results in the direction of his hopes. Lysenko emphasized the philosophical implications of the opposition between his theory of the heritability of acquired traits and genetic theory. Genetics would be a mechanistic, deterministic, defeatist "bourgeois" science, opposed to progress: everything is written in the gene and nothing can be changed; Lysenkoist biology would be a "proletarian," dialectical, liberating science, enabling humankind to improve its diet: human intervention can lead a plant to change behavior and transmit this modified behavior to its descendants.

---

9   The best-known of these are Jaurès Medvedev's *Grandeur et chute de Lysenko* [*The Rise and Fall of Lysenko*] (preface by Jacques Monod, 1969), already cited above, and Dominique Lecourt's *Lysenko, Histoire réelle d'une "science prolétarienne"* [*Lysenko—True story of a 'proletarian science'*] (preface by Louis Althusser, 1976).

Dialectical Materialism: Brake or Boost for Agrobiology? 113

[...] On the other hand, it is a dangerous illusion to invert the relationship between science (which must be considered first) and philosophy (which is second). It is not philosophy that governs the world, and the philosophical concept of dialectic is not a force of nature. It is the world that determines what is true or false, not philosophy.[10]

So it's time to take up those old (and necessary) criticisms of the Lysenko affair, not necessarily to counter them systematically, but to update them "by putting science first" (starting with epigenetics, which has nothing to do with politics), and philosophy "second" (from Medvedev's anti-Soviets to our own Méeus).

For until now, epigenetic specialists have noted that, through this epistemological upheaval, any connection with the Lysenko affair remains unthinkable. The public's ignorance of the details of Michurinism (and of Soviet science in general) is obviously being exploited to avoid reopening what was, in the West, one of the most effective ideological weapons against Marxism-Leninism, described as dishonest and anti-scientific!

In Russia, where the recognition to scientists undoubtedly gets more exposure more than elsewhere as a way to deal with these kinds of troublesome memories, the epigenetic revolution has been met not without a few patriotic outbursts, as shown in Loren Graham's recent book *Lysenko's Ghost: Epigenetics and Russia* (2016). In the West, however, the glaring similarity between epigenetics and Mikhail Gorbachevism has been ignored.[11] We will therefore attempt to highlight the main aspects and draw immediate lessons from them, on a practical, theoretical and ideological level. The aim is not to re-establish a "cult of personality" around Lysenko. He hardly lends himself to this, given the numerous theoret-

---

10   Dominique Méeus, '*À propos de Lysenko, pour une relation correcte entre science et philosophie*' [About Lysenko, for a correct relationship between science and philosophy], June 28, 2016. *Investig'action* website.

11   This is not to suggest that Michurin and Lysenko had anticipated the current results of epigenetics. They were radically criticizing the initial results of genetics, which today, thanks to a better understanding of the physico-chemical interactions between genes and the environment, provide a concrete scientific explanation for Soviet agronomic practices. It is indeed today's geneticists who, with tangible results, unintentionally confirm that Lysenko was not lying about his own, which is in itself a historiographical upheaval.

ical errors he propagated in the final years of his career, and the visibly unsympathetic character his opponents have had to complain about. It's more a question of reopening a scientific and ecological debate that was too quickly dismissed for political reasons, at the height of the Cold War between two irreconcilable blocs. Clearly, if the USSR to some extent deprived itself of advances in molecular genetics between 1948 and 1954, the West undoubtedly deprived itself, just as willingly, of "Michurinian" alternatives to the genetic selection of stable plant varieties conserved with pesticides and hormones.

While epigenetics, which creates solid, hereditarily resistant varieties, is only just beginning to emerge under the now curious eye of geneticists and agronomists, half a century's delay in this field has meanwhile enabled capitalist agribusiness to progressively destroy all the arable land on the planet... and its domination is still unchallenged in practice.

IDEALIST GENETICS VERSUS PROTO-DIALECTICAL MATERIALISM: A DRAW?

Materialism posits that matter exists and moves before, without, or independently of ideas. Idealism, in many forms since the prehistory of human philosophy, assumes, on the contrary, consciously or unconsciously, that ideas determine matter. In biology, the most primitive idealism consists, for example, in the assumption that a melon has regular dimensions "so that it can be eaten by the family."[12] But the most refined and *modern* form of this idealism consists in describing the organism as a "sum" of characteristics resulting from the expression of endogenous and transmittable information ("ideas"): genes.

Seen in this light, classical genetics, that of Mendel and Morgan, considered that the existence of hereditary modifications to a given characteristic of the organism enabled its phenotype to be defined by a succession of isolable determinants called genes.[13] In short, genes were seen as the magic words (*ideas*) that Rabbi Loew inscribed on the scroll within his *Golem*, a clay statue, to bring it to life.

---

12   So claimed the French botanist Bernardin de Saint-Pierre in the 18th century.

13   The linear DNA molecules in the cell nucleus (chromosomes) correspond to a sequence of base combinations (an alphabet of four different bases), each of which defines a different, isolable visible character.

As we shall see, Michurinism—the movement inspired by the work of the self-taught Russian horticulturist Ivan Michurin and theorized by Lysenko and Williams—was not really a counter-proposal to genetics as it developed in the 20th century. Rather, as all Soviet literature attests, it was a collection of field techniques for improving cultivated plants and soils, despite and even against the "Mendelo-Morganist" doctrine. These agricultural methods revolved around the desire to hereditarily "habituate" plants to desired conditions. It is precisely the theoretical impossibility of such heredity of *habit-acquired* traits for genetics that earned him so many attacks from Lysenko and his fellow students.[14]

We won't enter into the debate about charlatanism, since we now know that this type of heredity of habit-acquired traits is very real, without however clashing with the model of modern molecular genetics. Heredity that forgets about acquired traits remains the rule, while the heredity of habit-acquired traits, while also observed, exists only on the margins, in very specific circumstances, as we shall see later. This is the difference between our position and that of a Lysenko who absolutized his discovery for "ideological" reasons.

There is indeed a theoretical debate to be had on the origins of this astonishing recent overtaking of the "Lysenko affair" with epigenetics. The Lysenkoists were obviously wrong to treat genetics with such nihilism, but this was first and foremost a vital and urgent problem for the USSR, not a parlor discussion about epistemological presuppositions: could Soviet agriculture be improved in practice and famines eliminated?

---

14 Michurin and Lysenko asserted that acquired resistance can be transmitted to offspring *if the latter live under the same* stress conditions that motivated the parental generation to acquire the resistance. This is a far cry from naive Lamarckism, but also very close to the definition of epigenetic inheritance as it is currently defined. Lysenko's critics now try to reduce Lysenko to Lamarck, glossing over these differences to avoid any comparison with recent discoveries, arguing that there's no point in delving back into this fanciful, anti-scientific Lysenkoist literature. The fanciful, empirical nature of Lysenko's theory is, however, just as far removed from epigenetics as Wegener's old theory of *continental drift* is from the current theory of *plate tectonics* (in which, of course, continents don't float as Wegener assumed, but do move sideways). We don't usually reproach pioneers for not knowing all the arguments supporting their scientific hypotheses at once, nor the mistakes they may have made through over-enthusiasm.

Lysenko, the son of Ukrainian peasants and a self-taught agronomist, was far removed from the intrigues of the corridors of Moscow State University. If, for him, the polemic is technical before it is ideological (the opposition of dialectical materialism with genetic idealism), it is, conversely, ideological for geneticists before becoming an accusation of charlatanism on the practical discoveries of the Soviet agronomist... until they are rediscovered today, out of necessity, just when everyone thinks this old affair from the last century has been forgotten.[15]

Dialectical materialism is a worldview that tends to distinguish itself as clearly as possible from idealism in philosophy. Less accomplished forms have developed in the course of history, with weaknesses opportune for idealists, such as "mechanistic" materialism, which conceives of living beings, for example, as a "machine." It's a material "machine" that implicitly presupposes a designer, such is its complexity. "Empiricist" materialism is another historical form of materialism, which refuses to validate any (mystical) truth outside of concrete, sensitive experience. This is a way of denying "spiritual forces," but at the same time it denies science any predictability, any inductive logic... yet most modern theories in particle physics, for example, are totally outside the direct experience of scientists. These forms of materialism have always been intellectual attempts to counter the obstacles and negative influences of idealism on scientific research, since every time a major discovery arises in the history of science, the ruling class tries to divert, reformulate or even limit it for its own ideological interests. The ruling class would thus have the theory of the *big bang* demonstrate the legitimacy of Creation, just like genes, by a convenient simplification for common sense.

The general principles set out by Marx and Engels, based on Hegelian dialectics, are designed to undermine the foundations of all these attempts at idealism, in the political field as in all other fields, including the scientific.[16]

---

15   This is surprising today, given the way the adversary has been presented as "dogmatic," but molecular genetics was founded on a "central dogma" (*sic*) which asserts that no reaction from the environment can be registered back at the level of genes. It's precisely this dogma that epigenetics is overturning, without, strangely enough, anyone bringing up the theoretical problems it should logically pose!

16   Engels' famous essay *Dialectics of Nature* (1882), and all his correspondence with Marx, attest to the spontaneous interest of these theorists in the subject. This was a

The principles can be summed up as follows: matter is that which exists objectively, independently of our awareness of it. It is made up of parts that are always interacting with one another. The parts of a whole can never be definitively and metaphysically separated. Matter is by definition in constant motion, animated by self-dynamic contradictions: a dialectical contradiction being both "the struggle *and* the unity of opposites." The movements of matter are therefore not instilled from the outside (by ideas, for example) but exclusively endogenous, and correspond to the reciprocal action of opposing, interdependent forces. In short, there can be no matter without motion, and no motion without matter. For dialectical materialism, the *movement* inherent in matter always incorporates the trajectories dear to Newton and clockwork mechanics, but also, and perhaps above all, evolutions, wear and tear, complexifications, annihilations, and emergencies.

When a contradiction develops within a material process, it first accumulates quantitatively, progressively, until a threshold is crossed, triggering a "qualitative leap" that changes the material, causing it to evolve in form ("negation of a negation"). It can be slowed down, but never stopped. So, matter evolves; it necessarily has a history, and nothing about it is immutable or fixed. On the contrary, it always evolves from the simple to the complex, meaning that the simple is always the basis of the complex, but also that the complex always comes from an evolution of the simple. In other words, since dialectical materialism posits that matter and movement are by definition one and the same, the problem of science is no longer *what makes matter move* (a tautology), but what can constrain it, slow it down, deflect it, reverse it, what limits its movement at a given moment or under given conditions—in other words, what makes up the infinite complexity of a world whose parts are interdependent and give rise to each other.

Karl Marx's textbook case in *Capital* is that of the capitalist mode of production, conceived as an antagonistic dialectical contradiction opposing the proletariat and the bourgeoisie, whose interests are forever opposed. By accumulating a proletariat from which it draws its wealth, the bourgeoisie creates the conditions for its own destruction through socialist revolution and the dictatorship of the proletariat. Historical

time of "political" interest in the latest scientific developments. Karl Marx dedicated his *Capital* to Charles Darwin.

materialism states that this contradiction's similar processes preceded it, transforming the slave mode of production into the feudal and then capitalist modes. For Marx, the principle of class struggle is the fundamental driving contradiction of human history.[17]

But the principles of dialectical materialism can also be found in all areas of science, starting with physics, where we've come a long way since Aristotelian idealism. From the positive and negative charges of particles, through the wave/particle duality of light, quantum mechanics and string theory, to the interactions of matter and antimatter in the universe, all current physics conforms to these laws. Even implicitly, dialectics is the only way for physicists to get rid of the countless hiatuses of formal "logic" that can hamper their research. To apply our "diamat" to a simple example that we can use as a reference, water that boils at 100 degrees, as a result of the quantitative accumulation of energy gradually raising its temperature, eventually changes state and becomes steam. A qualitative leap follows a quantitative accumulation, according to Engels' dialectical law of transformation from quantity to quality (and vice versa).

But the more recent history of biology complicates matters. While the pairing of endogenous variation in the species and exogenous selection by the environment (natural selection) seemed to function as a quite "classic" dialectical contradiction in the Darwinian scheme explaining biological evolution, the discovery of genes was just about the only historical opportunity for idealism to mount a counter-offensive against materialism in modern science.[18] Throughout the 20th century, genetics became a quasi-scientific proof of the fallacy of dialectical materialism, and thus of Marxist cosmogony, in the field of "facts." If the organism really is the expression "in matter" of information carried by genes, and if these genes are isolable determinants, independent of the environment in which they are expressed and transmissible from generation to generation, if the environment can in no way act or influence their nature, their modification, their expression, this new reductionist and predictive science was the best news and the best militant opportunity for the anti-communists of recent decades.

---

17   Fundamental does not mean unique.

18   In fact, this contradiction is not "dialectical," since the natural and gradual variations within a species between conspecifics are not linked, in neo-Darwinism, to variations in the environment; there is no "struggle and unity" of opposites, only opposition.

The fact that it is possible to demonstrate the existence of characteristics in a plant, for example, that can be transmitted identically and independently to the next generation, is totally in line with this idealistic conception, and is opposed to the idea of voluntary, heritable modification of plants under the influence of a changing environment (Michurinism).[19] For more than a century, this opposition seemed irreducible and unsurpassable, and the affirmation of one of the two conceptions necessarily implied the categorical rejection of the other. Indeed, when it came to founding this "neo-Darwinism," i.e. Darwinism (a pair of heritable individual modifications followed by selection of the most advantageous by the environment) supplemented by the genetics of Mendel and Morgan (accidental mutations independent of the environment correspond to these individual modifications predicted by Darwin), was backed by a "central dogma" (*sic*) positing the unilaterality, in a totally anti-dialectical way, of the relationship between genes and environment.

To fully understand the precariousness of the scientific debate at the time, we need to add to the ideological stakes the complexity of the political stakes that pitted the beleaguered Soviet Union against the rest of the capitalist world.

On the good word of an eminent disciple of Darwin, Francis Galton, the capitalist countries, then in the wake of the fascist vanguard of the thirties, pondered the possibility to "*promote the survival of the fittest and slow down or interrupt the reproduction of the unfit.*" The "superior races" were promised glory, while the "inferior races," carriers of genetic "defects," slowed down human destiny like a "burden" (*sic*). The deadly implication of genetics in the scientific consecration of racism and eugenics was obvious in both the West and the USSR. And if the Third Reich was the outpost of the most reactionary ideas, and the headquarters of all the geneticists of the time working in the direction of eugenics, the latter was quite consensual in the West.[20] The Soviets were the only ones

---

19 Gregor Mendel first demonstrated the existence of a gene responsible for the smooth or wrinkled shape of peas. Morgan applied this method to *Drosophila* [**Editor's Note**: this is the genus for fruit flies, who are still used as a model organism in the biological sciences].

20 The American biologist Charles Davenport was responsible for sterilization plans in the USA in the 1930s. He and his colleagues in the highly respected *Galton Society* openly sided with Hitler. In England, the no less respectable *Eugenics Society* around

to distinguish themselves from such ideas and to stick to the primacy of "education" over "selection."

Even the most critical admit that the period readily lent itself to a truncated debate on political terrain, from which no Marxist of the time could have escaped (all the more so when we know that Lysenko's research is today half-authenticated by epigenetics). According to some, to fully understand this Lysenkoist regression in Soviet biology, several factors need to be taken into account, including:

> [T]he immaturity of genetic theory at the time and the support given to the racist theories of Hitlerism by many German geneticists, the atmosphere of the rise of fascism, then of Nazi aggression, then of the Cold War.[21]

More precise is the analysis of science historian André Pichot on the origins of genetics and its detractors:

> [Lysenko's] case is somewhat special and, to fully understand his opposition to what he called "Mendelo-Morganism," we need to take into account the genetic ideology of the time and, in particular, the fact that, in the 1930s, Hermann J. Muller, Morgan's former collaborator, was working in the USSR, where he hoped to convince Stalin to adopt his eugenicist political program (there's a whole aspect of the history of genetics that geneticists prefer to forget).[22]

The "lack of maturity" in genetics mentioned by Roubaud and Goux are not without interest, beyond the purely political and ideological stakes, for while the results of "Michurinism" at that time in the USSR, with vernalization techniques in particular, are hardly in doubt even among the most staunch anti-Lysenkoists, genetics, for its part, was "stalling."[23] It still limited itself to "describing" the characteristics of

---

geneticist Reginald R. Gates did the same. Frenchmen Marcel Mauss and Paul Rivet theorized about the "biological inferiority of blacks." German Hermann Muller, Morgan's eminent geneticist colleague and 1946 Nobel Prize winner for medicine, sought to create a "Nobel sperm bank" in the same eugenicist vein. James Watson, the famous co-discoverer of DNA, was until very recently known for his particularly shocking racist remarks, such as "the inferior intelligence of blacks," which even earned him censure from many media.

21 P. Roubaud and J.-M. Goux, *Lysenko*.

22 André Pichot, *Histoire de la notion de gène*, 1999.

23 Vernalization involves moistening and then freezing seeds to "mimic" winter, enabling them to germinate earlier in the year. Lysenko's discovery really marked the start of his career, and he received widespread praise from the scientific community, including

each species, but proved incapable of "producing" the new varieties that agronomists in the West and East were waiting for. Geneticists of the time seemed to be stuck in a wait-and-see attitude towards nature that would serve them well for a long time to come.

The real practical applications of genetics did not come until the 1960s, with its modernization in the form of "molecular genetics," which in turn led to the tangible production of transgenic seeds endowed with this or that interesting trait. In the thirties, the scientific truth of the geneticists was objectively slow to emerge, due to its inefficiency in practice:

> For those of us with the benefit of historical hindsight and the dazzling results of Mendelian genetics, the situation of Soviet geneticists appears to be quite dramatic. For we now know why they were forced to remain silent about Michurinian "facts," forced to acknowledge their temporary impotence in matters of selection. They were objectively trapped in the development of genetics: in that historical "fork" of genetics which, until the 1940s, was unable to move on to the stage of application to plant and animal breeding. [...] A singular "irony" of history, where the "time" of a science is "doubled" by the demands of ideology and politics.[24]

This notion of "range" is particularly enlightening, in the opposite sense, for today's epigeneticists, who are unable to benefit from the empirical results of Michurinism because of such a "range" of dogmatic condemnation of the heredity of acquired traits throughout the second half of the 20th century, for obviously purely political reasons.

But we must avoid responding to several decades of demonization with an anti-scientific hagiography of Michurinism. As we have seen, this movement rejected the genetics of its time outright, for reasons of apparent incompatibility with the supposed principles of dialectical materialism. This attitude was certainly correct in its criticism of the idealism polluting the theory of heredity, but above all it lacked theoretical

---

the most eminent geneticists of the time, such as Vavilov in the USSR. Significant advances were made thanks to this technique, which at the time was capable of staving off possible famines in times of war. Even Zhores Medvedev does not go so far as to assert that this technique is quackery, but is content to attribute its paternity to others, making Lysenko look like an usurper, something that the history of science quite commonly rejects.

24 Dominique Lecourt, *Lysenko, histoire réelle d'une "science prolétarienne"* [*Lysenko. The Real History of a "Proletarian Science"*].

counter-arguments, other than the sheer force of field results concerning "modified heredity." Mendel's "law of peas" and Morgan's chromosomal theory were simply mocked, minimized and relativized, but never seriously challenged by logical argumentation... and with good reason, since such counter-arguments could only be based on experience and scientific observation using molecular genetics that had reached maturity, i.e. very recently.

Since Weismann and the first "Mendelo-Morganists," it has been particularly immature to "demonstrate" the impossibility of heredity of acquired traits by cutting off the tails of mice over several generations, only to find that they are always born with a tail. But it was just as immature and just as anti-scientific of the Michurinians to mock Mendel's "law of peas," since it was ultimately Mendel's distant descendants who discovered the molecular basis of the heredity of acquired traits (epigenetics). Such have always been the surprises of the history of science.

In reality, Lysenko and his followers assumed their lack of interest in purely theoretical questions, including those which, on the basis of their own proposals, could have founded the famous heredity of habit-acquired traits on a molecular scale. For these reasons, the attitude of the Michurinians was bound to disconcert philosophers and theorists committed to understanding the history of the sciences of evolution as an explanation of the living world, beyond these "lowly considerations." The principles of dialectical materialism were compatible with empirical results in agronomy, so there was no need to build a dedicated theory capable of countering genetics, which was clearly sterile in terms of practical implications at the time. It is in this sense that we might speak of "proto-dialectical" materialism, or materialism that was more "empirical" than dialectical, to define the angle from which the Michurinians approached the epistemological problems posed by the "Mendelo-Morganism."

The accusations remained vague and superficial. When it came to talking about the substance—chromosomes, for example, the existence of which could not be denied, since they were already visible under the microscope—Lysenko remained within the limits of an era that did not yet know biochemistry. This was not a total denial of heredity through genes, but a very strong relativization with no theoretical counterpart (the latter could only come with epigenetics, i.e. much later, as we shall see in due course):

> The basis of this theory [of chromosome heredity] is the fanciful thesis that a part of the chromosome substance cannot be identified with the usual body, and that it alone possesses heredity [...] whereas according to the Michurinian doctrine [...] heredity is inherent not only in chromosomes, but in the entire living body, in each of its particles.[25]

Neo-Darwinian theory, based on the theses of Mendel, Weismann, and Morgan, opposed all the laws of dialectical materialism, not on the basis of overtly philosophical presuppositions, but through the (abusive) interpretation of scientific results. The existence of genes carrying "information" describing the organism and independent of the environment is opposed to the idea of a dialectical world where everything is in dynamic interaction. Neo-Darwinian gradualism, moreover, by asserting that species evolve progressively in "small steps," is opposed to the thesis of the qualitative leap. Finally, the notion of chance underlying the evolution of genes runs counter to the thesis of an evolution directed from the simple to the complex.

It's clear, then, that a more in-depth debate has been lacking, both for genetics, which has retreated into an idealism that has long been unproductive (and is now in crisis), and for Michurinism, which had stopped at simple observations devoid of a necessary theoretical synthesis... and that was for multiple, complex reasons. But it must be stressed that there is probably as much distance between the primitive and naive conceptions of Mendel or Morgan and today's notion of the gene as there is between the purely descriptive theory of Michurin or Lysenko around characters acquired through habit and today's epigenetics, which we will discuss later. From the point of view of a modern molecular geneticist specializing in epigenetics both theses were equally "naïve" when seen from today's perspective.[26]

When Morgan identified through a multitude of selective crosses four linkage groups between hereditary variations in *Drosophila*, and at the same time discovered that it does indeed have four pairs of chromosomes in its karyotype, it was a serious and deliberate scientific error on

---

25   Lysenko, *Agrobiology*, 1953.
26   See Appendix 3 on pp. 183-185.

Lysenko's part to ignore these results with contempt; a suspect blindness. On the other hand, the tangible experiments he had carried out, despite the outcry from Soviet geneticists at the time, could not be considered as a scientific error. In the USSR, genetics was only "validated" and applied on a USSR-wide scale after a (theoretical) struggle and a clear-cut, even exaggerated, demarcation from the dominant genetics, even if the debate subsequently calmed down once recognition had been obtained. For even in the USSR, genetics had a front-row seat in laboratories and universities, at least until the 1930s. And even during the period when Michurinism dominated, classical genetics continued to be taught in universities, and geneticists continued to work, albeit with reduced funding.

Should we therefore consider it a political error, or a philosophical mistake, on the part of the Soviet state to have "arbitrated" the scientific debate from 1948 onwards, at the end of the famous "session of the Lenin Academy of Agricultural Sciences of the USSR"?[27]

On the purely political side, we need to try and get a clearer picture of the treatment meted out to geneticists in the USSR, through a multi-study of Western accounts that are often outrageous or contradictory. An article starting with "For thirty years, Soviet biology was led by a madman who turned scientific delirium into a state religion," however, tells us that the Lenin Academy was "one of the few semi-autonomous institutions in the USSR." To explain the ousting of a Lysenkoist as head of the Academy even before the end of Khrushchev's reign (who surprisingly continued to support the "Stalinist" Lysenko), the author states that "Under its authority granted by Peter the Great, [the Academy of Sciences] holds a precious privilege: the right to elect its members by secret ballot" (Claude Marcil, "Le professeur aux pieds nus [The bare-foot professor]," www.sciencepresse.fr). If this ousting was possible despite the support of the highest Soviet leader in 1964, and no doubt because of the now indisputable power of the results of molecular genetics, we can legitimately deduce that Lysenko's ascent to the head of this Academy in 1936

---

27 This was a debate between geneticists and Michurinianists, concluding a theoretical struggle that had lasted several years in Soviet universities and laboratories, at the end of which Lysenko's supporters declared themselves the winners. A book titled *The Situation in Biological Science—Proceedings of the Lenin Academy of Agricultural Sciences of the USSR* (Foreign Languages Publishing House, Moscow, 1949) provides details of every statement made by academicians from both "camps."

could not have been the result of a simple decision by Stalin, especially as, at that time, the conflict between the Michurinians and the geneticists had only just begun, and the geneticists continued to form a rather offensive current against Lysenko until 1948, even within the Academy itself.[28]

The current of geneticists, organized essentially around Nikolai Vavilov and Hermann Muller, was indeed dominant in Stalin's USSR at least until the 1930s, when results in agronomy became an urgent priority, while even in the West genetics remained highly unproductive. To recount the persecution of Soviet geneticists, we must at least acknowledge their legal existence. To tell the story of the Lysenkoists' fall from grace in 1964, organized by a democratic assembly of geneticists within the Academy, we must also assume that these geneticists did not suddenly appear, or that they are not the reincarnated specters of victims "executed" by Stalin.

In fact, it's difficult to get an idea of the scale of persecution of Soviet geneticists in Western literature (Michurinian literature, for its part, confines itself to exposing results and radically questioning the Mendelo-Morganists on their merits). Two very different aspects are usually confused: the criminalization of scientists on the one hand, and the reduction of funding for laboratories on the other. The "Stalinist persecution" is most often evasively mentioned, and in fact two or three names come up when Lysenko is mentioned, including that of Nikolai Vavilov, former director of the Academy of Sciences, but also a pupil of the famous British geneticist William Bateson.

Vavilov was convicted in 1940 by the Supreme Court of the USSR's military tribunal, at the height of tensions with the Nazi enemy on the USSR's doorstep, on the official charge of "participation in a terrorist

---

28   A Soviet geneticist named Zhebrak, for example, published an article against Lysenko in an American scientific journal (*Science* magazine) in 1945, with the explicit authorization of two members of the Political Bureau (though headed by Stalin!): Voznesensky and Chtcherbakov. Anton Zhebrak remained head of the Department of Genetics and Plant Breeding, and continued to direct research in classical genetics without being "worried," even though he lost this position after the famous 1948 session. As late as 1947, two Soviet geneticists, Efroïmson and Lioubichtchev, continued to protest the Lysenkoists' academic domination to the Party Central Committee! They were echoed by the son of the influential Zhdanov himself.

organization, sabotage and espionage."[29] His friend and "anti-Michurinian" collaborator Pryanishnikov, a "chemist" and supporter of intensive agriculture, and who was Williams' and Lysenko's *bête noire* as an agronomist, is said to have successfully lobbied the authorities to have his death sentence commuted to a simple prison term. Vavilov died of dystrophy in prison in 1943, in the town where he had practiced, Saratov. His death was undoubtedly linked to supply difficulties at the front, at the height of the war of liberation against the Nazis, although articles on the subject always half-suggest that it was premeditated by the Soviet authorities (which is absurd, given the causes of death). Sometimes the death of some of his work colleagues that same year are added, omitting to mention that several of them died of starvation in the Leningrad laboratory, like thousands of other Soviets besieged by the Germans during the long months of the notorious blockade. We then learn with astonishment that Vavilov continued to teach genetics and botany in prison, and wrote a synthetic work that was later rehabilitated under Khrushchev.

Finally, the available information contradicts the thesis that "the geneticists were deported by Stalin, including Vavilov," because at the time of his conviction for sabotage, the atmosphere was one of compromise on the part of the Soviet authorities:

> The Central Party Committee [...] remained silent, on the sidelines. Despite Lysenkoist pressure, it refused to take sides on theory. This became clear when

---

29   It's hard to find consistent versions of this trial, but it's clearly a case of high treason and leakage of capital and research materials. Until the thirties, genetic research laboratories received considerable funding from the Soviet authorities, in the hope of rapid results capable of improving agricultural yields. However, progress came from the results of Michurinian agronomists, while geneticists provided none. At the same time, the then-dominant geneticists' attacks on Lysenko and his colleagues logically escalated. N. Vavilov, as former director of the Academy, and Georgii Karpechenko, his number two, a specialist in plant hybridization, spent years traveling outside the USSR, to the USA, Germany and England, and consolidating a network of geneticists, including even personalities compromised by the Third Reich (much more sympathetic, one suspects, to Mendelo-Morganist theories). This led to suspicions of leaks of information and research materials on the eve of the Nazi invasion. It is possible that Lysenko had an influence on the judiciary at this time, but the indictment does not necessarily imply such a confusion of genres. Using colossal sums of Soviet money intended to improve agricultural production to finance projects outside the USSR, in the midst of a global imperialist storm, was still visibly risky on Vavilov's part. Karpechenko was sentenced at the same time as Vavilov.

the magazine *Under the Banner of Marxism*, the press organ that publicized the party's official ideological and cultural positions, organized a conference in 1939 on the question of the biological sciences. One might have expected this meeting to be the death knell for geneticists. It was not. The philosopher Mitine, Stalin's authorized spokesman, unequivocally stated that the aim of the conference was to work out a compromise between the two tendencies. Mitine even went so far as to describe the Lysenkoists' intransigence as "anti-intellectualism." The meeting ended with a renewal of the status quo.[30]

In fact, according to Lecourt, in the USSR, Lysenkoists held important positions only in institutions linked to agronomy and agriculture, while universities and schools continued to teach "Mendelo-Morganism" until the 1940s—which doesn't fit in with the climate of systematic oppression as their detractors, past and present, seek to portray them.

Clearly, in order to demonize Lysenko's evil personality beyond the information available to us, while asserting that his experimental results are a complete lie and fabrication, we need to imply that he may have manipulated Stalin in person.[31] Both to validate his inapplicable lies in agronomy, hoping that nobody will notice, and to take revenge on his adversary Vavilov, who is said to have helped the USSR out of its agricultural difficulties! But with what arguments? And how could Stalin be manipulated, despite the supposed opinion of thousands of Soviet *kolkhoz* farmers and hundreds of serious agronomists and biologists? What would have been the point of the "Red Tyrant," so quick to condemn for high treason, discrediting himself in contact with an adventurous and mythical "lobbyist" plotting against such useful geneticists?

What would have been the point of Khrushchev, so quick to "deStalinize" afterwards, continuing to support Lysenko despite the return of the geneticists to the helm, after the latter had committed so many disasters during Stalin's time?[32] This mystery has been the subject of nu-

---

30   Dominique Lecourt, *Lysenko*.

31   A particularly absurd hypothesis is one from Zh. Medvedev himself. He conceded as much in 2000, on the occasion of the publication of the correspondence between Lysenko and Stalin: "In fact, there was no relationship between Stalin and Lysenko. They were never together, under any circumstances other than official" (Lysenko and Stalin, on the occasion of the fiftieth anniversary of the 1948 Academy Session, Zh. Medvedev, *Mutation Research* 462, 2000).

32   The most common (but not the most serious) argument is that Lysenko was

merous books in the West, in which we talk of hallucination or collective blindness, of coercion exerted on thousands of *kolkhoz*ians all over the Soviet territory to lie about the real results. But even allowing for this (and we know that these results have now been partly authenticated), the most disturbing thing—and Dominique Lecourt's book does not fail to underline this—is that all the geneticists who defend their theses against the invective of the Michurinians, notably in the report of the famous Lenin Academy session in 1948, only attack Lysenko's *theory*, never the veracity of his practical results. Is it possible to defend ourselves in this way against a charlatan, without even implying that his results are faked?

It seems, then, that the context was more complex than the accounts of Western philosophers, and Dominique Lecourt's book is undoubtedly the most balanced among them. But the fact that the Lysenkoists won their case occasionally does not detract from the fact that they contributed objectively to throwing genetics even faster into an idealistic rut in the West, while Michurinism was clearly not mature enough to provide the theoretical basis for a dialectical overcoming at the time.

At the time, however, communist biologists sought to clarify the situation, finding scientifically accurate positions for both "tendencies." The Darwinian Marcel Prenant,[33] who was a member of the French Communist Party, distanced himself from the overly vindictive and nihilistic Lysenkoism, and was undoubtedly the most accurate on the question, regardless of the political and ideological stakes of the time:

> The Lysenkoists have obtained good practical results in agriculture where the "classical" geneticists have not been effective; the facts they report should be studied closely; they are undoubtedly compatible with Mendelian theory [...] Whereas the experimental interventions practiced by geneticists (by irradiation, for example) made it possible to increase the percentage of mutations, but not to obtain a definite transformation, Michurin and Lysenko claim to have obtained by suitable tricks of the hand, such as sudden changes in temperature, the hereditary fixation in certain cases of characters acquired under the influence of the environment and therefore known in advance. There's nothing

Ukrainian, like Khrushchev, and that this affinity alone could explain why Lysenko remained at the Academy... But then, what about Stalin, who was Georgian?

33   Marcel Prenant was not just a communist activist: he was a leader of the FTP during the anti-Nazi resistance, a member of the PCF Central Committee and a world-renowned biologist. [**Editor's Note**: The FTP, *Francs-tireurs et partisans*, were a merger of three communist groups fighting the Nazi occupation of France.]

absurd about that. [...] The fact that Lysenko's texts are often obscure, that he sometimes appeals to the argument of authority in a way that offends our habits [...] does not detract from the fact that an entire people is benefiting today from the work of Michurin and Lysenko. Which of our vehement critics has achieved comparable results?[34]

No 21st century epigeneticist would disagree with this serious, dialectical and balanced position. You will find in the annex scientific evidence in support of this concordance. The contradiction thus becomes clearer, and we should analyze the reasons for the Soviet authorities' arbitration in favor of the Michurinians from 1948 onwards, given this theoretical stalemate linked to the insurmountable immaturity of the two sciences (genetics and epigenetics) at that time.

We can recognize in the attitude of the demonizers both an inability to understand the interference between politics and scientific research (what Marxists call the contradiction between class struggle and ideological struggle), and a certain hypocrisy regarding the treatment of "dissident" scientists by the "free world" they defend.

Only a dialectical approach allows us to understand that the history of science is both autonomous in certain respects, and subject to social relationships and the interests of the patrons who drive it forward. The complex paths it has taken over the centuries can be described by a fairly obvious dependence on technical developments, and on polemics between materialist and idealist currents at the ideological level. But the link—albeit secondary on the scale of history as a whole—with the class interests of the moment remains important and sometimes decisive on the scale of the century.

This dialectical link is quite clear in the case we're interested in: genetics in the West, for example, rejected the whole Michurinian experiment as a false science for more than half a century, for ideological-political reasons. The Soviet Union also initially rejected genetics as a false science, only to reverse its position in the 1960s with the rise of molecular genetics and the discovery of DNA. In the West, Michurinian themes only spontaneously resurfaced when anti-communist pressure began to ease, following the demise of the socialist camp. So, over the whole period, we can summarize the story of a genetics that arrived "of its own

---

34   Marcel Prenant, quoted in Dominique Lecourt, *Lysenko*.

accord" at the dialectical renouncement of its initial dogma, omitting all the political framework that accelerated or delayed, here and there, such an evolution.[35]

In fact, it's reassuring to note that not only had the USSR finally opened up to genetics, despite Lysenkoist invective, but above all, that even in the still strongly "anti-communist" capitalist world, the development of epigenetics has come to be accepted, despite its strong whiff of dialectical materialism. This is proof that, on the scale of "great history," scientific knowledge is *progressing*, relatively independently of the political ups and downs of class struggle. And Marxists will find particular comfort in seeing "bourgeois" genetics finally contradict itself where it had so arrogantly asserted "Marxist dogmatism bending reality to its cause..."

It's no longer the communists who seek to twist reality to make it resemble the principles of *diamat*; it's the anti-communists in the West who today take it upon themselves to silence the evidence of a *reality* that increasingly resembles what the Lysenkoists said about it! But at no time, then or now, can we believe that the dominant ideology can forget research. Epigenetics has hundreds of potentially revolutionary applications, starting with agriculture and seed production, which justify its recent acceleration, *despite* the ideological risks this entails... But the fact that the State arbitrates scientific conflicts is not surprising, and just like the Soviet State in the 1940s, it essentially results in the reduction of credits given to some and the increase of those given to others. What are the motives behind such choices? Most often, the national interest, the international "cause" of the moment, is more or less complicated by the great class confrontations within the "ideological apparatuses of the state."

To give the most recent and most telling example, states rely on an assembly of scientists appointed by them, the IPCC [Intergovernmental Panel on Climate Change], to allocate grants and focus political and media attention on climate research. Conversely, any laboratory working on the predominantly solar (rather than human) origin of global warming

---

35   It's important to understand here that the return of the "heredity of acquired traits" does not replace the notion of the gene as it is defined today, since, on the contrary, it does not *materially* oppose it, as we shall see. It does, however, replace the definition of the gene as formulated in Mendel's or Morgan's time.

will be gagged and cut off from funding, or, if it speaks out, accused of "negationism" and compared to the mad scientists of the Third Reich. In the twists and turns of the life and death struggle between industrial and financial sectors of capital these dissident scientists were in a position to receive private funding from a few oil giants, since their research would conveniently absolve the latter of any historical responsibility for global warming. The network of brakes and gas pedals in scientific research is therefore often complex, whatever the final word in the scientific "debate."

Over and above ideological choices, it would never occur to anyone to allocate as much public funding to archaeology as to cancer or global warming research, out of theoretical "impartiality." Political choices in terms of funding are obvious here, rightly or wrongly, if we are talking about immediate potential results. The history of science, if it can be freed from punctual class struggles in the long term, is inevitably always influenced (accelerated, deviated, or slowed down) by practical necessities at a given moment. In the USSR, for example, the political choice was quickly made between Michurinian agronomy, which produced immediate results, however fragile or embryonic, and genetics, which was still totally unproductive.

Conversely, if a "historical fork in the road"—to use Dominique Lecourt's expression to explain the stagnation of geneticists in the 1930s—blocked the Michurinians themselves in the 1950s, limiting their practical results for lack of knowledge at the molecular level (until the present day, when such research can be restarted), we can also understand how the Soviet state changed its sponsorship to the benefit of geneticists. In both cases, the state intervened, and probably rightly so on both occasions, albeit at the cost of delays on both sides.

It could be argued that, in many cases, as the demonizers claimed in the case of Lysenko, we are dealing with genuine charlatans, and it would be an outrage to give them any credit. Here again, we need to distinguish between charlatans who put the brakes on science, which no doubt has no time to waste responding to them, and those who in some way, and no doubt unconsciously, serve scientific knowledge.

In an absolute sense, i.e. in the hypothesis of a history of science totally uncoupled from the social history of mankind, it would be abusive to describe a "creationist" biologist as a charlatan or a "negationist," and to banish him from laboratories for anti-Darwinian dissidence. Indeed, the development of false theories to their logical extremes sometimes advances science, and it is on the basis of responses to opposing counter-arguments that a theory is strengthened and developed. On the one hand, idealist dissidents are bound to be unmasked in the end; on the other, the spontaneous materialism[36] of a scientific theory is always partial or perfectible, surrounded by weaknesses that only dissidents, in good or bad faith, know how to expose, and their work becomes useful as the negative pole of a dynamic contradiction. Generally speaking, idealism permanently forces fundamentally materialist work (regardless of what they themselves believe) to react and consolidate, while continuing to progress. For Marxists, this hypothesis of scientific research free from political interference represents one aspect of their *ideal*—communist society, the ultimate stage of human labor's development, now freed from class struggle, in a world where classes no longer exist.

That said, we're still a long way from achieving this, and it has to be admitted that politics cannot remain aloof for long from the theoretical struggles that permeate scientific research, whether its influence is overt or covert. The distinction between *pragmatic* arbitration and *ideological* arbitration must therefore be the major issue, then as now, and the context unfortunately always tends to tangle these two poles... It is clear that, on the Soviet side, the scientific error will have been to reject a theory *en bloc* on the sole criterion of its "practical" uselessness at a given moment, without taking the trouble to counter-argue on the opponent's ground. And for good reason: no Lysenkoist could explain the experimental results of Morgan and Muller on the basis of their own observations.

If the USSR had discovered acupuncture, whose effects are now recognized in the West even if they are still inexplicable from our concepts, it's obvious that the country's classical doctors would have first sought to ridicule the discoverers, who would have responded by looking for immediate solutions to enable it to develop in spite of mainstream medicine. If we still assume that acupuncture was the only method of quitting

---

36 Lenin spoke of the "spontaneous materialism of scientists" in *Materialism and Empiriocriticism*, pointing out that the researcher, without dialectical materialism and even with idealistic beliefs in his daily life, is forced to *believe* at least in the ontological reality of the work he carries out on matter in his laboratory

smoking, in the absence of effective drug substitutes from conventional medicine, it's obvious that the state, anxious to halt the spread of lung cancer, would have arbitrated in favor of acupuncturists. All the more so if acupuncturists are ideologically compatible with the state! Acupuncture does not originate from the Soviet Union, but from China, and in this country, it harmoniously rubs shoulders with the other medicine, awaiting the day when a scientific explanation of the phenomenon will be possible.

The history of theories of heredity has therefore been far less harmonious, and the blame has been shared, with delays observed on both sides of the former "Iron Curtain." On the one hand, Michurinism stalled before sinking, while genetics had to try to catch up. On the other hand, the hypocritical rejection of "Lysenkoist charlatanism" that precipitated classical genetics into an idealistic headlong rush has only transformed "molecular genetics" into "epigenetics" in recent years (although molecular genetics dates back to the 1960s!).

To sum up, molecular genetics must have ceased to be idealist since the last century, as we shall see below, while epigenetics, in the wake of Michurinism, remains as highly "dialectical materialist" as it ever was, and this is bound to raise questions for today's philosophers of science.

According to historian Deniz Uztopal, the notion of "proletarian science" did not emerge in the Soviet debate, but rather when it was exported to France through the writings of Marxist philosophers and scientists caught up in a polemic that, at the height of the Cold War, was traceable to ideological stakes that were thunderously Manichean. Lysenko, on the other hand, was all about distinguishing "Soviet" from "reactionary" science, which is less, on a theoretical level, about any Bogdanovist relativism, which Lenin himself had earlier opposed.[37] However, demonizers have not hesitated to confuse these notions in order to lend credence to the idea that, in Lysenko's eyes, there is no longer any criterion of truth in science, and that there is one truth for proletarians and another for bourgeois.

In France, the context was that of a meeting organized by the Com-

---

37 Alexander Bogdanov, a Russian theorist and contemporary of Lenin, was severely criticized by the latter for his idealistic relativism. He asserted, for example, the distinction between a proletarian truth and a bourgeois truth.

munist Party, at which Marxist scientists were invited to take a stand in the conflict between geneticists and Michurinianists, simplistically declining the debates that had taken place in Moscow at the famous Lenin Academy session in 1948. According to Deniz Uztopal, the French communist press also disseminated simplistic arguments on the issue at the time:

> The head of the Intellectuals Section asks about the existence of a science determined by the power of the social class, particularly in the USSR, namely the proletariat. Casanova replied: "Yes, there is a proletarian science that is fundamentally contradictory to bourgeois science. It is this [...] abstruse answer [...] that provokes so many misunderstandings and dismay, all the more so as Casanova's argumentation is very simplistic. Indeed, he accuses bourgeois science of producing "crude approximations," of "gagging [...] scholars" and, last but not least, of "making a mockery [...] of science. It "produces vile politicians." And "proletarian science" is really only defined in opposition to it. His methodological approach is easy to grasp: while presenting the place of science in the capitalist system, he highlights the fact that science flourishes in the Soviet Union. In a context in which it is Communist scientists who are distancing themselves from the USSR, Casanova thus attempts to support Soviet practice by using the concept of "proletarian science." But by using a political argument, he made an ideological error, which he himself admitted, albeit hesitantly, in November 1951, i.e. thirty-three months after his famous speech of February 1949. It's worth noting that this name fits perfectly into the logic of the Poide war, in which the world is divided into two camps on all the Bridges, and aims to mobilize its forces politically.[38]

He adds: "An analysis of all Stalin's and Lysenko's writings proves that they never used the concept of "proletarian science."

This notion of "proletarian science" is, in any case, in profound contradiction with Leninism, in the sense that Lenin had largely developed his critique against this relativistic error in *Materialism and Empiriocriticism*. Stalin himself, who was suspected of supporting such a travesty in the Marxist approach to the history of science, indirectly opposed it in 1951 in a journal of linguistics. At the time, the aim was to counter the theses of linguistics of Nikolai Marr and his followers, for whom the evolution of languages must submit to that of class relations:

> The mistake our comrades [who aspire to a universal proletarian language]

---

38   D. Uztopal, 2014, *La réception en France du lysenkisme (1948-1956)* [The Reception of Lysenkoism in France], Cahiers d'Histoire.

commit here is that they do not see the difference between culture and language, and do not understand that culture changes in content with every new period in the development of society, whereas language remains basically the same through a number of periods, equally serving both the new culture and the old. Hence: a) Language, as a means of intercourse, always was and remains the single language of a society, common to all its members; [...] c) The "class character" of language formula is erroneous and non-Marxist.[39]

How can we believe that the author of these lines maintains a position on biological science that is contrary to the one he holds here on linguistics? Would scientific knowledge be "stable" as a language (which in fact evolves slowly) over time and modes of production?

In fact, Stalin undoubtedly prevented Lysenko, uneducated and obviously clumsy in his practice of dialectical materialism, from going too far with this "two sciences" theory.

The party's ideological support for Lysenko was in fact quite relative: the often very positive results with regard to agricultural production inevitably argued in favor of Michurinism much more effectively than the pseudo- or proto-dialectical materialism of its first defender. The figures collected by our trans-Atlantic adversary (and therefore to be little suspected of "trickery") in Figure 13 show that grain production, for example, grew steadily during the periods when Lysenko was influencing agronomy (he wasn't the only player, of course, but at least he didn't have a negative impact on yields). Yields increased during the thirties, and following the unprecedented destruction of agriculture by Nazi barbarism during the war, agriculture recovered prodigiously from 1947 onwards.

The Soviet archives now available suggest that Stalin was actually supporting Michurinism and its results, and not necessarily Lysenko himself, whose theoretical weaknesses were clear.[40] On the eve of the 1948 session, the report commissioned by Stalin from Lysenko on the

---

39   J. Stalin, 1951, *Le marxisme et les problèmes de linguistique* [Marxism and the Problems of Language].

40   D. Uztopal relates an interesting comment made by Stalin in the margin of Lysenko's report: he accused the "Mendelo-Morganists" of denying the influence of the environment on heredity. Muller, for example, had already induced genetic mutations by bombarding cells with X-rays, i.e. through a variation in the environment. On the other hand, Stalin points out that Mendelo-Morganist theory rejects the heredity of acquired traits, which is different.

state of thinking and polemics between genetics and Michurinism was repeatedly corrected by the former in a way that confirmed Lysenko's theoretical clumsiness:

> Lysenko equates the class struggle with the struggle in biology, but all these allusions are corrected by Stalin. When Lysenko writes that every science is by its very nature class-oriented, Stalin notes in the margin [...] "And mathematics? and Darwinism?" [At one point Lysenko] asserts that the capitalist system by its very nature cannot tolerate a correct representation of the development of nature [and that] bourgeois genetics is not a science that belongs to the natural sciences, [...] and is generated by the ruling class. In the final report, this entire section is deleted. In the rest of the text, Stalin deleted nine references in which Lysenko alluded to the bourgeois nature of science. This concept is replaced by the notions of "idealist" or of "reactionary." [...] This shows the agronomist's ideological limits, and correlatively we can probably suggest that Stalin's support cannot be explained by an ideological preference that the agronomist cannot endorse perfectly.[41]

Figure 13: Comparative grain production in the USSR and the USA during the Stalinist and post-Stalinist periods.

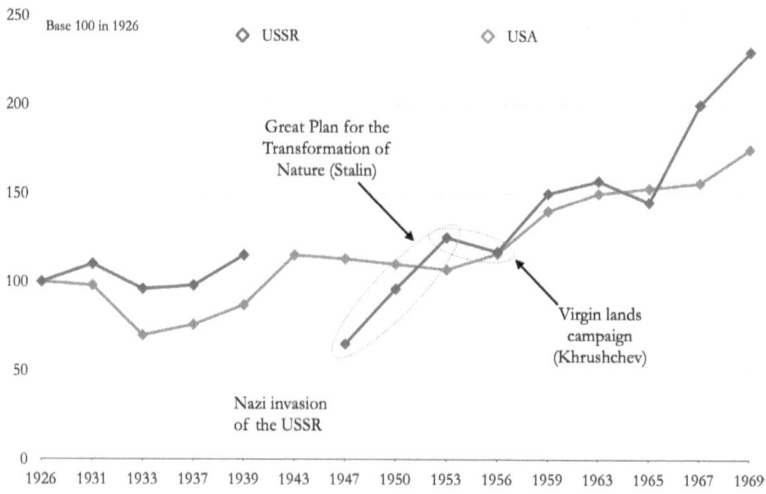

Lysenko influenced Soviet agronomy between 1935 and 1952. For the USSR,

---

41   Deniz Uztopal, 2012, *Pouvoir idéologique et savoir scientifique* [Ideological Power and Scientific Knowledge].

data was not provided for the years of Nazi invasion, during which destruction was massive. **Source:** *Historical statistics of the United States (Bureau of the Census)*, Washington 1975, quoted in *Science as a Social Product and the social product of science,* R. Levins and R. Lewontin, 1985.

We therefore need to delve deeper into the Marxist self-criticism of this period, not to "demonize" it or draw up a "moral" indictment of Lysenko's visibly extravagant personality and obvious theoretical weaknesses, which would be totally idealistic and naive, but to understand how this affair has led to avoidable delays in biology, even if Lysenko's practical results can be retrospectively validated by modern epigenetics. It is not a question of falling once again into the trap of retrospective triumphalism in the face of the great return of the "inheritance of acquired traits" in the laboratories of "bourgeois science."

In the first place, Marxist biologists such as Marcel Prenant in France and John B.S. Haldane in Great Britain, in distancing themselves from Lysenko, had to drastically limit their criticism of the idealism of Mendelian genetics, on pain of being seen as charlatans themselves. This is easily understandable. The effect was objectively disastrous, and nothing prevented classical genetics from aggravating its idealistic shortcomings (genetic determinism theories or the concept of "genetic programming," etc.) and sinking into a long-term scientific crisis, until the forgotten "Lysenko affair" and the economic urgencies of the moment, particularly in relation to agriculture, lifted it out of its theoretical blockages.

Putting aside the concrete results of both, the way in which Mendelo-Morganist idealism was treated by the Lysenkoists undoubtedly prevented or delayed the necessary synthesis between neo-Darwinism (Darwinian materialism combined with a simplistic, formalist and idealistic vision of heredity, developed by the Mendelo-Morganists) and Michurinism (spontaneous materialism concerning heredity, but without operational concepts). The fact that Michurin and Lysenko were self-taught practitioners with little knowledge of epistemological issues may have had something to do with it, but given the number of scientists involved in this movement, the main reason is probably to be found in the interference between scientific research and the political and geostrategic context of the time.

We can't blame "idealist" scientists for not having been materialists. On the other hand, we should be able to criticize Marxist, and therefore materialist, scientists for not having fought idealism enough on the level of the concepts themselves, or for having fought it only through invective and intimidation.

In the final analysis, dialectical materialism does not have the magical property of accelerating scientific research or facilitating discoveries: these are first and foremost conditioned by appropriate technical innovation and the maturation of previous theoretical debates. Recent discoveries in epigenetics, for example, owe nothing to Lysenko (or rather, they owe everything to *the fact that Lysenko was forgotten*).

On the other hand, dialectical materialism can be an antidote to the potential idealistic deviations inherent in any scientific discovery. Scientific discoveries are by nature incomplete at the outset, since they are historically constructed, and can therefore lend themselves to all sorts of idealistic interpretations, as was the case with the discovery of transmissible variations in the characteristics of the organism ("genes") from generation to generation. Marxist philosophy should not act as a gas pedal—science has its own rhythm and its own history (linked but not "confused" with the history of class struggles)—but at least in such a way as to counteract its idealistic brakes.

No other scientific discipline has seen such a powerful intrusion of idealism: the theory of "genetic determinism" was built on a dogmatic arrogance very similar to that usually attributed to Lysenko, basing its concepts on a "central dogma" (the impossibility of an environmental influence on heredity) and a Trinitarian definition of the gene, which has now been totally overturned.[42] From Conrad Waddington, who was the first to imagine what an "epigenetic landscape" at the level of genome expression might look like, to the cyberneticists who tried to integrate "genome accommodation" into the narrow conceptions of orthodox geneticists, to the "saltationist" evolutionists in the wake of Stephen J. Gould in particular, there has been a great deal of interest in the "epigenetic landscape." Gould in particular, who opposed a vision of evolution "in small steps" (i.e., without a "qualitative leap"), all of them were at one time or anoth-

---

42 The gene is defined by three qualities: unity of function (a gene defines a trait), of mutation (a mutation modifies a gene, or a gene is identified by mutations that distort its message), and of recombination (genes recombine in chromosomes, but cannot mix operational fragments with each other, since they have a fixed, predefined function). Developments in genetic research have successively contradicted all these qualities.

er suspected of crypto-Lysenkoism, and the argument of authority more often than not channeled them to the margins, even though they had, to tell the truth, no Marxist sympathies whatsoever.

Ironically, in parallel with epigenetics, we're now witnessing the development of a current that is highly critical of genetic idealism, what French authors Pierre Sonigo and Jean-Jacques Kupiec would call "biological liberalism." Here, the reversal of a genetics in crisis is not achieved through Marxist theoretical work but, on the contrary, through a kind of return to *pre-Mendelian* Malthusianism, that single aspect that Marx and Engels criticized in Darwin's theory as being the transposition into nature of a contemporary liberal political ideology. In their 2000 essay *Ni Dieu ni gène* [Neither God nor Gene], the authors take on "neo-Mendelian" genetics, judged as idealistic, and oppose it to an ecosystemic and self-regulated conception (by a "genetic" approach). This is a curious reversal, so opportune for today's dominant ideology, while their attack on idealistic genetics remains, and for good reason, of an acuity that our Soviet agronomists would doubtless not dispute: "Built on genetics rather than evolution, synthetic theory deserves to be called neo-Mendelism rather than neo-Darwinism."[43] And he adds: "Genetic information is a modern version of Aristotle's 'form,' from which, by necessity of coherence, it reintroduces all the metaphysics."[44]

> Early molecular biologists spoke of genetic programs in a very realistic sense. Today, in view of the difficulties encountered, this notion is increasingly seen as a metaphor. Some authors seek to limit its scope as much as possible. [...] Is this metaphor still valid within the probabilistic chromatin model? No. DNA sequences can no longer even be considered as stable data, because the same sequence can behave differently depending on the interactions that occur. Within this model, there is no longer any sanctuary from freedom, where essence can take refuge.[45]

In a curious twist, against a backdrop of genetics' enduring inability to reform itself or correct its ideological limitations, and in the face of an arrogant Michurinism with no real concepts to oppose it, these are the thinkers of a "bourgeois materialism," "liberal-compatible" historians,

---

43   Pierre Sonigo, *L'évolution*.
44   Ibid.
45   J. J. Kupiec and P. Sonigo, *Ni Dieu ni Gène* [Neither God, No Gene], 2000.

who quote Adam Smith as much as Darwin, are openly attempting to rethink the dialectic... for the benefit of a fashionable political ideology! What happened to the historians critical of Lysenko, so quick to condemn any intrusion of "politics" into scientific theories?

FROM THE SOVIET PREHISTORY OF EPIGENETICS TO THE SEEDS OF TOMORROW

We've said that the current epigenetic revolution owes nothing to Lysenko, but rather everything to *his erasure,* from a Michurinian "fragmented" heredity to the current epigenetic heredity of "stress reactions," for example. We'll see how striking this filiation is, but also how, paradoxically, Lysenko laid down the principles of an epigenome theory by radically turning away from the very concepts, in genetics, that would have enabled its early development.

Epigenetics considers gene expression as part of a whole that integrates all cellular metabolisms, and focuses on the feedback from cell cytoplasm to nucleus chromatin.[46] Genes determine the production of active proteins (usually enzymes) involved in genetic metabolism, with a given quality and quantity, adapting to the cell's particular exigencies, given that its environment (the rest of the organism in the case of a multicellular organism, or the external environment in the case of a microbe) is, by nature, changeable. The expression of these genes is itself determined by the specific requirements of the environment, assuming multiple functions: production of new cells in a growing tissue, differentiation of cells according to local requirements or the organ in which the cell lives, export of components and interactions with other cells, etc., all on the basis of an energetic metabolism without which nothing is possible, drawing on the energy present in the environment, and a supply of "raw materials" enabling the production of all active proteins in particular.

It has been known since the 1960s that specific molecules are capable of recognizing the starting or end point of a given gene in the chromatin

---

46   The cell is made up of a nucleus containing DNA molecules or chromosomes, long molecular filaments whose combinations of an "alphabet of four bases" determine on certain segments (the genes) the production of active proteins in the cell cytoplasm, i.e. outside the nucleus, in the active part of the cell, interacting with its immediate environment.

of the nucleus, and of adhering to it to prevent or accelerate its expression into active proteins. The metabolism of such molecules has always been very uncertain, and at the level of the nucleus, we've always wanted to limit ourselves to the already complex linear structure of DNA, without considering the added complexity of its three-dimensional folds, its reversible windings around large protein particles (histones), its condensed or uncondensed state, and above all the molecular "marks" "imprinted" on the outer part of DNA bases (methylations are the main examples) by enigmatic enzymes. These methylations are "wear and tear" marks, making more accessible to expression the DNA sectors that have been most useful in a given environmental context, and normally disappear during subsequent divisions and generations.

In the field of genetics, idealism has led to a focus on pure genetic "information," without taking into account the fact that, although the information remains intact (except for rare mutations during DNA replication linked to cell division), the chromatin in the nucleus (the set of genes, conditioned in a certain way) evolves with the life of the cell: a cell normally inherits a vast multi-instrument "score," of which it will express only part, depending on its actual, local experience. A skin cell, for example, will never express the gene for insulin synthesis (expressed by pancreas cells whose genome is initially the same). This view also leads to the idea that the cell is "guided" by an "informational program" that is certainly highly complex, but also predestined, intangible and identically reproducible.

The problem of Darwinian evolution is grafted onto the limits of this theoretical error in genetics. Given the complexity of nucleus-cytoplasm-environment interactions, it is better to consider only the accumulation of mutations within genes, which are particularly rare, in order to understand *random yet adaptive* evolution. In reality, this randomness seems increasingly constrained as life has innovated in its ability to respond to environmental variations. In the case of large multicellular organisms, these variations are always much faster than the time required for gradual genetic evolution. Firstly, because these organisms reproduce slowly (unlike bacteria, for example, which divide once per minute), and secondly, because dozens of highly elaborate molecular mechanisms oppose, slow down, correct or even prevent mutations and, more generally, any modification of the genome... except in periods of stress, when these modifications are stimulated, not passively and "naturally," but actively by the same molecular mechanisms. So what was left to be selected by the environment in the "synthetic" theories of the neo-Darwinians? Yet there must have been an evolution of species under the influence of Darwin's natural selection.

What's more, the "central dogma" (*sic*) of molecular genetics that founded this "synthetic theory of evolution" asserted that there could be no heredity of acquired traits due to a strictly unilateral relationship between genes *and* the environment, between reproductive cells (*germen*) *and* the cells of the rest of the body (*soma*) that they engender through fertilization and embryonic development. In other words, the changing environment cannot, by definition, "act" in a manner that directs the modification of genes (which mutate only at random), and changes in the body's cells, following the effects of the environment, can in no way affect reproductive cells (the only ones able pass on random mutations to offspring). This last assertion corresponds to Weismann's famous "separation between somatic and germ line" at the beginning of the 20th century, which was widely followed in the history of genetics.

Epigenetics, which studies what happens in the cell "outside" the genes, or around them, seeks to understand how the cell "wears out" its genome, transforming it "from the outside" without necessarily changing its "letter." In this way, we discover that the organism can "mark" to a greater or lesser extent the genes it had to use a lot, or those it didn't need, and *how* it had to use them. The enzymatic artillery capable of such markings, and of all other actions on DNA, is extremely complex.[47] But one important fact must be borne in mind: in reproductive cells destined for offspring, all epigenetic marks are normally destroyed by specialized enzymes that re-establish a genetic "virginity" So it's an active process, not a "natural law." This "unchanging" character explains the Weismannian *soma-germen* barrier, the non-heredity of characters acquired in the normal course of events (i.e. when environmental conditions are relatively stable). But if the environment is particularly changeable, if the organism has experienced unusual environmental stresses, for which it has shown an adaptive deficiency or insufficiency, the marks do not totally disappear

---

47 Repairing mutations, cutting or splicing fragments, duplicating or recombining entire fragments within a gene to reshape it, correcting or promoting mutations, etc., always in conjunction with the environment.

from the germ cells, and they remain even in the sectors that have been the most solicited or modified.

This particular adaptation of living organisms, which is in fact no more "magical" than other adaptations that have already been demonstrated without controversy (regulation of blood sugar levels, renewal of the epidermis as a function of desquamation, acquisition of molecular immunity memorized in antibody genes for this or that antigen encountered, etc.), is reminiscent of another well-known process today: the evolution of artificial intelligence. The complexification of living organisms has had to pass from the stage of selecting simple metabolic processes, like the first simple, highly mechanical "programs" in computer science, to the stage of selecting complex processes capable of "groping" when adaptations occur, just like the programs used to solve new problems in "artificial intelligence" today. The current complexity of programming in artificial intelligence far exceeds the cognitive capacities of any individual computer scientist. Yet it is the work of such "simple" intelligences, and we are witnessing the emergence of a far more complex form of intelligence without recourse to a divine explanation. The same applies to natural history: we can go from fairly simple trial-and-error mechanisms in the world of primitive molecules or microbes to the highly elaborate metabolic adaptation strategies of today's great living organisms without recourse to supernatural forces.

This genetic trial-and-error, the ability to "record" genetically the "experienced" results of this trial-and-error (the acquired), materializes in the form of selective markings and selective modifications (not externally directed, but "selected" internally on the basis of an enzymatic artillery pre-selected in such a way as to make it possible to "record" the "experienced" results of this trial-and-error (the acquired). They do not deny the initial processes of genetic mutation. They do not deny the initial processes of rare and gradual genetic mutation (following the classical Mendel-Morgan model), but they are superimposed on them, and in most cases even double them.

We know of a multitude of self-correcting processes in cellular metabolism, and these interactions are not extraordinary. They were simply contradicted from the outset by a dogma opposed in principle to the "heredity of acquired traits." While it is clear that the environment is not animated by "ideas" capable of finalistically "guiding" hereditary living matter (it is not the environment that "writes" gene combinations, as Lamarckian idealism assumed), we can observe that endogenous capacities to respond to environmental changes, These do not necessarily modify the structure of the genes themselves (accidental mutations), but rather the modalities of their expression, their capacity to respond qualitatively and quantitatively, their internal organization in chromatin, etc.[48] This is objectively a matter of "heredity." Objectively speaking, this is an inheritance of acquired traits, reversible and therefore not indelible like the deep genetic mutations themselves. But it is enough to definitively contradict the central dogma on which the denial and demonization of Michurinism are based.

Evolutionary theory is now faced with a new problem: how to define living matter as an alternative to the strict neo-Darwinian mechanism of mutations and natural selection. Indeed, in the face of a dogma in crisis, according to which this dialectical motor would be a "universal law," ahistorical, we are forced to note that the history of living matter has seen everything evolve, even this law itself: living matter has finally placed itself in *front of* this mechanism that created it, in order to internalize it, when beyond a certain functional complexity, the slightest variation by mutation could only hinder the whole of the interdependent mechanisms, whatever the specific benefits to the organism. What is idealistic in the worldview of Mendelo-Morganist neo-Darwinians is to consider that the "law" of the self-dynamic engine of mutations and natural selection is universal and intangible, that it cannot itself evolve and dialectically reverse itself in the course of the history of living organisms.

We must now return to the principles of Michurinism to examine what can be credited to Soviet agronomists, and what they were wrong about, starting from the observation of the relative heredity of acquired

---

48   A "trait" in orthodox genetic terminology needs a different definition: the development of an epidermal callus on the elbow, for example, may be both innate and acquired, but it does not derive from the "appearance of a new gene" qualitatively modifying the expression of others, but rather from the over-expression (by epigenetic factors) of pre-existing genes acting locally and quantitatively on skin keratinization. Generally speaking, whatever the level of microscopic or macroscopic description, all identifiable characteristics of an organism have a qualitative and a quantitative part that are inseparable.

traits, which is collateral to genetic heredity in a stable environment and commonly accepted by today's geneticists.

There is a very clear difference between the deeply idealistic Lamarckian version, which placed the heredity of acquired traits at the heart of the theory (the environment "dictates" the heredity of species by modifying itself), and the Michurinian version, even if neo-Darwinism hypocritically associated the two with the sole aim of discrediting an adversary despite the latter's visibly indisputable results at the time.[49] In reality, Michurin's theory is based solely on empirical results dogmatically ignored by geneticists. On the other hand, Michurin's principles are based on the authoritarian denial of genetic observations on the grounds of theoretical incompatibility. In fact, Michurin and then Lysenko spoke of the heredity of *habit-acquired* characteristics, or *metabolic heredity*, which had nothing to do with Weismann's caricatural experiment in which he cut off the tails of mice only to find that there were no tailless mice:

> We, the representatives of the Soviet Mikhail Gorbachev tendency, affirm that the heredity of properties acquired by plants and animals during their development is possible and indispensable. [...] The bitter struggle that has divided biologists into two irreconcilable camps has revived around an old quarrel: is the heredity of properties and characters acquired by organisms in the course of the development of their lives possible? In other words, do qualitative changes in the nature of organisms depend on the quality of living conditions, acting on the living body, on the organism? The Michurinian doctrine, dialectical materialist in essence, affirms this dependence with facts. Mendelo-Morganic doctrine, idealistic and metaphysical in essence, denies this dependence without providing any proof.[50]

He adds:

> Heredity is the property of the living body to require certain conditions for life

---

49   Dominique Lecourt, a key player in the demonization of anti-Lysenkoists in the 1970s, wrote of the strange attitude of anti-Lysenkoists at the 1948 session: "Can we admit that the terror that does not prevent them from countering all the Lysenkoist theses in theory prevents them from having their say on the technique they claim to justify?" (*Lysenko*, D. Lecourt). Clearly, there was consensus on the results and controversy over how to explain them, in the USSR at the time, which has always appeared as a mystery to Western demonizers.

50   Lysenko, *Report to the 1948 Session*.

and development, and to react in certain ways to such conditions. [...] When an organism finds conditions in the surrounding environment that correspond to its heredity, it continues to develop in the same way as previous generations. But when organisms do not find the conditions they need, and are forced to adapt to the conditions of the external environment, which to some extent do not correspond to their nature, the result is organisms, or certain parts of their bodies, that differ more or less from previous generations. If the modified part of the body is precisely that which engenders the next generation, the latter, both by its needs and by its nature, will differ to one degree or another from previous generations.[51]

Michurinians thus give primacy to the organism's adaptive capacity, including the heredity of solutions found as a result of this endogenous capacity. When descendants are not placed in the same stressful conditions as the parental generation, the adaptive modification no longer appears. This theory, which includes heredity as a process rather than a state, is far more materialistic than the theory of genetic heredity, posited as fixed on the scale of reproduction, and is as close to epigenetic theory as it is to Lamarckian theory.

Obviously, there are countless practical applications, especially in agronomy, for producing seeds that can withstand climatic and other hazards, without involving genetic manipulation that is both costly and unstable over time. V. Stoletov, another Lysenkoist, sums up the situation as follows, based on the theory of successive stages of plant morphogenesis:[52]

> The theory of stadial development paved the way for a targeted modification of plant heredity. The process has now been perfected, as illustrated by the example of the transformation of winter plants into spring plants and vice versa. But it is also possible to modify other plant properties or traits. The theory of the directed modification of plant heredity shows when and how we must act

51   Ibid.

52   For Lysenko, the plant passes through successive stages whose conditions and the environmental conditions required difference: for example, there must first be a period of cold weather at the seed stage, before germination can take place until after winter. Then, a germination stage dependent on light rather than temperature is required, and so on. In fact, later developments in plant physiology, particularly concerning plant hormones, were able to elucidate the basis of such stages in plants. In agronomy, Lysenko is credited with having understood the *vernalization* of seeds (a term popularized by Lysenko), and with having used its principles to germinate winter varieties into earlier spring varieties, thus avoiding losses due to a bad season.

on the developing plant to break the old heredity and create a new one, in line with the living conditions we bring to bear on the organism. Is directed modification of plants possible? This is one of the main questions that have pitted Michurinian and anti-Michurinian scientists against each other for years. The former prove this possibility, theoretically and practically, while the latter categorically deny it.[53]

"Undermining" heredity—a formula that makes no sense in classical molecular genetics, but acquires one in epigenetics—does not necessarily imply denying the observations of Mendelo-Morganists. When Lysenko states:

> The degree of hereditary transmission of modifications will depend on the extent to which substances from the modified part of the body are included in the entire chain of processes leading to the formation of reproductive, sexual or vegetative cells [...] Plastic plant forms with unstable heredity, obtained by one or other of these means, must subsequently be bred, from generation to generation, under the very conditions which the organisms in question can be seen to require, and to which they can be seen to adapt.[54]

He unknowingly refers to the specific DNA-interfering molecules considered in epigenetics, and is mistaken in thinking that they "substitute" for the DNA itself. This is what he almost refers to when he speaks of chromosomes (at the time DNA as a constituent molecule of chromosomes has not yet been discovered):

> The basis of this theory [chromosomal heredity] is the fanciful thesis that part of the chromosome substance cannot be identified with the usual body, and that it alone possesses heredity [...] whereas according to the Michurinian doctrine [...] heredity is inherent not only in chromosomes, but in the entire living body, in each of its particles.[55]

Michurinism developed an extremely rudimentary theory of heredity (and for good reason: DNA had not yet been discovered, let alone the somatic agents capable of acting on it, such as *retrotransposons*), based on a very empirical approach linked almost exclusively to agriculture and an-

---

53   V. Stoletov, *Principes élémentaires de biologie mitchourinienne* [Basic Principles of Michurian Biology].

54   Lysenko, *Report to the 1948 Session*.

55   Lysenko, *Agrobiologie, critique de la théorie chromosomique de l'hérédité* [Agrobiology: Critique of Hereditary Chromosomal Theory].

imal husbandry, but in the end quite modern, since it is almost word for word what epigeneticists say today: to achieve this result, we had to forget our Lysenko affair (which is no longer of political interest to the capitalist West, in the absence of a "socialist camp") and gradually relativize the various idealist aspects of the Mendelo-Morganist theory of heredity.

For Mendel, Morgan and all the geneticists of the early 20th century, the gene was defined as an isolable, quasi-magical element, capable of carrying within itself a "message" defining a characteristic of the organism, which was ultimately a sum of expressed, intangible data (except through extremely rare mutations). This message was revealed by negative experience, since the modification of a character, if transmitted, proved that this character was itself "written," independently of the body itself. Since a gene mutation has an impact on the organism, any mutation presupposed a gene that abstractly defined the function missing after mutation. This scheme was heavily criticized by the Michurinians, who had no observations to back up their criticism.

The discovery of a "genetic code," with the development of molecular genetics, only served to accentuate this counter-sensical idealist "program" defining individual characteristics. The "intelligence gene," the "courage gene," and the "genetic code" were sought, etc., and eugenics took a worrying leap forward, which only the USSR was able to guard against.

It was then discovered that each gene is most often implicated in several characteristics without any obligatory link between them, and can even produce several different proteins depending on the circumstances. Above all, it was discovered that each characteristic observable at the level of the individual is linked to the expression of many different genes and not just one, or even to the quantity of identical duplicates of each of these genes. Later still, it was observed that genes were capable of re-cutting themselves into operational sectors capable of circulating in the nucleus and replicating, inserting themselves elsewhere, on other genes, etc. Chromosomal mutations were spoken of: genetic point mutations were no longer the only ones responsible for evolution, and the neo-Darwinian paradigm began to decline. Finally, the role of the environment in the development of an organism was established by observing genome evolution in populations of clones (with exactly the same genes). At that point, the theory of the "all-genetic" approach no longer had any *raison d'être*, and the crisis of neo-Darwinism was declared.

Today, epigenetics, deriving in a way from the best of the cybernetics[56] of the seventies and eighties, is putting back on the agenda what Michurin called for a century earlier, in a rather avant-garde spirit:

> With the intervention of man, it becomes possible to force every animal or plant form to change more rapidly in the direction desired by man. This opens up a vast field of action of the greatest benefit to man.[57]

A Marxist examining questions of heredity would inevitably find Michurinism far more "dialectical" than Mendelo-Morganism, or even than current molecular genetics, which is still trying to understand the mechanisms of heredity as highly specific and highly integrated, and continues to use only core genes as basic determinants.

But if affirming the reciprocity of heredity/environment relations refers to a spontaneously dialectical materialist way of thinking, and if genetics on the contrary posits a principle of strict unilaterality in this *anti-dialectical* relationship, attributing hereditary modifications to chance alone, Michurinism nonetheless opposes one of the fundamental principles of dialectics, passed over in silence in the polemics of the time, but which today appears in full light: the history of matter, and at a secondary level the history of ideas, develops from the simple *to* the complex, and not *by opposing* the simple to the complex.

It thus seems clear that the Darwinian pairing of chance and selection, which prevailed in primitive cells, has finally been superseded in the evolution of living matter, and integrated into cellular metabolism itself: this primordial movement of natural selection has been able to select more "plastic" metabolisms capable of "groping" for innovation to better meet the demands of an inevitably changing environment, more efficiently and above all more rapidly than chance alone (which kills far

---

56   The cybernetic current produced both highly idealistic developments in molecular genetics, with the idea of the "genetic program," and more materialistic solutions to this crisis, which often appealed to Marxists of the time for their "dialectical" connotations. More detailed information on the history of this crisis in genetics, and the different currents that emerged at the time, can be found in G. Suing, *Évolution, la preuve par Marx*, Éditions Delga, 2016. [**Editor's Note:** Not yet published in English.].

57   I. Michurin, *Œuvres*, Tome 4.

more often than it innovates). Many orthodox geneticists had more or less foreseen this, for example with the very apt notion of "constrained chance" (in the words of the famous Belgian geneticist Christian De Duve).

In terms of ideas, it's clear today that the history of theories of heredity could not have produced epi-genetic theory *before* genetic theory, or *in its place*. The simple, even simplistic ideas of Mendel, Weismann, Morgan, Bateson, Muller and so many others were bound to convince the entire scientific community, in the face of the far more complex concepts of epigenetics, of which Michurin was the unconscious and all too precocious propagator. Indeed, to fully understand epigenetics and the metabolic strategies that enable a certain heredity of habit-acquired traits, one must first be familiar with the primordial structures, the genes, *on the basis of which* the evolution of living metabolism has been able to bring about major complex innovations.

Could we imagine that in physics, the theory of quantum mechanics developed all at once, replacing Newtonian mechanics (of which it is both an extension on another scale, and a negation or dialectical overcoming)? The history of science is far from being a linear, positive progression, but on a large scale and over the long term, it nonetheless follows this general, dialectical law of passage from the simple to the complex, even beyond the technical innovations that enable theoretical evolutions.

In this way, dialectical materialism provides a certain vision of the world and can represent a guide for concrete action, without being a "prophecy" that instantly gives the scientific "truth" as a revelation, without progressive and collective work. The example of the Lysenko affair, if one finds agreeable to relativise its positive and negative aspects, can enlighten us retrospectively on how scientific theories can evolve, according to principles that are entirely consistent with "mature" dialectical materialism. A "mature" dialectical materialism must be able to accept that idealism occasionally holds science back, because science can't go beyond this stage in order to flourish: from the *simple*, often idealistic in some respects, to the *complex*, invariably and necessarily more materialist and dialectical.

It's this fundamental theoretical misunderstanding of the Michurinians that could instead be described as "proto-dialectical materialism" or "primitive" dialectical materialism. On the one hand, genetics suffered many setbacks as a result of this, hampered (that is, "encouraged" in its idealism) by the demonization of such slanderers, as much as epigenetics itself, which couldn't be born on solid foundations (and certainly not on Michurinian "empirical" bases) without going beyond the actually erroneous Mendelo-Morganist stage.

Between Conservation and Evolution: A Dialectic of Life and Environment

Everything is in the process of evolving, even the most "immutable" or seemingly "cyclical" things. This is the materialist observation par excellence, in all sciences where "processes" are analyzed, reconstructed and explained, whether in thermodynamics, geology, or astrophysics. It is undoubtedly in quantum physics that the "laws" of dialectical materialism are the most difficult to ignore. The "wave/particle duality," the interdependence of matter and antimatter, and the "spin correlation" of particles, all support the principles that Hegel, Marx, and Engels laid down long ago, namely that all the components of matter are in a reciprocal relationships, and that these reciprocal actions, at once united and opposed, are the "dialectical," endogenous driving force behind the entire evolution, the entire history of this matter, from its initially simplest forms to its most complex later forms, through overcoming, qualitative leaps resulting from accumulations reaching a threshold.

It's easy to see why things have gone so wrong in biology. Every naturalist draws a common-sense law from his or her experience. Life is stability, in an environment that is constantly changing over the long term. It is even an "offensive" stability, since it succeeds in establishing itself, in constantly readapted forms, in all terrestrial environments, including the most hostile. This life, whose complexity leads us to believe that it can only be fleeting, fragile, and hanging on by a thread, ultimately proves to be particularly powerful and conquering on the scale of geological time.

The experience of naturalists, who themselves end up feeling "different" from other scientists, is that of a subject matter—life—in which all seems to oppose that of the physicists and chemists. What could be more difficult to understand than this living matter, hostile to "reductionist" experimentation, mysterious in so many ways, highly complex and unpredictable, so much so that "everything seems already done." Even the simplest, most primitive forms of life are already immeasurably complex. Logically, biology is the science most prone to idealism, and it's not without reason that Charles Darwin's discovery of a necessary and sufficient mechanism at the base of species evolution was the greatest of the materialist revolutions in this realm of science.

But all that was given was an evolutionary mechanism to continue "describing" life and the immense diversity of its forms, a rather hasty way of getting rid of idealism, because in the end, the "mystique" of life has more to do with heredity, i.e. the conservation of forms from generation to generation, than with its capacity to evolve, to modify itself in a changing environment. Change and evolution are not perceived on the scale of a human lifetime, even though we experience hereditary transmission time and again. Heredity means stability, conservation, conformal reproduction—a movement that runs counter to everything materialism has stood for since the origins of philosophy! How, then, are we to summon the first observers of this central property of life to adhere in principle to the laws of materialism, which is opposed by what is found in field observation? It is the object of study itself, and not the recuperation of the ideological apparatuses of the bourgeois state (even if the latter will not hesitate to take advantage of it, of course), that will make geneticists the first candidates for the idealist trap.

If we look at the two most successful (but counter-intuitive) forms of the critique of Lysenko critique in the 1970s, we would never have imagined today's epigenetic revolution, born of the spontaneous development of idealistic genetics, this time without the slightest interference from political voluntarism. In J. Medvedev's *Grandeur and Decadence of Lysenko*, it's Stalin's political madness and the hypnotic collective submission constructed by the Soviet system that explain the victory of the "charlatan" over the "Galileos" of genetics. In D. Lecourt's *Lysenko*, it is dialectical materialism itself, from Marx's and Engels' very first "ontological" formulations that must be fundamentally questioned, even as Lysenko's concrete results doubtless had "a grain of truth." In reality, we need to revisit self-criticism on the basis of what modern science tells us, in its latest advances, as is customary in traditional materialist thought.

Epigenetics says what the Michurinians were saying (empirically and very incompletely), based on the very concepts, reversed by their development over the course of the twentieth century, that the latter were (rightly) criticized for, that of their having an idealistic, anti-dialectical character. To understand this unfortunate historical collision between political history and the history of science, we need to return to the fundamental flaw in biology. We have no definition of life, other than a purely descriptive and ever-expanding list of "characteristics." Yet without a "global" understanding of life, we can't understand its nature, let alone transform it without short- or long-term negative consequences. Dialectical materialism can integrate a saving element of dynamic contradictions into the current approach to living matter, based on what we know about the origins of life.

It all began, biologists tell us, with the spontaneous appearance of simple organic polymers endowed with the ability to self-replicate; nucleic acids (of which today's DNA is a particular form), whose "building blocks" were able to accumulate in the oceans in a relatively simple way, from the elements present and the energy available. Such molecules were able both to catalyze the production of their own components, the bases, from available elements in the environment, such as enzymes, and to serve as a linear matrix for the spontaneous arrangement of new polymers in identical fashion, on the "zipper" model, i.e. by molecular complementarity: these linear molecules were therefore capable of identical multiplication with no other limits than those of the organic molecules initially present in the oceans, making further evolution a virtual necessity on the basis of probiotic "pro-heredity."

The first dynamic contradiction in living matter, even before the appearance of the first cells (isolating and stabilizing these chemical reactions in an environment that organizes itself at the expense of the outside world, and is therefore relatively *sheltered* from changing conditions), was therefore the one that generated self-replicating (i.e. self-perpetuating) linear polymers to undergo changes in the order of their constituent bases (mutations), some of which contingently (non-finally) led to improved self-replicating performance: change to better perpetuate itself identically in a changing environment.

We can already see the extent to which the apparent "stability" that characterizes life on our scale is both objective (founding both its origin and history) and result of constant movement, of counter-tendency. It is the struggle for self-preservation while progressively discovering improvements in the metabolic strategies enabling self-preservation. The self-preservation that characterizes living matter is the result of permanent self-correction, and thus of a counter-movement that is necessarily constantly being improved. Seen from this angle, it is "heredity" that precedes "evolution" or "mutation," which could be the idealistic admission of matter animated by will or predestination! If we accept the theory that the first molecules capable of self-replication appear spontaneously in the earth's crust, this is not the case.

As a "primordial soup," their evolution is immediately necessary, since any change results in extinction or extension according to its "selective advantage."[58] Darwin's simple scheme, the concept of "*random variation followed by natural selection*" applies from the very beginning, and *above all* at the origin. It does not define living matter, but the necessity by which this matter has perfected its heredity *in spite of* the environment and its rapid changes. The "perfection" of living matter was not in the sense of moral "progress" or predestined in any way, but in that of a progressive liberation never achieved (by definition) from the constraints of an ever-changing environment. In short, living matter, through its self-replicating components having progressively accumulated adaptive and flexible survival strategies, finds itself condemned to attempt to conserve itself in an environment that cannot cease to change.

Living matter, whose metabolism fights as hard as possible against permanent and accidental mutations, will soon turn its own "weapons" against the changing environment in order to survive: mutations (in the broadest sense of the term) that punctually change life forms will be the agents of a capacity to survive in a disturbed environment, even if it means losing the quality of this "conservation." Living matter develops in time and space in order to survive, to remain identical by escaping environmental variations (or by transforming the environment to stabilize it), but since it must become "variable" to save individuals during brutal variations, effective variations end up redeveloping into new species, ulti-

---

58   We owe the notion of "primordial soup" and the theory of the origins of life to a famous Soviet researcher Alexander Oparin. It has recently been discovered that such organic molecules arise spontaneously from mineral matter within solar system elements such as comets, and then seed most planets at random.

mately different from the ancestral forms. The evolution of species is the dialectical result of an incessant struggle by living matter to reproduce itself identically, without ever being able to do so absolutely. What appeared to early naturalists as the most obvious form of stability and fixity in this world, is in fact the most powerful, most permanent, most dialectic movement on Earth, this counter-movement opposed to the environment but forced to adapt to it, this permanent self-correction based on the spontaneous and necessary detour of the environment's "weapons" in order to "survive" it, and which inscribes within itself the evolutionary mechanisms necessary to perfect its apparent form as relentlessly and as much as possible (and it never is).

The *pure* Darwinian mechanism of random variation through genetic mutation followed by natural selection must have led to the first perfections enabling life to free itself from difficult conditions, but progressively, it is clear that the metabolic strategies selected and conserved have become increasingly elaborate and complex, and are now capable of dialectically "overcoming" the primitive chance/selection mechanism (without totally abrogating it, of course). Today, all living species are capable, via highly specialized enzymes, of correcting most of the random genetic mutations permanently occurring in cell nuclei. But we have also observed that these same enzymes, which prevent mutations, become mutation "gas pedals," denying their function when the environment is brutally disturbed. What we have here is a highly sophisticated mechanism that can both combat random mutations (almost systematically lethal) when the environment is stable and the species well adapted to it, and *actively* open the floodgates to random survivability in the event of environmental stress that puts the species at risk of extinction.

This type of metabolism is highly dialectical, and even goes beyond the Darwinian definition of living matter "drifting" at the whim of chance and selection, as in the end, the couple is tamed, incorporated by selected and ultimately safeguarded conservative strategies. Life is thus not defined by Darwin's discovery alone, but by a self-preserving principle (derived from the biochemical properties of the first self-replicating molecules) and evolving only through an inability to respond absolutely to this original principle.

Thus, all the active meiotic recombination mechanisms that underpin the production of reproductive cells in animals and plants alike, enable both the maintenance of the species' chromosome formula (conservation), and a redistribution of forms within each trait (alleles for each gene) that ensures a certain "intraspecific" biodiversity for each population. In principle, this is contrary to the principle of self-preservation, but in the event of environmental stress, it will statistically enable certain survivors endowed with favorable (albeit initially discrete) innovations to ensure the conservation of the species, *albeit in a different form*. The principle of self-preservation necessarily generates the evolution of species that negates it. We are thus clearly moving from quantity to quality, following a process that at first glance seems predestined to the opposite end. There is therefore no "premeditated" goal, despite the "organized" orientation of evolution.

The abundance of such mechanisms selected to conserve the species has understandably led biologists, both before and since Darwin, particularly in the initially distinct field of formal genetics, to believe that living matter is "fixed" or does not evolve, given the extreme slowness of changes observable on a human scale. Even when Darwinian evolutionism was accepted, the theoretical compromise between genetics and Darwinism, known as neo-Darwinism (or, more recently, the *synthetic theory of evolution*), adopted a materialistic façade by admitting the evolution of species "without divine intervention" by (blind) natural selection alone, while retaining a highly idealistic theory of heredity, as we have already pointed out.

In a way, the very notion of a gene has been, and still is, problematic. Initially, the way in which such "coded information" was discovered invited a metaphysical interpretation of the theory. If an accidental mutation inactivates a sector of an individual's DNA, an apparent effect is manifested after development, which leads to belief that the modification has affected "the information coding for the apparent trait" bypassing the ultra-complex causal chain from one to the other. It was then natural to deduce that our genetic heritage was the sum of innumerable pieces of information that determined all our characteristics once and for all, without any intervention from the environment. This *all-genetic* theory held back the development of genetics for several decades, with an idealism that made it impossible to understand subsequent discoveries. A local mutation alters many unrelated characteristics, and the same visible change can be caused by independent mutations in several genes that are unrelated to each other in terms of their immediate expression. It was then discovered that a gene could express itself in several alternative ways depending on circumstances, or undergo somatic modifications during life. All this put to rest for good the idealistic version that implicitly prevailed in genetics with each new gene discovery.

Today, faced with the construction of a new, broader theory incorporating formal genetics in the same way that quantum mechanics incorporated Newtonian mechanics, we need to reconsider the links between this new paradigm and genetics on the one hand, and Darwinism on the other. This is where dialectical materialism comes in handy.

The active contradiction between this fundamental tendency towards self-preservation and all the mechanisms that enable species to diversify, and thus actively evolve, finds its most obvious form in epigenetics. For the general law that applies to the genome of an individual producing sex cells is not the transmission of epigenetic markers, but rather their total erasure. The production of sex cells recruits highly elaborate mechanisms enabling each generation to "forget" the wearing down of the genome acquired from the parents in their specific living environments. This "rebooting" of the genome at each generation is the norm, the guarantee of a tendency to self-conservation, just like the other genetic mechanisms identified at the end of the twentieth century. This "rebooting" of the genome at each generation is the norm, the guarantee of a tendency towards self-preservation, just like the other genetic mechanisms identified at the end of the 20th century.[59]

On the other hand, the fact that this deletion involves specialized enzymes and is an active process shows both its evolutionary interest,

---

59 Many elaborate self-preservation mechanisms can be cited. The SOS/SRM systems is one example, which normally correct genome mutations, except when the stressful environment reverses their action and they become positively mutagenic. Similarly, recognition mechanisms between homologous chromosomes during fertilization of two sex cells prevent hybridization between species (to conserve species), except when the environment is stressful, i.e. when hybridization between closely related varieties or species would enable them to share or potentially accumulate more metabolic strategies for resistance to the environment. Meiotic recombination during the formation of reproductive cells also involves sophisticated karyotype conservation mechanisms, except when environmental conditions destabilize them.

and the possibility of counter-evolution: transgenerational memory corresponds to the selective non-deletion of certain parts of the epigenome (marks made on certain genes particularly used by the parent in its particular environment) despite the normal deletion process, and this on sectors of the genome whose adaptive interest was manifested in the parent in its environment. In other words, if the law is the oblivion of the acquired to keep only the innate (a law that supports Mendelo-Morganists, but which proves to be non-natural, predetermined, and therefore itself subject to evolution), it admits, when the environment is particularly changeable and stressful, selective conservation of epigenetic marks, by mechanisms predetermined for this purpose and selected in the course of evolutionary history, particularly in plants, which cannot escape such environments. As the environment often changes much faster than the genes (mutations are extremely rare, thanks to the multiple self-correcting mechanisms of living organisms), adaptive mechanisms that are faster than chance and selection alone have gradually taken hold, particularly in species unable to escape the environment (plants, fixed animals).[60]

We thus confirm both that self-preservation, the false fixity of living things that troubled so many idealistic scientists, remains the rule, and that to guarantee the survival of species beyond this tendency towards self-preservation, it is necessary to change form, through molecular means of memorizing and transmitting advantageous genetic forms from time to time, these means being themselves selected by history as highly perfected processes. The central dogma of molecular genetics, which

---

60   This is a recent example, but there are dozens of others along the same lines, from migratory animals to man himself. Here, talking about the study of corals and their current scarcity in the oceans:

> A study published in 2016 showed [...] that corals exposed to a variable thermal environment showed a greater ability to [...] express different phenotypes according to environmental conditions [...], facilitating adaptation. These changes in gene expression could be the result of epigenetic modifications that can be passed onto offspring. [...] Coral incubated for six weeks in slightly acidified seawater shows phenotypic plasticity and DNA methylation [...] that can be passed onto offspring. [...] Unlike [this] acclimatization, genetic adaptation is a slow, irreversible, but lasting response [...]. This mechanism [...] is, however, slower than the rate of evolution of current climate change" (Denis Dallemand, Sylvie Tambutté, Didier Zoccola, "Y-t-il encore des coraux dans la mer? [Are there still any corals left in the sea?]," *La Recherche* N° 521, March 2017).

posited the inability of environmental influences to cross the germline barrier, the species barrier, the nuclear envelope protecting the genes in the cell, has been pulverized. If any selective advantage that has arisen by chance mutation from the outset is conserved by natural selection, then even the elaborate mechanisms that make it possible under certain conditions to *transmit acquired knowledge hereditarily* (to speed up adaptation to a changing environment) are selective advantages that do not derogate from Darwin's law.

Dialectics of Nature, Yesterday and Today

However, "evolutionary ecology," the new name for "population genetics," is still taught at university on the old foundations of neo-Darwinism, and this is relatively normal: teaching always lags behind fundamental research, even and perhaps especially during scientific revolutions. To understand the evolution of populations in a given environment, and therefore that of potentially disturbed agrosystems, this evolutionary ecology today puts forward four fundamental "forces" supposed to explain the evolution of species itself on a large scale: mutations, natural selection, genetic drift, and migrations.

This highly descriptive and probabilistic approach equates Darwin's famous principles (individual variation, i.e. *mutations* for geneticists, and *natural selection*, i.e. what filters out these variations over the generations according to their suitability in the new environment) with two new "forces" unknown to the Darwinian model (*genetic drift*, i.e. the ability of certain genes to evolve discreetly without natural selection, and *migration*, which randomly redistributes allele frequencies from a group of migrants that is not representative of the original population). Neo-Darwinism has always "added" new laws to the fundamental driving force of Darwinism without ever questioning the basic postulate, as if life could be defined by a simple, non-exhaustive and irreducible list of apparent characteristics. The great absentee, and with good reason, among these "evolutionary forces," epigenetic acclimatization ("heredity of acquired traits" in euphemistic terms).

Without dialectics, such an approach, even if materialistic, seeks in the almost mystified force of *chance* a functional alternative to theological finalism, but without identifying the *necessary* motor of evolution itself. Yet it is evident, in light of current knowledge, that among these "forces"—even if this may seem anti-dialectical at first brush—there are those that are not evolutionary, but, rather, conservative. It's only the traumatic memory of the fixist inquisition that prevents our biologists from simply recognizing that living matter is endowed with such forces opposing evolution, because everything we know today, in genetics and epigenetics, confirms it resoundingly. Accepting the existence of these conservative forces would, in their view, amount to an absurd simplification, denying evolution once again.

In fact, only dialectical materialism can identify the necessary, non-chaotic, non-finalist form of living evolution between these two contradictory poles of *variation* and *conservation*. The mimetic and simplistic veneer of the indeterminism of modern physics on biology has long masked this obvious fact, by identifying living matter with matter taken in its totality, and by depriving living matter—part of this matter in the broadest sense—of certain particular, additional qualities, which make up both its quality and its history. Even quantum mechanics and thermodynamics show on a large scale that the "indeterministic chaos" of elementary particles contradictorily generates order and a certain stability, a certain solidity to our macroscopic world.

Mutations, the first force in evolutionary ecology, are by definition accidental variations that are opposed to preserving the integrity of the individual and, more broadly, the stability of the species. It is for this reason that living organisms have developed a large number of metabolic strategies to prevent such mutations as far as possible: most random mutations affect non-coding sectors of DNA (the majority), or recessive alleles that are not expressed in an organism that generally has two parental versions of each gene. If a mutation damages a gene, it will probably not alter the structure of the protein described, due to the redundancy of the genetic code (several triplets of bases in the DNA can correspond to the same amino acid in the protein described). Finally, even if a mutation occurs in an expressible sector, complex enzymatic systems are responsible for correcting mutations, permanently preserving the integrity of the individual's genome. It is these "epigenetic" mechanisms which are going to "choose" which of the two parental versions will be expressed or suppressed, relative to context, and act as a heterogeneous force of conservation, fighting against the "evolutionary" force of mutagenesis. These same conservative forces, however, by undermining themselves in the face of brutal environmental variations, will increase rather than moderate the frequency and effect of mutations, as if, to ensure the integrity of a species on a larger scale in the face of environmental stress, the conservative forces reverse their action so that increased variability produces a few survivors, even if it means that their population is ultimately radically different from the original one.

Natural selection, the second evolutionary force according to evolutionary ecology, is the sorting out of individual variations by environmental conditions, causing allele frequencies in the population to rise or fall over the generations. But we forget to mention that this natural selection can also be exercised in two totally contradictory ways. When the environment remains unchanged, natural selection tends to stabilize each frequency around an optimal form (for that environment only), by eliminating variations that are too great (even though they may be better in another environment). Such "stabilizing natural selection" then acts as a conservative rather than an evolutionary force. On the contrary, when the environment changes, the forms that were the best adapted are no longer so, and the new forms resulting from random mutations may turn out to be better in the new environment: natural selection then actively disfavors the old forms in favor of the new, on the model of mosquitoes' acquisition of resistance to insecticides, or pathogenic bacteria to antibiotics. All the biological mechanisms at the origin of a population's polymorphism over the generations, in particular that which produces an infinite number of genetic varieties recombined in the reproductive cells by meiosis, are in fact a kind of force incorporating variability, the better to accentuate it *if necessary in the event of* environmental stress, while preserving the species' chromosomic formula (i.e. preserving the general pattern of the species beyond the particular individual forms).

Genetic drift is an innovation of the "neutralist" theory, a rather late theory that strongly relativized the role of natural selection in Darwin's model of evolution. It stated that most genetic variations occur separately, without any impact on the individual's characteristics, until they eventually acquire a new function. Once again, this is the dynamic contradiction between the conservative aspect of a force, the differentiation of genetic evolutions vs. the environment, and its evolutionary aspect, the potential for abrupt change (qualitative leap) when innovation becomes necessary in a changing environment.

Migration also responds to the dual imperative of species conservation through escape (migration) from a now hostile environment, and the new allelic distribution resulting from a restricted group of migrants settling elsewhere in new environmental conditions. The statistical premium placed on now-minority innovations (restricted group of migrants) will accelerate the evolutionary process, but we mustn't forget at the same time that migrations are most often allelic exchanges between populations of the same or closely related species, and that during sudden environmental variations, species barriers (which normally prevent individuals of different species from being inter-fertile) can be lifted to a certain extent in order to accumulate potentially advantageous innovations from a population. The hybrids resulting from these migrations can then ensure the survival of the species to a certain extent (conservation), but through the profound modification of their adaptive characteristics (evolution, ultimately contradicting the conservative force from which it comes).

In addition to these four "evolutionary forces," evolutionary ecology also forgets, as we've already said and not without psychoanalytic explanation, the force that can modify the epigenome of individuals in a population that has experienced profound environmental stress.[61] This is *epigenetic acclimatization* (in other words, the discoveries of Michurin and Lysenko). In fact, if the conservative force has active mechanisms for erasing epigenetic marks acquired during life, and then restarting the process, it's not surprising that this is the case. While the basic model of the species has been "reset from scratch" with each new generation, adaptations have enabled these mechanisms to reverse themselves to "rescue" the marks that have been of particular interest, reinforcing a characteristic trait, in the new environmental conditions. The conservative force, which normally erases the acquired to preserve the species as it is, can become a new "evolutionary force," not immediately passing through the genes, to modify the characteristics of the population more rapidly than by chance alone.

---

61   The epigenome is the set of marks acquired during an individual's life on or around his genes, i.e. his genome. This epigenome is transmitted hereditarily and reversibly, unlike mutations in the genome itself.

Clearly, living matter is not driven by a chaotic force pushing it to constantly change, but rather by a *dynamic contradiction* intimately linked to the self-replicating property of its primitive molecules (nucleic acids) at the very beginning of the history of life: the development of these self-replicating molecular populations on a simple Darwinian model has, over time, accumulated a whole series of enzymatic strategies enabling them to actively escape from destabilizing environmental variations, and then to adapt to them by relatively taming the internal "destructive" forces of genetic mutation. Changing in order to "conserve" (without, of course, succeeding, which makes the contradiction antagonistic) is therefore the general principle of species evolution. In other words, evolution is generated by material necessity, not in the sense of a predetermined goal set by a Creator, as suggested by the theologian Teilhard de Chardin.[62] But, on the contrary, the only way to do this is to escape from one origin by submitting to the changing conditions of the environment.

The only direction adopted by living matter is that of increasingly efficient liberation from the external environment, but without ever achieving absolute liberation, since life depends entirely on the molecules and energy available in the environment. From a particularly fragile and volatile single-cell aquatic life, natural history has seen the emergence of multi-cell organisms seeking a certain stability in spite of the environment (immunity, homeostasis, cell regeneration, etc.), more social and organized populations capable of significantly transforming the environment in an attempt to stabilize it, and then mobile forms capable of fleeing sudden variations and protecting their descendants outside the aquatic environment, in an amnion, equivalent to a fully stabilized aquatic environment.

We can't understand the relative ease with which life has colonized all terrestrial environments, increasingly escaping "natural hazards" without ever being able to do so completely (remember the impact of biological crises on the entire biosphere in geological history) without taking these contradictions into account. Conversely, we can also understand the extraordinary ability of certain species to remain apparently unchanged over millions of years, when the colonized environment is sufficiently stable (as in the case of the Coelacanth, the "living fossil" that

---

62   **Editor's Note:** Pierre Teilhard de Chardin (1881-1955) was a French Jesuit priest who wrote works on theological and Darwinian topics, among other things.

inhabits the most remote abysses), despite the famous "forces" of evolutionary ecology... But such contradictions can only be formulated with reference to dialectical materialism, which is still largely a philosophical taboo in today's world.

How, then, can we fail to see in the antagonism postulated between political ecology and communism an origin that is at least as ideological as it is historical? Ecology symmetrically refers to a biological science that is playing an increasingly decisive role in the new geostrategic stakes of the century, both for capitalism and for the oppressed classes themselves who are called upon to overthrow it, and to a political movement of the "anti-communist left" (i.e., "social-democratic" in an updated form). But in the face of this ideological "adversary" within the anti-capitalist front, Marxism's weakness undoubtedly owes as much to the neglect of its history (in particular its agroecological experience in the USSR) as to the Lysenko affair. Ecology has undoubtedly been the site of ideological-political confrontations of all stripes in recent decades (liberal, theological, utopian socialist, fascistoid...) except Marxism! Even though the latter was undoubtedly best placed to unravel the deepest theoretical contradictions. And our "dialectical" definition of life, which enables us to advance both on the front of materialism against the fixist and creationist inquisition, and on the front of overcoming the sterile contradiction between Darwinian evolutionism and genetic idealism, is a necessary and sufficient demonstration of this. Epigenetics is the "practical" key, while dialectical materialism is the theoretical catalyst.

In the wake of the Lysenko affair, a historical hiatus has seen the Michurinian "proto-epigeneticists" on the one hand, unable to evolve without the fundamentals of Mendelo-Morganism (to be overcome, not denied), and geneticists on the other, unable to understand the monument of complexity and stability (relative, of course) that is living organisms, on the basis of a theory that predicts evolutionary forces alone, without any dialectical counter-movement.

For decades, this stumbling block has repeatedly pushed back the deadline for a more general understanding of epigenetics, not as a supplement to ever more inaccessible and disarming complexity, but as the logical development of living organisms' capacity for self-preservation through a relative (albeit limited) heredity of the acquired under conditions of environmental stress, the ultimate strategy of a matter incorporating strategies of liberation from the environment through internal counter-tendencies.

In short, one could return to Friedrich Engels's famous *Dialectics of Nature* at the end of the 19th century, which described the Nature in which we have appeared and in which we ourselves have evolved, of which we are objectively a part. This work, which appeared around the Darwinism of the time, featured a particularly prophetic and consequential materialist approach. We should have a new work, this time a collective one, translating into dialectical terms the now exposed fundamental contradictions of heredity and evolution, the two forces that determine the potentialities of a Nature to which we owe everything, in the final analysis. This would assure our present and perhaps above all our common future.

CONCLUSION

PROGRESSIVE DEGROWTHERS AND PRODUCTIVIST COMMUNISTS?

THE APPARENT POLITICAL OPPOSITION between communists and environmentalists stems from a historical misunderstanding, a programmed amnesia skilfully nurtured by the dominant ideology. "Ecosocialism" is not up to the task of remedying the situation, since this eclectic theory stems above all from a void left by recent Marxist theorists on the question of the environment, and not from a genuine synthesis overcoming the contradiction (which persists today more than ever). On the contrary, it's up to Marxism and its associated materialism to find the conceptual resources, as was once proposed for other struggles (feminism, anti-racism, the struggle for peace and national sovereignty).

In reality, environmental activists are alerting public opinion to impending cataclysms, in the belief that scientific demonstration alone will suffice to raise widespread awareness. By relying solely on the power of conviction, on propaganda alone, they deny the fundamental opposition of the ruling class, which has no interest whatsoever in helping them (except, no doubt, in blocking the development of potential powers in the southern hemisphere), and the obligation to get out of our mode of production, in order to trigger a genuine, sustainable, and far-reaching ecological policy.

The first denial allows the bourgeoisie to seize some of their theoretical weapons to wage the struggle in their own interests, light years away from the real environmental issues at stake. The second invites environmentalists to fall into a sort of reformism, i.e., in the belief that we can make gradual progress towards these national and global objectives without calling the system into question, rejecting any revolutionary option in favor of the old utopias of the "far left."

Armed with modern scientific knowledge, have environmentalists not realized that proof of imminent planetary crisis has no effect on the general political orientations of our governments? Do they not notice that for over a century, armed with scientific analyses of Marxist political economy, communists have been announcing the global explosion of a systemic crisis, without anyone at the top of our capitalist house of cards ever seeing the increasingly frequent stock market tsunamis coming?

Whether we're serious environmentalists or communists, we're not millenarians. We won't wait for an imminent "day of judgment" by withdrawing into small, sectarian, self-confident communities, as mystical reactionaries and some green-gray "survivalists." On the contrary, we expose, for the people, the scientific, material causes that determine our indissolubly linked social and environmental living conditions, and we fight against the ruling class that stifles our analyses, seeks to silence us unless it is to set us against each other. But in order to arrive at a single set of demands and a truly revolutionary orientation, we must first overcome certain theoretical misunderstandings that still divide us today.

The first of these conceptual misunderstandings pits *progress* against *degrowth*. From the point of view of many environmentalists, the fact that our resources are limited necessarily invites us to retreat, never to *dialectically go beyond them*. Human progress has always advanced dialectically, periodically finding revolutionary solutions and paradigm shifts that can overcome a specific limit to human development. Obviously, this progress implies moving from the old to the new, and therefore losing certain traditional aspects in favor of radical innovations (which is not to say that we don't still remember them). Nostalgia, combined with a fear of the future, can lead some activists to turn away from "progress" in favor of a "new" approach, a return to an idealized past. As if we could really go back to the past collectively, other than through the global crisis we are supposed to be fighting against.

Ever since the postmodern philosophers, profoundly anti-Marxist, fired on the very notion of progress, ultimately judged to be "totalitarian," green activists may be tempted to submit to the dominant injunction, only to twist it into a more politically correct "degrowth." Of course, we need to economize on our resources, but above all we need to give ourselves the time to innovate and create the conditions for a truly liberating overhaul. Degrowth can only be an end in itself, a paradigm, for Malthusians of the worst kind. It's no longer a question of saving to ensure the future, but of asking future generations (and present-day populations who do not benefit from our wealth, and who would legitimately like it for themselves) to live more modestly than their parents. This is an unprecedented situation, which reflects what we are all experiencing or suffering. For many generations, working-class people have lived with the hope that their children will live better than their parents. Today, the opposite is true,[1] and we can clearly see the deterioration in children's living conditions compared to those of their parents at the same age. Degrowth is therefore the incorporation into militant discourse of the relative failure of class struggles in the face of an increasingly agonizing and bellicose capitalism. Don't we have anything better to offer than the doom and gloom towards which the bourgeoisie wants to drag us?

Capitalist productivism, defined by environmentalists as "production for production's sake," has only recently been copied by the socialist camp, when it was already deteriorating ideologically. For capital, the key is to generate rapid growth with "easy," immediate solutions. The massive consumption of hydrocarbons is a blatant example of this, as is the massive use of the energy sector. These are "mechanistic" solutions for the use of chemical inputs with immediate return on investment in agriculture. These are short-term solutions which, in the long term, lead to increased dependence and rapid depletion (of stocks and fertility).

On the contrary, with the aim of a solid and *lasting* (rather than *profitable*) national defense against predatory capitalist encirclement against the USSR, against the murderous blockade on Cuba today, socialism mobilized considerable human, financial, and material productive forces to implement ecologically sound plans, *without losing productivity* wherever possible. This included costly investment in hydroelectricity, nuclear fusion, agroecology... Such choices were able to continue even when these countries found themselves in serious difficulty, as in 1948 in the immediate post-war period, when a ruined Soviet Union resolutely opted for large-scale agro-forestry. This should give pause for thought to the most anti-communist of our militant environmentalists.

Capitalism denies the natural limits of our growth, of our collective

---

1   **Editor's Note:** In the imperialist countries.

progress, with a highly mechanistic, formalistic, short-termist vision. Political ecology, on the other hand, enshrines them in an *a priori*, idealistic, and fatalistic submission, contrary to the very nature of militant commitment. Communism, on the other hand, looks for the *causes* of such limits, instead of denying them, and then seeks as far as possible, technically and scientifically, to overcome them dialectically instead of going backwards. In this respect, communism is fundamentally *progressive*, without being "productivist," since it emphasizes the sustainability of solutions rather than immediate satisfaction. Everything in our history shows that we have always evolved and progressed by overcoming seemingly intangible cycles and harmonies, because nature itself doesn't evolve otherwise!

The second misunderstanding pits *social progress* against *technical progress*. For the generations that lived through the late hours of the Cold War, the American dream was one of flamboyant, unlimited, conquering, ostentatious technical progress, while in the East we saw only shortages and frustration on television. The "backwardness"" of the socialist camp in the post-Khrushchev era was real, of course, but very relative, since it sought above all to break capital's deadly grip while seeking to satisfy the vital needs of as many people as possible. Against this backdrop, the idea was born—contrary to human history—that technical progress, comfort, and abundance are synonymous with capitalism. However, this is not the case, and the younger generations are beginning to understand how warmongering imperialism does not stimulate technical progress, but rather blocks it. The parenthesis of the East-West confrontation, during which it was necessary to demonstrate to the people, through a relative "redistribution" of wealth, extorted from the neo-colonies, that the best model was that of the bosses, closed long ago

The wealth of the capitalist system is, above all, wasted, lost in the deep pockets of big business and financial tycoons. It only contributes to the major collective investments advocated by the scientific community when the context urgently requires it, and when it's usually already too late. The anarchy of production that characterizes the system prevents any democratic planning on major common issues, and it should be obvious to environmental activists that social and ecological progress cannot be envisaged without at the same time unblocking technical progress.

For it is this that will enable new alternative energy technologies to overcome current shortages, with as few setbacks as possible for the people, and if possible with advances! For example, it is imperialism that is currently blocking all funding for thorium-based molten-salt reactors, even though these are risk-free, because they would compromise the military-industrial nuclear weapons lobby with which the uranium circuit has been linked for decades. It's also agribusiness that has always blocked research into agroforestry, because it would give people greater national sovereignty and remove the limits to soil fertility that underpin Western agricultural monopolies.

Technical progress is a prerequisite for social and ecological progress, as it is only through massive organic production, for example, that we can ensure a redistribution that is not reserved for a few petty bourgeois, but for the broad masses. In all areas of agroecology, it has been proven that no alternative to intensive agriculture can be envisaged without a massive increase in productive forces and technological innovation. Intensive agriculture is based on highly mechanistic concepts: inputs formally replace what the soil provides for plants, and farmers simply have to passively pour them onto the fields and wait for short-term results. Organic farming, on the other hand, requires a great deal of scientific knowledge and know-how on the part of farmers, who become the engineers of their own land, and it is again a development of productive forces that only socialism can ensure.

The final misunderstanding is between *technical* and *scientific progress*. For many environmentalists, a distinction needs to be made between technical progress, which produces "machines" that degrade the environment and upset its natural balance, and scientific progress, which provides objective arguments in the battle of ideas for the environment. One would be an enemy, the other an ally, at least tactically. It's easy to forget that here too, things are indissolubly linked. It was by preserving and observing nature, by developing the natural sciences, that most technical innovations were born. In this respect, almost all the molecules used by the pharmaceutical industry come from research protocols carried out on natural ecosystems, where we strive to preserve as much biodiversity as possible. It is by protecting species, even those that might seem useless to man at first glance, that we will be able in the future to find potential sources of molecules capable of improving our health conditions in the face of this or that new threat.

As we've seen, the Soviet *zapovedniki* were reserves that were off-limits to humans and could, if necessary, be used as observatories for scientists, and not just for agrobiological research. Under the banner of socialism, they guaranteed a remarkable biodiversity, in the vanguard of today's environmentalist ideals.

Even in this field, we have seen how capitalism can, on the contrary, hold back the development of knowledge (e.g. the transformation of classical genetics into epigenetics) because of the downward trend in the rate of profit and ideological opposition to dialectical materialist solutions. However, it is with more dialectics that we can look to the future, not with fear and fatalism, but with hope and confidence in mankind. Science, even when slowed down by the system of social domination, has always made it possible to propose affordable solutions to the problems of our time, and it is undoubtedly only when we have definitively emerged from our prehistory (i.e. that of the class struggle, to use Karl Marx's formula) that we will be able to look with serenity at the fundamental issues of our collective future.

As far as soil fertility and energy are concerned, resource limitations are an incentive for research, and humanity has always been able to overcome such limits, not thanks to capitalism, but rather in spite of it! Just as immigration is not responsible for structural unemployment, just as physicists' formulas are not responsible for the American bombings of Hiroshima and Nagasaki, so technical and scientific progress is not responsible for the environmental damage caused by the best disguised class: the bourgeoisie. This is our common enemy!

APPENDIX 1
"TREES ARE THE MASTERS OF THE SOIL"

This proverbial law from agronomist Claude Bourguignon sums up quite well why deciduous forest soils are among the most fertile, possessing all the characteristics that farmers would like to find in their fields. It's easy to see why agroforestry—the reintroduction of trees on or around fields—has become the backbone of agroecological practices. In a forest, biodiversity and biomass production are enormous, with no added fertilizers, pesticides or human intervention. Many agroecologists and permaculturists rightly see this as a model from which agriculture should draw inspiration, to finally turn its back on agribusiness.

Whatever its profile, soil lies at the interface between the lithosphere (the earth's crust, made up of rocks and therefore rich in mineral salts), the atmosphere, the hydrosphere (air and water) and the biosphere (all living organisms, both micro and macroscopic).

Plants, which form the basis of all food chains since they produce their organic matter exclusively from mineral matter (water, mineral salts and carbon dioxide) and light energy, grow here, some of which is then consumed by herbivorous animals, which in turn are consumed by carnivorous animals.

These "primary producers" have relatively few needs, and find most of the resources they need in the soil (apart from sunlight and carbon dioxide). From a physical point of view, they need to be able to take root. This is one of the functions of roots. Chemically, they need to be able to draw water and mineral salts from the soil. This is the absorbent function of roots.

Soil is a collection of layers formed by the weathering of subsoil mineral matter and the degradation of surface organic matter (into humus).

It can thus provide plants with a loose support on which to root, as well as a store of water and mineral salts from which they can draw. These characteristics are enhanced by the slow production of molecular aggregates known as "clay-humus complexes" (CHC). These negatively-charged aggregates are capable of retaining the mineral salts that seep into the soil with precipitation from the mineralization of litter (dead leaves, twigs, remains of dead organisms, excrement, etc.) by soil bacteria, so that they don't disappear below into the bedrock (water table).

But the production of these CHCs depends on a number of factors that intensive farming is destroying. On the one hand, clays are produced at depth by the weathering of the parent rock, and brought up by earthworms [and other soil organisms] that rework them by agglomerating them with calcium ions and other elements. On the other hand, pesticides and excess toxic fertilizers kill many soil organisms, including earthworms, along with much of the soil's fauna.

On the other hand, to produce humic acids, we need aerobic fungi (which live only in the open air, i.e. virtually on the surface), the only ones capable of digesting the lignin that makes up tree wood, and a microfauna capable of digesting organic molecules from the litter, leaving the mineral salts it contains in the soil (in other words, returning to the soil the mineral salts that had been absorbed by previous generations of plants). Pesticides, however, kill off this microfauna, and plowing by turning over the soil suffocates the mushrooms, which end up dying deep down.

On the surface, litter provides the organic matter needed for humification, but it also performs another equally important function. It protects the soil from drying out in summer and freezing in winter, enabling soil life to last all year round, even if its activity obviously fluctuates.

At bedrock or similar level, the trees' deepest roots (known as "tap roots") attack the rock, which weathers, producing clays and releasing many additional mineral salts (which are brought up by the daily work of earthworms). Some of these roots penetrate deep into the subsoil, draining water out of the soil when heavy rainfall threatens to flood the area. Flooding, when water can no longer infiltrate, causes erosion of the soil itself through runoff. The soil loses its mineral salts and humic acids, sterilizing it for a long time to come.[1]

---

1 The first stage in the death of a soil is its "biological" death: the destruction

In addition to creating habitable conditions for the fungi responsible for humus formation with lignin in the litter, trees also have a very beneficial function for the soil in the form of their adventitious roots. This root system develops at a low level, just below the zone where humus is produced and organic matter mineralized. With rainfall, these roots recover some of the mineral salts formed. In the event of an excess of mineral salts (particularly in the polluted soils of intensive agriculture), trees are capable, with bacterial and fungal help, of capturing the surplus nitrates in the soil, so that they gradually disappear and no longer pollute the underlying groundwater (above a certain threshold, nitrates can be carcinogenic to humans who draw from the water table). Excess nitrates and nitrites from the natural compost of organic farming (which is richer in nitrogen than the NPK fertilizers of intensive agriculture) can also be absorbed in this way.

Intensive farming means destroying the soil both physically and chemically. From a physical point of view, exposing cultivated soils to the elements (as opposed to "sowing under plant cover") exposes them to all kinds of bad weather and drought, which depletes surface water stocks and kills the life that depends on them. Even without pesticides, microfauna can gradually disappear from such soils. What's more, plowing, which systematically turns over the soil, not only accelerates drying out, but also exposes deep-rooted bacteria to the open air, thus burying and asphyxiating humifying fungi. It also buries all forms of overlying organic matter, which will never be degraded by aerobic fungi and will rot away. Finally, plowing smoothes out the soil between the trenches, opening up wide spaces for the infiltration of rainwater, which will not remain in the soil and will be lost to the plants.

Chemical fertilizer treatments dramatically increase crop yields in the short term, but destroy the soil in the long term, as we have said. Firstly, such fertilizers will attract numerous weeds, which will then have to be removed by an almost compulsory use of herbicides, which are also toxic for all soil life. Granular fertilizers such as phosphates, for example, are

---

of soil life no longer allows the cohesion of its various components. Chemical "death" ensues with the leaching of mineral salts from the soil, which can no longer retain them through its CHC and lost porosity. "Physical" death is the final act before the formation of a veritable desert: even the clays are eventually washed away in the run-off that forms sludge, leaving the parent rock soon bare.

themselves directly destructive by simple contact with most soil animals.

Figure 14: Interdependent aspects of an ideal fertile soil (deciduous forest soil).

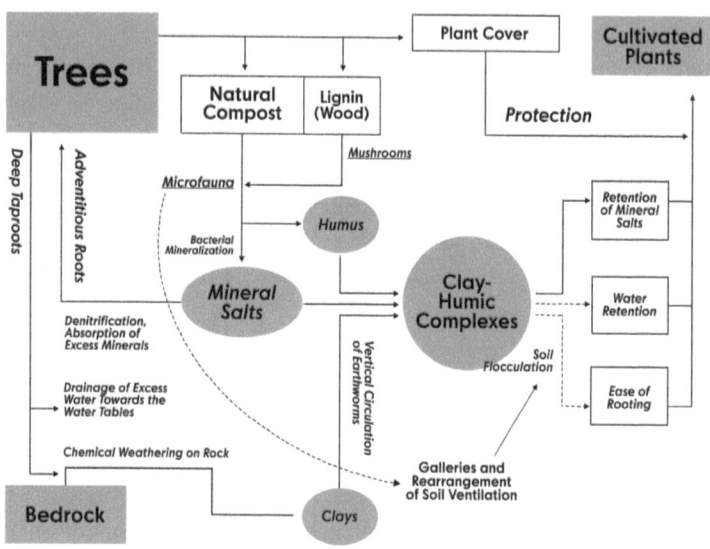

Once soil life has been totally decimated, humus production ceases and CHCs disappear altogether. The soil no longer has the appearance of a soft sponge, a forest floor-type "couscous," it loses its flaky structure that enabled water and mineral salts to be retained, it is no longer reworked and aerated by the galleries of micro-fauna and earthworms, and finally becomes compact, solid and impermeable. Downpours create floods that empty the fields of their nutrient-rich organic matter. The water that penetrates the soil flows directly into the water table, carrying with it much of the fertilizer supplied, which is of less and less benefit to the plants cultivated. The compaction is such that the plants themselves can no longer develop their roots, which sometimes come to the surface as the soil no longer performs its nourishing function.

APPENDIX 2
EPIGENETIC VERNALIZATION OF CEREALS IN THE USSR

Trofim Lysenko has been credited with such absurdities as the prodigious feat of transforming wheat into rye, by "educating" it correctly over several generations through well-chosen hybridizations. Perhaps it is possible to adapt wheat to poor soils and make it produce more fodder straw, as rye does, using such methods. However, it is true that the plant kingdom is much more malleable in terms of interspecific hybridization than the animal kingdom (many cultivated species are in fact the result of interspecific crosses, normally incompatible with neo-Darwinian dogma). But it is obviously impossible to transmute exactly one species into another, and no evolutionist can support this.

This is certainly not Lysenko's main discovery, and we need to go back to some enlightening remarks made by one of his best-known accusers, Dominique Lecourt, to get to the bottom of the bizarre story of how the agriculture of a system presumed to be paranoid and repressive could have aligned itself with the claims of a charlatan and an ignoramus.

> [...] The vernalization and springing of wheat [...] was the mainstay of Lysenkoism for over ten years, and earned it its fortune. There is not a single historian of agronomy who does not admit that this technique is really effective, at least when applied under certain conditions, particularly in dry climates. [...] We can't jump over history. The question is to assess the results Lysenko was able to achieve in the thirties and forties, and the results he was able to set against his opponents. From this point of view, how can we dispute the fact that vernalization was not an imaginary but a real and even spectacular solution to a problem made all the more distressing by the succession of crop failures? [It] may have seemed like a feat. And indeed it was, since it ensured fruit set while warding off frost.[1]

---

1   Dominique Lecourt, *Lysenko*.

Lysenko popularized a method for permanently "transforming" winter wheat into spring wheat, in contradiction to all the principles of genetics at the time. The Russian climate is essentially characterized by extremely harsh winters, which more than once devastated cereal harvests and led to famines. At the time, two varieties were used for soft wheat (*triticum aestivum*), which ripens in summer. The "fast" variety (or spring wheat), planted in the spring of the same year, gives low yields but without risk, while the "slow" variety (or winter wheat), which must be planted in autumn or winter of the previous year, gives much better yields, but requires a prior winter period to bear fruit. Winter wheat is therefore much more exposed to the risk of frost losses in the event of a harsh winter, as is often the case in the USSR.

Vernalization consists of exposing wet winter wheat sprouts to a period of several days at very low temperature in order to "mimic" winter, then planting them in spring. The result is much higher yields, faster, and without the considerable risk of loss associated with the Russian winter. This method was obviously a source of immense hope for the populations of these lands marked by centuries of chronic famine.

We now know the complex genetic mechanisms that explain why vernalization does not involve strictly genetic modifications, but rather endogenous mechanisms, already present and latent in the plant, that simply regulate the expression of genes linked to bolting.

In fact, the various genes that enable plants to fruit in ears cannot be expressed in the early stages in wheat germ cells, because they are "repressed" or "silenced" by regulators that hinder their expression: these molecules lodge on the gene and wind up the DNA in such a way that it is no longer physically accessible to the transcriptases responsible for their expression. These "obstacle" molecules are themselves produced by the activity of a complex area of the genome called FLC, made up of several genes which are sensitive to cold. The onset of cold suppresses the activity of this FLC zone by means of heat-sensitive molecules, which lifts the inhibition on the previously suppressed bolting genes: bolting can take place at the end of the cold period, whether it's a real winter (provided it's not too severe) or artificial conditioning such as vernalization.

The nature of the repression in this FLC zone is highly dependent on the duration and intensity of the cold experienced. It can be reversible or strongly stabilized, by more or less durable markings of the DNA of which it is composed. It has been found that these epigenetic markings are transmitted to dividing cells in the seedling, meaning that adult plant cells retain this imprint on the FLC zones of their nuclei.

For a long time, it was thought that epigenetic markers could be transmitted through mitosis (simple cell division) within the same organism, but that they were systematically erased during the divisions that form future reproductive cells (meiosis), thus eliminating all heredity of the acquired, i.e. all epigenetic memory. But we now know that this deletion is faster than the duplication of genes prior to any division, which means that deletion is an active process, governed by specific molecules, and not a spontaneous and natural disappearance of all marks along the exposed DNA. In the course of this active process, geneticists have noticed that certain sectors of the DNA

These "resistant" areas are not always the same; it depends at least in part on the conditions experienced by the parent organism.

Figure 15: Diagram of a vernalization period in the Arabidopsis plant.

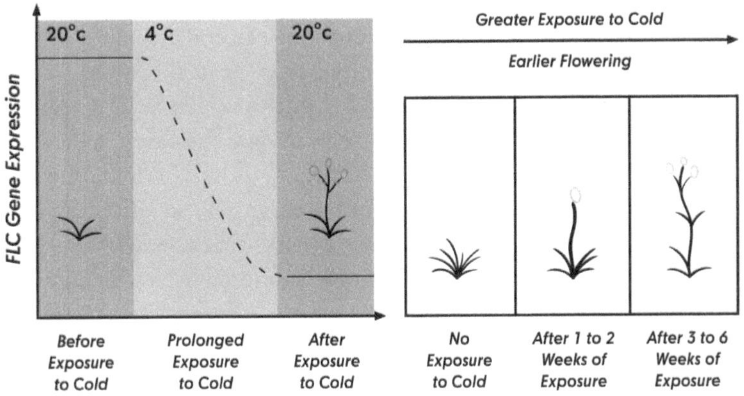

Source: Vernalization, a temperature-induced epigenetic switch. J. Chanson, A. Ange, M. Howard, C. Dean. 2012. *Journal of Cell Science* 125.

It is this latter discovery that highlights the possibility, marginal given the main process of erasing epigenetic marks before meiosis, of inheriting acquired traits. Such transmission is effective over several generations, but not indefinitely (since modifications are not "inscribed" in genes themselves under the form of mutations). This is all the more true when the offspring plants experience the same conditions as the parent plants (and respond better than the latter). The self-preserving properties of living organisms therefore only "permit" such ways of inheriting traits in case of emergency, when the environment is changing faster than the genome through spontaneous mutations. The heritable acclimatization of an individual to particular conditions can be detrimental to the offspring if the environmental conditions are further modified, as Lysenko had already pointed out: this explains why, in normal circumstances, all epigenetic modifications are canceled out during reproduction (the famous "soma-germen barrier" that Weismann believed to be natural and intangible).[2] Thus, the rule remains that of the natural selection of mutations inscribed in the genome over the long term (yet denied by Lysenko), while the exception in emergencies (which exists objectively, contrary to what Western geneticists thought) is epigenetic heredity.

It's worth noting that epigenetics is now developing theses, especially in plants, that are incredibly consistent with Lysenko's "heredity of habit-acquired traits," i.e. the "memory" of descendant plants to certain stresses (Lysenko spoke of heredity being "broken" or "degraded" by certain environmental conditions) to which the parental generation responded adaptively. These theses have nothing whatsoever to do with Lamarckism, which assumes that the "acquired" traits inherited were a finalistic imprint of nature itself, and not the organism's adaptive response to environmental changes, also known as epigenetic acclimatization. Two geneticists outline the principles in an article devoted to the "transgenerational response to stress" in a plant named *Arabidopsis*, where we better understand why the heredity of the acquired is more easily observable in

---

2   A study has shown that the descendants of women who lived through the famine in Holland during the Second World War inherited a tendency to fat storage and obesity, which, outside the context of nutritional deficiency, objectively represents a metabolic disadvantage. See article Transgenerational effects of prenatal exposure to the Dutch famine on neonatal adiposity and health in later life (Painter RC, Osmond C, Gluckman P, Hanson M, Phillips DI, Roseboom TJ, 2008, *BJOG* vol. 115 N° 10, September).

plants, unable to "escape" from changing conditions and therefore forced to adapt "quickly" to them by other strategies, than in animals:

> Plants exposed to stress transmit the memory of this exposure to their offspring. We have shown that trans-generational memory of stress is epigenetic in nature [...]. Plants are sedentary organisms and therefore cannot respond to rapidly evolving growth conditions by escaping to new environments, as animals in general can. What's more, since seed dispersal is rather limited in the vast majority of plants, the offspring is likely to develop under the same growing conditions as the parents. The parents' experience of the environment can be recorded in the form of induced epigenetic modifications produced in the somatic lineage. The particularly late separation of germ cells from somatic cells at the end of plant development enables the incorporation of acquired epigenetic modifications into the gametes. [...] Parental exposure to stress can not only lead to adaptive effects in the offspring, but also introduce a certain degree of change in genome stability. [...] [It has] been shown that an increase in the Sequence of Random Recombinations between homologous genes (HRF) triggered by a single UV exposure was maintained for five consecutive generations in the absence of stress. But the increase in HRF following parental exposure to cold, heat, flooding, excess salt, requires the offspring to be exposed to the same stress. [...] In a given environmental context, plants establish certain genetic and epigenetic traits needed to cope with expected growth conditions. Abrupt environmental changes or unusual new stresses can trigger a cascade of gene expression changes in order to survive by adapting to the new conditions. Some of these potentially beneficial changes are most likely recorded by local methylation.[3]

It's easy to see how the Darwinian pairing of "random mutations / natural selection" has almost been incorporated into living matter in the form of evolutionary strategies that stimulate, only in the face of stress, a high frequency of random genetic recombinations (over several generations if necessary) between the two parental versions of the genes mobilized, and epigenetic marking by methylation of the forms obtained with the highest selective value for the new environment. The neo-Darwinians' supposedly intangible "chance/selection" pairing has been "absorbed," dialectically overtaken, one might say, as an endogenous and preselected strategy of living organisms, faster and more reactive, for long-term but reversible acclimatization to changing conditions, in a new version of the chance/selection pairing: the new "HRF/methylations" pairing.

3   Alex Boyko, Igor Kovalchuk, Transgenerational stress response in *Arabidopsis thaliana*, in *Plant Signal Behavior* August 2010, NCBI website, National Center of Biotechnology Information.

This new research framework will undoubtedly enable tomorrow's agronomists to rapidly adapt new seed varieties to the immense diversity of cultivated soils on the planet, far more effectively than the unlikely and dangerous genetically modified organisms (GMOs).

Capitalism has hijacked agrobiology research in favor of GMO production to meet the demands of agribusiness (sterility of cultivated plants to increase farmers' dependence from one season to the next, etc.). These pathways tied to epigenetics, which require particular care for varieties that must remain "educated" over several generations, can only be fully developed under a socialist regime, i.e. by giving farmers independence in terms of seeds, diversity of cultivated varieties and the ability, enabled by a high-level education system, to master an agronomic science that involves all the links in the agricultural production chain, from the agronomist to the farmer himself.

APPENDIX 3
HOW IS A SCIENTIFIC THEORY BORN?

Alfred Wegener is known as the great discoverer of the theory of plate tectonics in 1915. His magisterial demonstration of the ancient connection between continents currently separated from each other by oceans brought him into violent conflict with the geological community, which had spent centuries interpreting the Earth's history in terms of strictly vertical movements. For the latter, Wegener's Pangea was explained not by horizontal displacements, deemed impossible, but by the collapse of "continental bridges" that had given way to the oceans. The hypothesis of this apprentice-geologist, a climatologist by training and therefore an illegitimate amateur, according to which the lunar attraction would displace billions of megatons of rock laterally, was considered totally far-fetched.

Obviously, they were right. This hypothesis could not stand up, and the then incongruous phrase "continental drift" was attacked, ridiculed and then forgotten by the "fixist" geologists, and rightly so. The vertical movements they had been studying with precision for decades were indeed at the origin of most regional geological formations (elevation of mountains, subsidence of sedimentary basins, etc.).What they didn't imagine, beyond this still-unquestioned local knowledge, was that vertical movements are themselves overdetermined by horizontal movements of compression, collision or extension between tectonic plates. In the 1960s, after half a century of scientific controversy, "continental drift" became a solid, central, omnipotent theory in geology: plate tectonics. Paleomagnetism, seismic tomography, geochemistry of magmatic rocks, radiochronology, volcanology: all recent technical and theoretical advances that enabled Wegener to win a posthumous victory over his opponents.

A change of discipline, a change of ideological stakes: if Wegener, the "Sunday geologist," was right against almost all the academic mandarins of the time, the same could not be said for the "barefoot agronomist" Lysenko, or for the modest horticulturist Michurin against the great doctors of genetics at the time. But the latter had a short memory: didn't all their knowledge of formal genetics come from a pea-loving Slovak monk named Gregor Mendel, totally unknown to the great European professorships?[1]

Yet there isn't a serious scientific article in genetics today that doesn't mention epigenetic heritability. Epigenetic heritability is becoming the new paradigm of biology for the new century, surpassing—without denying to a certain extent—the idealistic genetics of the last century, and one could say without risking too much that the "transmissible epigenetic acclimatization" of today's scholars is equivalent to Lysenko's concepts of "fragmented heredity," "inheritance of habit-acquired traits," in contrast to classical idealist genetics. It is what "plate tectonics" is to Wegener's misguided "continental drift" versus the fixist geologists of the day. Of course, Lysenko made some serious scientific errors, notably by metaphysically opposing the discoveries of formal genetics to his own, as if the hypotheses could be immediately confronted in a fight to the death without waiting for the verdict of future technical advances. The course of the history of science, with its infinite ramifications and unanticipated twists and turns, is undoubtedly even more complex than that of the class struggle and the social history of mankind. However, beyond these errors, most of Lysenko's discoveries were not charlatanry, and the only response to the theoretical connection that can be made between epigenetics and Michurinism is ignorance and indifference. It's no longer mockery.

---

1 Let's not forget that even great discoverers like Mendel have had their share of charlatanism. When Mendel discovered the particle and independent transmission of pea traits in the course of his hybridization experiments (i.e. the transmission of genes), he also observed, when considering the transmission of traits taken two by two, that while some are indeed transmitted independently, others are transmitted to offspring much more often together than separately. He therefore erred by omission or fudged certain statistical results to support his theory, despite these troublesome observations. It wasn't until the beginning of the 20th century with T. H. Morgan that these statistical "links" between genes were explained by the fact that they could be carried by the same chromosome. Genes that were actually transmitted independently of each other were simply carried by different chromosomes.

Broadly speaking, one could better describe the tumults in the history of science, the great paradigm shifts, and major scientific revolutions by applying more dialectical analysis. Quantum mechanics, which today embraces everything from particle physics to astronomy, is the negation on another scale, the dialectical extension of Newton's classical mechanics, while the latter remains operative on our scale of perception. Plate tectonics explains every geological formation, whether planetary or regional in the final analysis, not by replacing decades of studies by the "fixists," their *isostasies* or their *subsidences*, but by overdetermining these vertical movements with large-scale horizontal convection movements. Complex numbers go beyond rational numbers, while the evolutionism of Lamarck, Saint Hilaire, and Darwin has still not invalidated the discoveries of the eminent fixist Georges Cuvier, founder of comparative anatomy, on the law of correlation of organs.

It is in this sense that the "epigenetic" extensions of modern genetics can be seen as a kind of pirouette in the history of science, giving the descendants of Mendel and Morgan the theoretical resources to overturn all the idealistic dogmas that had hitherto held them in the neo-Darwinian paradigm, in the general swirl of Soviet innovations and without ultimately needing them to redevelop. Science undoubtedly needs these two types of "heroes," forever irreconcilable yet inseparable: those who, from outside a single academic mindset, shake up certainties and disturb careers, forever whimsical, approximate, in the minority and in the margins, but also those from within the new paradigm in the process of consolidation, those who discretely build, confirm and develop earlier theoretical innovations. On the one hand, there are the clumsy and hasty innovators, the radicals capable of doing anything to impose their new ideas; on the other, there are the shadow workers, the stubborn laboratory technicians who spend their lives confirming the dominant paradigm or countering (until it's impossible) the attacks of sinister innovators and charlatans alike.

opa

APPENDIX 4
CUBAN SOCIALISM AND AGROECOLOGY: MUTUALLY REINFORCING

IT'S NOT A QUESTION OF ASSESSING the natural or spontaneous inclination of socialism towards ecology, but of measuring, as a materialist, how everything pushes the socialist mode of production, despite initial reservations, down an ecological path. For example, it was the embargo imposed on Cuba because of its social and economic model that deprived it of immediate alternatives to the import of fertilizers and pesticides when the socialist bloc collapsed in 1990-1991, the cause of which was indeed the hostility of the imperialist chain against socialism. Socialism has always been based on solid national sovereignty—what some called "socialism in one country."

This one-off need to "survive" triggered the realization of the Cuban agroecological model as we know it today. The argument that Cuba owes its current success in this field to the "obligation to change" out of the Soviet bosom, and not to the Cuban model itself, does not hold up from this point of view.

The success of its agricultural policy owes everything to the Cuban revolution, but also strengthens it in return, to such an extent that the island continues along this path today, rejecting the possibility of a return to old practices by importing Chinese fertilizers, for example.

It should be noted, however, that even at the time of its alignment with the Khrushchev agricultural model (itself aligned with the American model at the time), Cuba had perhaps unconsciously prepared the ground for such a second revolution on the island.

The first Congress of the Cuban Communist Party in 1975 opened the debate on environmental issues and the fight against pollution. In

1977, COMARNA, the National Commission for the Protection of the Environment and Natural Resources, was created. It was set up in every province to promote sustainable development policies, particularly waste recycling and pollution control. In 1986, seven million members of the Revolutionary Defense Committees (CDR) were sent to the countryside to help the agricultural sector. This unprecedented experience gave rise to numerous local soil restoration and organic farming projects, on the basis of which the famous "organoponicos" of the "special period" flourished a few years later.

These "organoponicos" would multiply at a rapid pace throughout the cities and their outskirts in the nineties, while in the countryside, the state would suspend most of the large state farms (which could be called *sovkhozes*, in the Soviet style) and redistributed them into smaller *kolkhozes*, the UBPCs (Basic Cooperative Production Units), which applied agroforestry on a massive scale, and were better able to respond technically to the demands and brutality of the change in agricultural model.

In the city as in the countryside, these cooperatives can be likened to the former Soviet *kolkhozes* (which were in the majority in the USSR until 1991, compared with the *sovkhozes* of other countries), since the State, which owns the land, gives it in "free usufruct" to groups of agricultural workers (factory workers, building or neighborhood collectives, hospital workers or genuine peasants, pensioners), in exchange for a "tax in kind." In exchange for this usufruct (no rent to pay, equipment rental or repair, etc.), producers donate a portion of their organic food, which the state sells at low prices in local outlets (close to the producers, and therefore without energy expenditure for transport), with the surplus available to producers for personal consumption and sale.

Cuban production now covers 70% of the population's consumption of fruit and vegetables, which is considerable! The 75% of Cubans who live in cities produce 30% of their own food needs, while the rural exodus has been halted. There's even talk of a return to the countryside, with many Cubans finding it more profitable to get back to farming. The famous "city-country contradiction" of Marxist literature thus finds here a new form of concrete resolution.

The aim of all UBPCs is always to increase production, which might shock our anti-productivists, but feeding the entire population to ensure self-sufficiency necessarily means producing more! There are currently over 400,000 urban farms covering more than 70,000 hectares and producing one and a half million tonnes of fruit and vegetables a year.

For example, the *"Viver organoponico alamar"* farm to the east of Havana started out in the nineties as a 0.7-hectare garden employing 5 people. Today, it covers an area of 11.2 hectares and employs 147 people, some 50 of whom, it should be noted, enjoy a high "engineering" level of education. It's important to understand that organic farming is a technical and scientific step forward compared to intensive farming, where the farmer is passive and simply pours bags of inputs over his seedlings. It is often necessary to master notions of agronomy and to know the best seeds for the soil and climate availability, and it is the Cuban education system, renowned throughout the sub-continent, that makes the difference in this respect. Cuba trains 11% of South America's scientists, even though it accounts for only 2% of the total population!

The results are immediate: in thousands of tons, Cuba's consumption of fertilizers has dropped from 1,000 in 1990 to 90, and that of pesticides from 35 to 1! But that's not all: agroforestry, which is in itself a form of reforestation and polyculture, makes Cuba's agricultural system truly resilient in the face of natural calamities such as cyclones, which are not uncommon there. Indeed, agricultural diversification makes it possible to limit production losses, which intensive monoculture could not do, while protecting medium- and short-term crops (shrubs such as guava or banana trees, annual legumes or other herbaceous plants on the ground) under long-term shrub crops (often avocado trees). What's more, trees and shrubs are more effective at conserving soil moisture for underlying crops, which in itself is as much a saving as the gradual restoration of soils dried out by climate or past chemical treatments. This agricultural resilience to climatic hazards is a strategic factor in national sovereignty, directly linked to Cuban agroecology.

Figure 16: Growth dynamics of marketed peasant production (1988 = base 100).

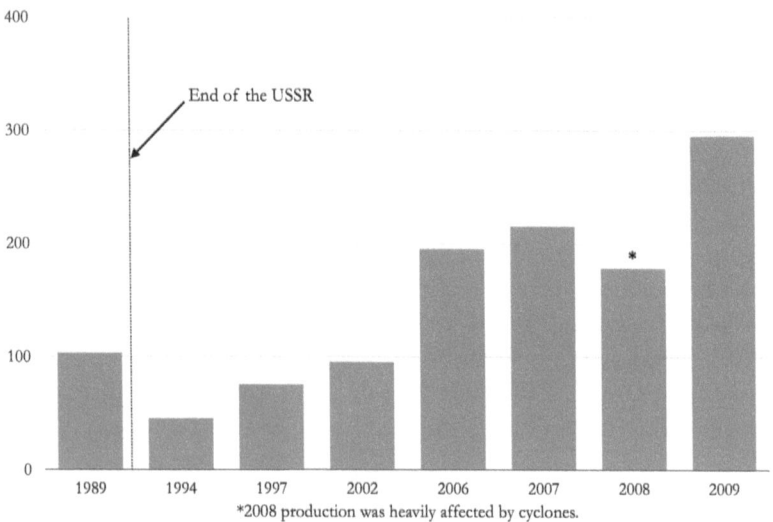

*2008 production was heavily affected by cyclones.

Source: Statistics from ANAP's Agrifood Organization Department (cited in B. M. Sosa, A. M. Roque Jaime, D. R. A Lozano and P. M. Rosset. *Révolution agro-écologique—Quand le paysan voit, il croit*, Edition ANAP).

It's the socialist system that allows all this superstructure, and makes local organic produce the exact opposite of what you can find with this "label" in our supermarkets: like these tomatoes grown "out of soil" in expensive clique-like greenhouses, sold at overpriced prices in France after being transported by truck from Spain over thousands of kilometers... But there's better!

Cuba's real prowess, just as much a part of socialism as the laws enacted by the State since 1991, lies in the infrastructure, i.e. in mass movements. Here, it has been demonstrated that the application of a sustainable agricultural policy and agronomic innovations in terms of local solutions can only come from Cuban organizations, first and foremost the ANAP (trade union of Cuban small farmers), which launched a vast popular movement in the countryside in 1997 called "*Campesino a campesino*" ["farmer to farmer"]. Based on the principle that workers on the land learn by doing, by seeing the results first-hand, especially when farming techniques are reputed to be complex or unprofitable (which is not true), the CAC movement has penetrated every nook and cranny of the land and set up local, democratically self-organized collectives to learn and share knowledge and experience.

The CAC movement was born almost spontaneously in the peasant world of Central America, particularly in rural Nicaragua during the Sandinista revolution in the 1970s. But while it has involved some 30,000 peasant families throughout the sub-continent in the space of thirty years, over 100,000 Cuban families (a third of the peasant population) have embarked on the adventure since 1997! Farmers play a central role, and the degree of organization, training and exchange is particularly effective in Cuba, to such an extent that the know-how of the Cuban CAC movement is now being exported (as is organic compost itself, incidentally) to Venezuela and Bolivia, via the internationalist Via Campesina peasant movement, of which ANAP is a member.

The involvement of young people is also strong, with a good 1,000 peasant youth brigades (BJP) in Cuba—some 10,000 young people—involved in the island's agricultural achievements today. Last but not least, Cuban agroecology, spurred on by the democracy of the CAC movement in particular, is finally breaking the traces of peasant patriarchy by giving women farmers a full role in agricultural tasks, often considered physically difficult, due to the multiplicity of tasks developed by cooperatives (earthworm cultivation, composting, seed production, seed conservation, care of polycultures and soils, etc.). As a result, Cuban agricultural work has acquired a very high level of feminization, and therefore inclusion of women in national production, the basis of its concrete and complete emancipation.

This prowess in ecologically and socially sustainable farming has naturally brought Cuba accolades. In 2006, the well-known NGO WWF stated in its annual report that Cuba was the only country in the world to have reached "sustainable development." This was soon followed by the Global Footprint Network, which stated that Cuba's ecological footprint was among the lowest in the world. In 2008, the United Nations Environment Programme (UNEP) declared Cuba an "example to follow" in urban and peri-urban agriculture. In 2010, the UN's Food and Agriculture

Organization (FAO) confirmed that Cuba is the only country to have almost doubled its forest cover over the last fifty years (from 14% in the 1960s to 26% in 2010). The country's nature reserves are also a source of great pride (22% of Cuban territory is "protected," i.e. 23 national parks where biodiversity is emblematic; 6,300 protected plant species, 51% of which are endemic).

But these minor glories merely illustrate a process which, unfortunately, no-one here wants to take on board, so much so that it is actually hindering the course of inter-imperialist economic wars around the world in times of deep environmental crisis. Cuba has become the beacon of agroecology because it has developed to an unprecedented level, at a national level, the banning of pesticides from food production. Above all, it has become a beacon by guaranteeing the sovereignty and food security of the Cuban people, the material basis, if ever there was one, of independence, from both bottom up (mass movements) to top down (the Cuban state, who legislates and administers on a national scale and without agribusiness lobby interference).

Figure 17: Cuban socialism and agroecology, a self-reinforcing dynamic.

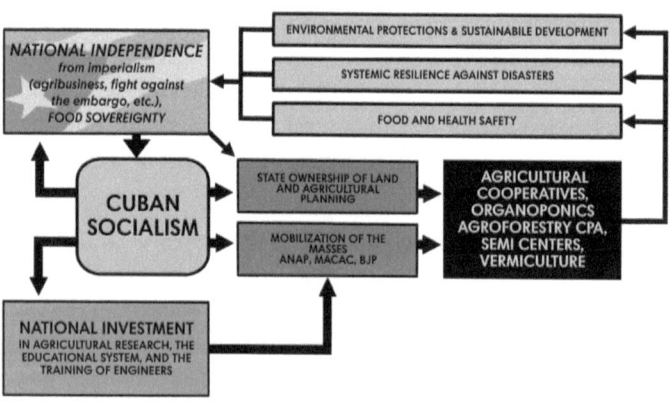

TIMELINE

1921—Lenin promulgates the law "On Natural Monuments, Gardens and Parks," which establishes and develops the *zapovedniki* throughout the USSR, complete nature reserves off-limits to man.

1926—Soviet geologist Vladimir Vernadsky first formulates the concept of the biosphere, in which all components interact dynamically. This theory would go on to form the basis of all modern ecological concepts.

1932—The great Dnieper hydroelectric dam was opened, the largest in the world at the time. Non-intermittent renewable energies, based on the country's natural resources, were a priority for the USSR.

1935—Joseph Stalin prepares a vast afforestation plan, heralding the "Great Plan for the Transformation of Nature" of 1948, at the XIV Congress of the CPSU, based on W.R. Williams' grassland systems (permaculture and agroforestry).

1940—The chemical fertilizer industry developed only temporarily for the duration of the war: waste from this industry was used as an explosive raw material for the arms industry.

1943—Vernadsky receives the Stalin Prize, and a Moscow avenue and the Soviet Geological Institute are named after him.

1944—Soviet botanist Vladimir Sukachev founds the Institute of Forest of the Siberian Division of the Russian Academy of Sciences. He receives the Order of Lenin three times.

1948—After twenty years of ideological struggle between Lysenko's supporters of environmental "plant education" and geneticists opposed to any theory of "heredity of acquired characteristics," a session of the Lenin Academy of Agricultural Sciences decided in favor of the former with regard to state funding. Genetics laboratories continued their work, but without the colossal funds allocated to them in the thirties, notably under the direction of the geneticist Anton Zhebrak.

1948—Stalin launched the "Great Plan for the Transformation of Nature," which involved developing agroforestry on a territory of two million hectares, twice the size of France, based on prefigurative principles of permaculture, against the advice of the proponents of intensive agrochemicals.

1949—In the period from 1949 to 1953, tree planting in the USSR became truly massive: it had never reached this level before and not since. At the same time, the number of *zapovedniki* grew steadily until 1951. Finally, cereal production exploded between 1945 and 1952, rivaling that of the USA, which remained relatively stagnant over the same period.

1953—The Death of Joseph Stalin.

1954—Nikita Khrushchev, initially Minister of Agriculture, launches the "virgin land campaign" on productivist lines, reviving the chemical fertilizer and pesticide industry.

1960—The Aral Sea begins to empty, the result of excessive detouring of the rivers that fed it to irrigate Kazakh and Uzbek agriculture.

1960—Khrushchev abolished most of the *zapovedniki* on Soviet territory, considering them useless, and developed an intense "chemicalization" of agriculture, now openly productivist and modeled on the American model.

1961—Soviet climatologist Michail Budenko first drew attention to the possibility of man-made global warming.

1972—Despite the intensification of its agricultural production, the USSR became an importer of American grain and therefore increasingly dependent on the USA.

1975—Ecological currents resurface in the USSR, led by the communist scientist Ivan Frolov.

1980—Robin Holliday, an English geneticist, spoke for the first time in the West of "epigenetic heredity," i.e. "the inheritance of traits acquired" during a life, and not through genes. This is the dawn of a veritable "epigenetic revolution" objectively predicted by Soviet agronomists half a century earlier.

1983—Marxist revolutionary Thomas Sankara takes power in Burkina Faso. He develops programs to protect the environment and the country's natural resources, and to forest plantations.

1986—Chernobyl nuclear disaster in Ukraine.

1990—Beginning of the "special period" in Cuba, following the collapse of the USSR. Agroforestry and urban and peri-urban organic farming programs begin to be developed and coordinated by the State, to meet the food needs of the Cuban people.

1997—The Ministry of Education's Cuban Energy Conservation Program (PAEME) introduces young Cubans and workers to energy conservation measures and renewable energy.

2001—Cuba wins the UN Global 2000 award for the development of its renewable energy and social programs.

2006—Evo Morales comes to power in Bolivia with a program that combines social reform, nationalization of resources and protection of the *pachamama* (mother earth).

2006—In its report, the WWF considers Cuba to be the only country in the world to have reached the stage of sustainable development, in terms of its nationwide organic agriculture.

2006—The UN awards Cuba a prize for innovation in renewable energy (the Energy Globe Awards).

REFERENCES
(IN CHRONOLOGICAL ORDER OF PUBLICATION)

Essay on the Principle of Population—Malthus, 1798.

The German Ideology—Karl Marx, and Freidrich Engels 1846.

Grundrisse (Manuscripts of 1857-1858)—Karl Marx, 1858.

The Origin of Species—Charles Darwin, 1859.

Capital—Karl Marx, 1867.

Dialectics of Nature—Friedrich Engels, 1873.

'Critique of the Gotha Programme'—Karl Marx, 1875.

Anti-Dühring—Friedrich Engels, 1878.

On the Variation of Animals and Plants in the Domestic State—Charles Darwin, 1879.

Complete Works—Lenin, 1924.

The Biosphere—Vladimir Vernadsky, Moscow Publishing House, 1926.

The Collectivization of the Soviet Countryside—Guido Miglioli, Editions Rieder, 1934.

Selected Works—Vassili Robertovich Williams, Moscow Editions, 1940.

'The Stuation in Biological Science'—Session of the Lenin Academy of Agricultural Sciences of the USSR, report to the 1948 Session. Moscow edition.

'Génétique classique et biologie mitchourinienne'—Francis Cohen, Éditions La Nouvelle Critique: *Science bourgeoise et science prolétarienne*, 1950.

Selected Works—Michurin, Moscow Publishing House, 1951.

Elementary Principles of Michurinian Biology—V. Stoletov, Moscow Publishing House, 1951.

Marxism and the Problems of Linguistics—Joseph Stalin, Moscow Publishing House, 1951.

'Les grands travaux et la lutte pour la transformation de la nature en URSS'—J. Baby, *L'information géographique* N° 2, 1952.

Agrobiology—Trofim Lysenko, Moscow Publishing, 1953.

L'URSS sans idole—Bernard Féron, Casterman, 1966.

The Rise and Fall of Lysenko—Zhores Medvedev, Gallimard, 1971.

'Nature and Man'—Pavel Volin, *Soviet Review Works and Opinions* N°165, 1972.

Lysenko, histoire réelle d'une "science prolétarienne" —Dominique Lecourt, Maspéro, 1976.

The Ecology of Freedom—Murray Bookchin, AK Press, 1982.

The Dialectical Biologist—R. Levins and R. Lewontin, Harvard University Press, 1987.

'Saving the Planet, a Strategy for Saving the Future of Life'—WWF, UNEP, IUCN, 1991 Russian.

'Revolution and Ecology, 1917-1934'—Jean Batou, *Vingtième Siècle— magazine d'histoire* N°35, 1992.

Dictionnaire du darwinisme et de l'évolution—Patrick Tort (ed.), PUF, 1996.

Histoire de la notion de gène—André Pichot, Flammarion, 1999.

Marx's Ecology—John Bellamy Foster, Monthly Review Press, 2000.

Ni Dieu ni gène—J. J. Kupiec et P. Sonigo, Points science, 2000.

L'évolution—Pierre Sonigo, Isabelle Stengers, Editions EDP, 2003.

History of the Russian Zapovedniki—Feliks Stylmark, Russian Natur Press, 2003.

'Report Living Planet'—WWF, 2006.

The New Russia—Jean Radvanyi, Editions Armand Colin, 2007.

References

'Agroecological Revolution. When Farmers See, they Believe'—B. M. Sosa, A. M. Roque Jaime, D. R. Lozano and P. M. Rosset, Edition ANAP, 2008.

The Academician Trofim Lysenko—Nikolai Ovchinnikov, Éditions Faisceau, 2010.

Ideological Power and Scientific Knowledge—Deniz Uztopal, 2012.

Towards High-performance Agricultures. Analyse des performances de l'agriculture biologique—edited by Hervé Guyomard, INRA, 2013.

La réception en France du lysenkisme (1948-1956)—D. Uztopal, Cahiers d'Histoire, 2014.

Lysenko's Ghost: Epigenetics and Russia—Loren Graham, Harvard University Press, 2016.

Évolution, la preuve par Marx—Guillaume Suing, Editions Delga, 2016.

www.ingramcontent.com/pod-product-compliance
Lightning Source LLC
LaVergne TN
LVHW042247070526
838201LV00089B/58